MUSCLES AND MORALS

Muscles and Morals
Organized Playgrounds and Urban Reform, 1880–1920

DOMINICK CAVALLO

UNIVERSITY OF PENNSYLVANIA PRESS
Philadelphia
1981

This work was published with the support of the Haney Foundation

Library of Congress Cataloging in Publication Data

Cavallo, Dominick, 1946–
    Muscles and morals.

    Bibliography:
    Includes index.
    1. Playgrounds–Social aspects–United States–
History. 2. United States–Social conditions–1865–
1918. 3. Child welfare–United States–History.
I. Title.
GV429.C38   790'.06'80973   80 –50689
ISBN 0–8122–7782–1   AACR2

Printed in the United States of America

To my parents,
Anthony and Margaret Cavallo

CONTENTS

ILLUSTRATIONS

PREFACE

Books, like people, are not necessarily what they appear to be, and it behooves an author to make clear from the start what his book is about and, equally important, what it is not about.

This book is a history of efforts made by urban social reformers during the years 1880 to 1920 to transfer control of children's play from the children and their families to the state. To achieve their goal, reformers urged municipal governments to construct playgrounds where the play of city youngsters could be supervised and controlled. The reasons for making children's play a concern of the state are numerous and complex, and the implications of state control had cultural and political ramifications that extended far beyond the playground. Reformers believed supervised play altered the personalities of young people, improved their abilities to deal with the pressures of city life, lessened ethnic conflict, and, perhaps most important, changed prevailing perceptions of male and female sex roles.

This book is not a history of American sport or recreation. Nor is it a study of the role of team games in American society. There is little discussion of individual games and no analysis of the distinctions between play and sport. My subject—my only subject—is what I call the movement to organize children's play, and its cultural and political implications.

ACKNOWLEDGMENTS

The pleasure of thanking those who helped complete the journey from dissertation to book is sufficient reward for undertaking a trip that is sometimes terrifying and always tedious. I would be remiss, however, if I neglected to acknowledge those whose negative influence inadvertently produced positive results. The historical profession, like any other profession, has its share of petty, insecure individuals, people who would close the academic gateway to the American past on those who do not share their social or cultural values. I thank those historians who would have every Italian student of this nation's history whistle an American tune before they allowed him to practice his craft; their personal and scholarly values forced me to look elsewhere for direction. Besides, I can't whistle.

Fortunately there were others. Robert Marcus sparked my interest in the cultural history of children's play during his American History seminar at the State University of New York at Stony Brook. His insightful suggestions, as well as his doubts about my interpretations, were both helpful and welcome. David Burner read both the dissertation and the revised manuscript and saved me from a number of errors. Fred Weinstein's reading of the dissertation was very perceptive, and he provided me with a useful bibliography of significant psychological works. I am especially indebted to Mel Albin, who never let friendship interfere with his responsibility to tell me when I was off the mark. His criticisms were always incisive and usually on target. Barbara Finkelstein, Robert Devlin, Paul H. Mattingly, Gerald M. Platt, and Glen Zeitzer read all or part of the manuscript and provided helpful comments. I hope the final product does justice to their efforts.

There were others whose kindness and assistance made the task easier than it would otherwise have been: the reference staff at the State University of New York at Stony Brook, especially Richard P. Feinberg; Andrea Hinding of the Social Welfare History Archives Cen-

ter, University of Minnesota; Charles E. Hartsoe of Virginia Commonwealth University; and the library staffs at the Russell Sage Foundation, Smith College, Springfield College, and the Recreation
Association of America. As every author knows, a good editor is a
priceless asset. I was fortunate to have the manuscript read by four
unusually perceptive editors at the University of Pennsylvania Press:
Jane Barry, Sam and Alice Steinruck, and Patrick O'Kane. And special
thanks to Martin Van Lith, who, as usual, did the driving.

Finally, there were those who made it possible. This book would
not have been written without the encouragement and love of Helene
Bauman. When discouragement verged on despair, as at times it must
during a seven-year project, she kept me from embracing that black
comfort. My parents, to whom this book is dedicated, gave more support
and made more sacrifices than I can recount or repay. I hope this book
serves as a first installment.

"Now, what I want is, Facts. Teach these boys and girls nothing but Facts. Facts alone are wanted in Life. Plant nothing else, and root out everything else. You can only form the minds of reasoning animals upon Facts: nothing else will ever be of any service to them. This is the principle on which I bring up my own children, and this is the principle on which I bring up these children. Stick to Facts, Sir!"—Charles Dickens, *Hard Times*

I hope that here in America more and more the ideal of the well-trained and vigorous body will be maintained neck by neck with that of the well-trained and vigorous mind as the two co-equal halves of the higher education.—William James

Introduction: The Movement to Organize Children's Play

"Child saving" was perhaps the most widely supported reform movement in the United States between 1880 and 1920. However vehemently social reformers disagreed among themselves about other issues, nearly all of them supported a host of child-saving efforts aimed at rescuing city children—especially working-class, ethnic children—from a cluster of social and economic hazards. These dangers included economic exploitation generated by unregulated capitalism, moral chaos and alienation created by unrestricted immigration, and threats to law and order fostered by an unsupervised adolescent street culture. Child-saving efforts were wide-ranging. The movement embraced publicly supported child welfare programs, such as child labor legislation, compulsory education, and medical inspection programs in public schools, as well as voluntaristic, nongovernmental efforts, including the creation of a host of boys' and girls' associations, such as the Girl Scouts, Boy Scouts, and Camp Fire Girls.[1]

One facet of child saving during this period that blended public and voluntaristic approaches to child welfare, and that has received little attention from historians,[2] was the movement to organize the play activities of city children and adolescents on supervised, municipally owned playgrounds. Between 1880 and 1920, a politically diverse group of reformers I call "play organizers," most of whom were progressive educators, social settlement workers, and child psychologists, analyzed children's play and tried to transplant it from city streets, where it was, they thought, unorganized and uncontrolled, onto supervised playgrounds. In the process they generated important ideas about the relationship between a structured play experience and child development. They viewed organized play as a vital medium for shaping the moral and cognitive development of young people. Equally important, organized play, particularly team sports for adolescents, was seen by reformers as an ideal means of integrating the young into the work rhythms and social demands of a dynamic and complex urban-industrial civilization.

By 1910 thousands of city playgrounds across the country had organized programs for children. Social reformers, under the auspices of the Playground Association of America, founded in 1906, felt that these playgrounds would be a cure for a variety of festering urban maladies. The play movement was one of the most dynamically led child-saving efforts—its leaders and advocates included Jane Addams, Jacob Riis, Lillian Wald, and Graham Taylor—and also one of the most generously funded. Between 1880 and 1920, municipal governments spent over one hundred million dollars for the construction and staffing of organized playgrounds.

The word "organized" had two specific meanings for play advocates. First, it signified the desire to structure the youth's play experiences on supervised, well-equipped playgrounds owned and operated by city governments. Organized activities in these facilities ranged from sandcastle-building by four-year-olds to adolescent team sports; furthermore, the games were carefully designed in accordance with the latest discoveries in biology and psychology and the latest innovations in the new field of playground management. The organization of play also had implications for public policy. Although the play movement was spearheaded by voluntary organizations, notably social settlements and the Playground Association of America, its leaders hoped to make the control of play a state responsibility. They wanted municipalities to own and operate playgrounds and to institutionalize government control over play by incorporating physical education courses into the school curriculum. Play organizers spent a good deal of time and money persuading city officials that play was too serious a business to be left to children and parents. Particularly after the founding of the Playground Association of America, their efforts were enormously successful, and by 1920 children's play, like their formal education, was increasingly supervised by the state. The organization of children's play, then, refers to attempts by public and private institutions to supersede parental control in this area of the child's life.

The word "organized" had a second and equally important meaning in the play movement. Inviting young people to use organized playgrounds was more than a strategy for removing them from parental supervision or providing them with healthy exercise. Modern biological and psychological theories of child development had convinced play advocates that playground experiences were means through which the young developed specific cognitive skills, moral tendencies, and social values. Play organizers argued that a connection existed between the social-training techniques employed on playgrounds, especially during adolescent team games, and the creation of a distinct personality type. It is important to understand how that personality was supposed to function. We cannot know whether play organizers succeeded in creating that personality, but we do know that they assumed that their social-training methods worked and would, therefore, have a specific impact on the youth's personality, as well as a profound impact on the country's political and cultural future. The team player's personality represented play organizers' vision of the ideal twentieth-century citizen, worker, and neighbor. The social training practiced on playgrounds with organized activities, then, was a means of "organizing" the city youth's personality; that is, the playground was a vehicle of political socialization. To understand the social and political aspirations of reformers, we have to analyze how they attempted to organize the youth's personality.

The first question to be explored here is why the play movement existed. As Professor Eugen Weber pointed out some years ago, the historian of attitudes toward play cannot assume that motives for promoting physical activities are self-revealing. "Physical training," Weber wrote, "always begs the question: training for what?"[3] Certainly, in analyzing the motives of play organizers we cannot overlook their most obvious child-saving interests: the moral and physical well-being of youngsters who lived in damp, dirty, congested tenements. How could city youngsters, wondered Jane Addams, thrive physically or morally when they lived in tenements where sheep were slaughtered in basements, where two or more families lived in a single apartment, where tuberculosis flourished, and where even incest went unpunished?[4] Vigorous outdoor exercise was hardly a cure for these conditions, but it could mitigate some of the physical hazards spawned by overcrowded and unsanitary housing.

Along with their interest in the physical well-being of children, Progressive Era reformers exhibited a well-documented aversion to the "asocial individualism" they associated with unregulated capitalism and entrepreneurial aggressiveness. They perceived team sports as ideal media for teaching young people the nonindividualistic ideals of cooperation, group loyalty, and the subordination of self to what play organizers called the "social whole."

The wish to counteract both the physical foulness of the slum and the moral corruption of the capitalistic individualism that built it certainly influenced play organizers. These social conditions alone, however, account for neither the play movement's existence nor its uniqueness among child-saving enterprises. Social reformers had resources in addition to team games and organized play for counteracting the moral evils spawned by individualism and slum life. For example, the activities of the Boy Scouts, Girl Scouts, and Camp Fire Girls promoted health and gave the city child a respite from his or her congested environment through excursions into the countryside. The emphasis on group direction in these and other institutions, such as student self-government organizations in public schools, encouraged cooperation and group loyalty at least as effectively as team games.[5] We must seek the sources of the play movement's unique contribution to child saving in other factors.

I argue that reformers saw team sports as child-saving devices because their psychological theories of child development assumed that a link existed between carefully organized physical exercise and both moral vitality and cognitive alertness. Play organizers believed that structured and supervised play experiences strengthened the youth's moral fiber as much as they fortified his body. They were convinced that a supervised program of rigorous muscular conditioning would determine what a youngster valued and how he organized his thoughts. Proper physical training, they argued, instilled values and aptitudes that allowed the city child to meet the challenges of his stimulating and often dangerous environment. Above all, play organizers believed that such training was an effective method of promoting stability in the child and reform in American society.

It is essential to understand why play advocates believed muscular conditioning was so important. While they held a wide variety of political and social views, most play organizers adhered to psychological, biological, and pedagogical theories of child development and training that held that muscles and muscle control were the primary links between the child's "inner" realm of idiosyncratic feelings and his "outer" world of social encounters. The musculature was not simply a lowly servant that dutifully executed the commands of the higher faculties, mind and conscience. Unlike faculty psychologists, play advocates believed that no hard and fast boundaries separated the child's moral, intellectual, and physical faculties. These faculties formed a single integrated system where each was an equal partner of the others. External conditioning of one faculty automatically affected the others. Since, according to play organizers, the musculature was the most accessible, easily trained and controlled of the three faculties, it was the one most readily influenced by social conditioning. In short, control the muscles and you control the mind and conscience.

On organized playgrounds the confluence of moral and cognitive elements into a flow of controlled muscular activity could be seen in the behavior of what play advocates called the "efficient" or "ideal" team player. During a baseball game the player's moral intent—his willingness to obey the rules of the game—and his cognitive analysis of the game's events and the responses demanded of him were welded into an undifferentiated and fluid muscular response. Play organizers assumed moral intent and cognitive analysis dissolved into, and became inseparable from, muscular activity during the game. Henry Curtis, director of the Washington, D.C., playground system from 1905 to 1909 and a nationally known leader of the play movement, described how this happened during a baseball game.

> One boy is on first, and another is on second. A fielder gets a liner in the middle field. Shall he throw the ball to first, or second or third? Shall he try to touch the runner and make a double play? *He must decide in a quarter of a second and act upon that decision instantly* or he will never make a successful player. If his judgment is right, handkerchiefs are waved and he is generously applauded; if he makes a mistake, he is hissed and called a fool. . . . the game imparts to the mind an alertness and vivacity which are essential to any large success either in business or society. [Italics added.][6]

The player was not supposed to interpret the implications of the game situation and then act. There was no time for deliberation. The team's success—and his teammates' evaluation of his behavior—depended upon the player's split-second alertness: he had to be instinctively poised to act. In other words, his muscles had to do his thinking for him. This demanded a merger of the player's analytical powers, moral control, and physical skills into an integrated and relatively unemotional flow of coordinated muscular action, a moral and cognitive physicalism, whose consequences could be objectively analyzed by teammates and spectators.

For play organizers, physicalism was a form of social training in which the youth's subjectivity was deemphasized. In order to perform effectively he had to analyze the meaning of a game situation quickly and objectively, and then act decisively. The "facts" of the game, not his subjective moral predispositions, had to guide his behavior. A disciplined physicality, which blended cognition, moral awareness, and muscular coordination, was seen as the most socially desirable expression of his moral intent and social aptitudes. The efficient team player was one whose private moral realm was reduced to his muscular reactions. Play organizers designed their social-training techniques with an eye toward equating physical appearance with moral intent. On the organized playground, in theory at least, if you knew what a player did, you knew what he was. The theory of moral and cognitive physicalism reduced the player to his overt, analyzable behavior.

It is not surprising that Henry Curtis, and other early twentieth-century urban child savers, focused on physical activity and the need to respond quickly and decisively to physical sensation in their social training methods. They were, after all, urban reformers, and even those reformers who were not anti-urban perceived the city as dangerously overstimulating. The child's audio-visual senses were inundated by an incessant stream of sensation.[7] To make matters worse, by 1910 most inhabitants of New York City, Boston, and Chicago—the centers of the play movement—were immigrants and their children. Their strange modes of speech and dress were supplemented by stranger religious and social values. Organized play programs were aimed at these "foreign" populations. Play organizers differed in their attitudes toward immigrants. Most play advocates agreed, however, that unrestricted Asian and southern and eastern European immigration generated social disorder and existential disorientation—for both immigrants and longtime residents. The more crowded and "foreign" cities were, the more it seemed as if city dwellers were strangers (and, therefore, mysterious and threatening) to each other.

Although the moral and cognitive physicalism promoted on playgrounds could not lower the decibel level in cities, it might make the youth more capable of coping with the urban jumble of sights, sounds, and smells by honing his perceptual faculties and by training him to respond decisively to unexpected sensations—just as the team player had to be poised to react to unexpected game situations. Moreover, physicalism might lessen the pervasive tensions that, according to play organizers, existed between ethnic groups, because it de-emphasized the significance of the individual's private realm of culturally determined values. The player's behavior, his willingness to obey the rules of the game, and his ability to get along with teammates were more important than his ethnic origins. Regardless of his ethnic or class background, the team player was what he appeared to be—he was his behavior. In addition, play organizers stressed those aspects of team games and team membership that were thought to be ideal social training for young people in a society becoming more organizational, bureaucratic, and corporate each year. They emphasized the importance of observing the rules and regulations of the games, as well as the need to subordinate personal ambition for the good of the team.

A second important feature of the play movement was its influence on the modern adolescent experience. Some behavior patterns we think of as typically adolescent, while not necessarily originating in the period between 1880 and 1920, were cultivated by the social-training techniques used by play organizers and other Progressive Era child savers and educators. This is especially true of the extreme form of adolescent peer-group conformity so prevalent among twentieth-century American youths.[8] Such extreme conformity is not an inevitable psychological adjunct of adolescence, but a pattern of behavior deliberately instilled in American youths. The team experience was consciously designed by play organizers to generate an extreme form of peer dependence in adolescents.

This policy evolved for a number of reasons. By 1880 "modern adolescence" had existed for perhaps half a century,[9] and few urban institutions existed to help the youth traverse the rocky road from adolescence to adulthood.[10] The peer group was supposed to fill this void by providing moral guidance and social direction to young people when they were not under direct adult supervision. To an extent, peer-group direction was designed as a substitute for family supervision, which play organizers thought an inept agency of discipline and social control. Advocates of play generally saw the plight of the urban ghetto youth in the darkest terms: he ran wild in the streets while his overworked, ignorant, or negligent parents sat in dark tenements unaware of his activities. For this reason play advocates perceived the peer group as a community-controlled institution providing adolescents with values and skills that were not being transmitted by the urban, especially ethnic, family.[11]

Play organizers could not, however, guarantee the behavior of the peer group. They encouraged peer direction because they thought its social expressions would be managed by institutions controlled by adults, like the playground.[12] Play organizers did not foresee the possibility that the peer group might eventually break away from adult control, and evolve into a "youth culture," or possibly even a counterculture. In the course of the twentieth century this is precisely what happened.[13] Play organizers, of course, did not create adolescent peer conformity; peer direction had existed among American and European youths since the eighteenth century.[14] Play organizers simply tried to control adolescent peer conformity for their own ends.

We can understand those ends only by linking playground social training to its potential effects on the youth's personality, especially in the moral and cognitive areas. During the past decade, historians of the child-training techniques of Progressive Era social and educational reformers have asserted that progressives wished to manipulate the child in order to make him a contented, productive, cooperative citizen of an emerging corporate state. According to these historians, reformers wanted to instill conformity in, and guarantee "social control" of, urban young people.[15]

Progressive Era child savers were indeed manipulative and obsessed with the desire to control the young. There is nothing, however, uniquely "progressive" about these wishes. All forms of socialization are manipulative and seek social control of the young. These labels tell us nothing specific about the intentions of child savers during this period.

Playground child training was a complex affair. It was designed to create a new equilibrium between a series of binary values and sensibilities, such as individualism and cooperation, initiative and caution, and—despite the emphasis on peer direction—personal freedom and group control over the individual. Reformers were convinced that a twentieth-century urban civilization could not enjoy economic prosperity or political democracy if its social and economic interactions were based upon what they saw as the unrestrained "survival of the fittest" individualism of the nineteenth century. Play organizers were equally certain, however, that economic prosperity and social progress could not be secured in a collectivist society. Playground social training, therefore, was designed to create a new and viable middle ground or equilibrium between individualism and collectivism. Play organizers stressed social order over individual freedom, cooperation between groups instead of competition between individuals, and peer-approved goals rather than individual aspirations. They did not, however, want to destroy the individual's freedom, his economic initiative, or his quest for advancement; they wanted to foster a new balance between these values and their counterparts, a balance that would harness individual drives to communal ends.

In chapter 5 I draw a psychological profile of this new equilibrium as it was expressed in the personality of the ideal adolescent team player. By "ideal" team player I mean one who embodied in unadulterated form the values promoted by play organizers. I do not claim such a person existed. The psychological profile is an attempt to expose the ideology of play organizers and describe, in terms of personality characteristics, their version of the ideal twentieth-century American citizen.

Whether these child-training techniques were successful is another matter. Children do not necessarily incorporate values they are exposed to in schools, homes, religious centers, or playgrounds. Moreover, playgrounds were not run like public schools; children were not given grades that became part of a permanent, historical record. We have no way of knowing what actually transpired during team games —what the youngsters saw, felt, or thought about their experiences. We do know, however, what play organizers wanted them to experience. If the psychological profile is impressionistic and drawn from one-sided data, it nonetheless provides important clues about how specific social-training practices can alter the psychological balance between binary sets of values. This approach uncovers the motives and goals of play-organizing child savers more effectively than the use of ahistorical terms such as "manipulation" and "social control."

The tensions between binaries such as freedom and order, and individualism and cooperation, referred for the most part to the economic order. Many Progressive Era reformers believed unregulated economic individualism was ruinous to social order and individual stability. When these binaries are viewed within the context of playground social training, however, it becomes clear that their meaning transcended both the economic order and the playground itself. The concern with economic binaries was but one ideological layer in a series of behavioral binaries, each linked to the others by a compelling cultural fault line, which led ultimately to the issue of masculine and feminine social roles. The ideal team player's personality represented a balance between other binaries, such as rationality and intuition, and initiative and passivity, that could be mobilized for economic ends but were not solely economic in nature. Many play organizers assumed that all the bipolar sets of values and sensibilities mentioned were rooted not in economic interactions, but in a primeval existential split between feminine and masculine predispositions. Generally, women were characterized as passive, domestic, emotional, intuitive, and self-sacrificing; men were perceived as aggressive, worldly, rational, empirically oriented, and self-interested. Because of their temperaments and intellectual orientations, men were ideally suited for competing in political and economic activities, while women were generously endowed with emotional and intellectual proclivities that made them incurably domestic and maternal.

The notion that sexual characteristics determined behavior and social roles was, of course, an axiom of mid-nineteenth-century thought.[16] What makes the play movement so interesting in this regard is that play organizers designed, though not always consistently, social-training methods that were supposed to harmonize and integrate traditionally bipolar masculine and feminine traits into the personality of the ideal team player—who was, by the way, a male adolescent.[17] The reasons for this shift toward integration of stereotypical sexual-social characteristics, which was the heart of the play movement's ideology and reason for existence, are discussed in chapters 5 and 6.

Finally, the play movement invites our careful study because it is an excellent example in microcosm of how Progressive Era child savers, and reformers generally, tried to forge social reform through administrative techniques. Reformers of that period are well known for their tendency to equate social amelioration with effective bureaucratic administration.[18] Play organizers tried, however, to bureaucratize more than processes and programs, that is, play and playground administration. They were equally intent upon making young people operate in an efficient, regulated, and organized fashion. Play organizers' ideas about how to administer things tended to penetrate their attitudes toward child training and human behavior in general. Their mission, as they saw it, was to train the urban young to think and feel in a regulated, efficient manner. The ideal team player was a thing, a process, and, like any other process, he had to be efficiently organized in the interests of social order and harmony.

These strategies for analyzing the movement to organize children's play uncover three important aspects of the relationship between child training and social reform in the years 1880 to 1920. First, the psychological profile of the ideal team player demonstrates that it is not enough simply to state, as some historians have, that Progressive Era reformers equated social amelioration with efficient bureaucratic control by the state over an ever-increasing number of activities. Implementing social improvements, through bureaucratic or other methods, is one thing; educating society's children to adapt to, and perpetuate, the bureaucratic model is quite another. Historians should also study how reformers during the Progressive Era tried to orient young Americans toward life in a bureaucratic society—a society, that is, where even the most private problems and aspirations were subject to public scrutiny and administrative regulation.

How did play organizers teach young people to relate their personal problems to public issues? How were they trained to look to public agencies, rather than to their families, for guidance? How did playground social training harmonize traditional American values, particularly the ideal of the free, enterprising, upwardly mobile individual, with the constraints upon individual freedom that inevitably accompany bureaucratization? Put another way, how did the personality created by playground social-training methods harmonize with the values of both the nineteenth-century enterprising American and the twentieth-century organization man? The psychological profile of the ideal team player links reform ideology, particularly the desire of reformers for bureaucratic efficiency, to child-training techniques designed to prepare the young for life in an organizational society.

Second, the psychological profile demonstrates that the child psychologists and educational and social reformers involved in the play movement wanted young people to be autonomous as well as group-directed. Both tendencies were emphasized in playground training. The ideal team player was not simply a conformist or an example of what David Riesman, in *The Lonely Crowd,* called other-directed. The player was other-directed, but that was only one feature of his personality. Playground training wove conformity and autonomy into a multidimensional personality that reformers believed was not only radically different from what they saw as the dominant personality traits of nineteenth-century Americans, but also perfectly suited to meet the stresses and challenges of twentieth-century urban-industrial society.

Finally, the analysis of the reform dimension of playground social-training methods demonstrates that attempts to create a specific personality type had broad cultural ramifications. The values and sensibilities instilled in the player did not exist in a cultural void. A person is not simply trained to be kind or aggressive, rational or intuitive, autonomous or group-directed, and so on. He is usually trained to incorporate particular values and sensibilities into overarching behavioral styles, particularly those involving sex roles. This was evident in playground social training, for the changes play organizers tried to effect in the player's moral and cognitive styles reflected other, seemingly unrelated, cultural changes they wanted to foster as well, especially with regard to sex roles. The psychological profile of the ideal team player sheds light, then, on aspects of social reform between 1880 and 1920 that transcended the organized playground.

The subject matter is complex, and the methods used to interpret it are unorthodox. In the interest of clarity I have divided the book into three sections. In Part One, chapters 1 through 4, the play movement is approached as a social-political reform effort. The ideas and aspirations of play organizers are presented with a minimum of interpretation, for it is essential that the reader obtain an unadorned picture of the play movement from the perspectives of its founders. Part Two interprets those perspectives. Chapter 5 contains the psychological profile of the ideal team player. Chapter 6 consists of an extensive psycho-biographical study of a prominent play organizer, Jane Addams. The purpose of this chapter is to analyze the relationship between changes in nineteenth-century sex role prescriptions, as expressed in Addams's life, and the social-training methods employed on organized playgrounds. Finally, the concluding section is a synthesis of key issues discussed in preceding chapters. In this section the cultural implications of playground social-training methods are discussed, along with the historiographic implications of my interdisciplinary methodology.

PART ONE

Organizing Children's Play

Inside the playground an absolute and peculiar order reigns.
JOHAN HUIZINGA

We are learning in a new field, what was taught by the economic world a generation ago; like industry, recreation has become a matter of public concern; *laissez-faire* can no longer be the policy of the state.
—Michael Davis, 1910

1

The Organization of Children's Play:
Institutional Phases, 1880–1920

On 23 October 1917 in Washington, D.C., Secretary of War Newton D. Baker delivered a speech to officials of the Army's division of recreation, the National Conference on War Camp Community Service (WCCS). WCCS was organized earlier that year by Baker and officials of the Playground and Recreation Association of America, the country's largest and most prestigious recreation association. According to Baker, the purpose of WCCS was to provide recruits with "wholesome" social activities and recreation during the emotionally difficult weeks following their induction into the army. Baker told his audience of professional recreation workers that WCCS should "hold up" traditional moral standards to recruits uprooted from family and community ties. By sponsoring team games, Bible classes, and supervised dances, WCCS would provide the "one . . . great social restraint" missing from the lives of uprooted and thus morally "confused" inductees: "the sanction of personal approval of the people with whom they have to deal."[1]

In Baker's view, both the creation of WCCS and its role in the war effort were logical culminations of the movement to organize the play of urban young people, which, he indicated, had begun some seventeen years earlier. In 1900, as in 1917, one of the major social problems in the United States was the existence of millions of uprooted people who for one reason or another had been wrenched from family discipline and from community "restraints" upon their behavior. Baker, a former progressive mayor of Cleveland and an acknowledged authority on urban affairs, said the difference between the two periods was that in 1900 the social dislocation had been caused by the peculiarities of American city life rather than by war. The influx of millions of non-English-speaking aliens during the last two decades of the nineteenth century, as well as the physical contours and residential mobility characteristic of American cities, had generated an atmosphere of moral anonymity.[2] In Baker's view, the absence of moral accountability and behavioral restraints was symbolized by the inability of city parents to control, or even keep an eye on, their restless, street-wise children.

> A boy in the country was known to everybody in his neighborhood. His misconduct was marked. The boy in the city could be a saint in the first ward, where he lived, and a scapegrace in the tenth ward, without anybody in the first ward discovering it. There was an absence of that pressure of neighborhood opinion . . . which was evident in the countryside where conduct was more obvious.[3]

Children playing on the sidewalk on New York's Lower East Side.
(Library of Congress)

The play movement began when urban reformers "discovered" that the organization of children's play, especially supervised team play for male adolescents organized by social workers on municipal playgrounds, would insulate youngsters from pervasive city vices, act as a deterrent against juvenile crime, and provide adolescents with the supervision and moral purpose missing from their lives. According to Baker, the play movement was a vital agent of social reform because it instilled moral values and social aptitudes that helped prepare youths for the perils, prospects, and imperatives of city life, and did so in a manner that promoted the behavioral restraints he associated with community life in the nineteenth-century American small town.[4]

Clearly, Baker thought the urban playground was more than a place where youths exercised, found refuge from the physical and moral perils of the city, and occupied themselves during hours when they were removed from parental and school supervision. For Baker and other urban reformers the movement to organize children's play was not so much a reform undertaken on the child's behalf, as was legislation limiting the employment of children, but a medium created to reconstruct and control his moral values.

While Baker's emphasis on the social utility of organized play accurately reflected the attitudes of fellow reformers, the enormous success of the play movement in the first two decades of the twentieth-century was the product of more than good intentions. The institutions created by play organizers to administer playgrounds and to propagandize the value of organized play were equally important. Contrary to Baker's opinion, the organizational phase of the play movement began nearly two decades before 1900.

PRELUDE: PLAY AND SPORTS IN THE MID-NINETEENTH CENTURY

Before discussing the origins of the play movement proper, it might prove useful to contrast early nineteenth-century attitudes toward play with Baker's ideas. Baker lived in a post-Darwinian world where biologically oriented child psychologies emphasized the developmental character of the life cycle. Childhood was defined as a psycho-physiologically determined stage of life, utterly distinct from other life stages, with its own "laws" of development and behavior. Every aspect of the child's life, including play and morality, had to be molded in accordance with the child's phase-specific needs and capacities. Consequently play and morality were qualitatively different experiences for children and adults: beings at opposite ends of the developmental spectrum could not be measured with the same psychological yardstick.

By contrast, while pre–Civil War Americans viewed the child as distinct from the adult, they often perceived the difference as quantitative rather than qualitative: children were less than adults—physically and mentally immature—but not necessarily distinct beings. Prewar generations seldom linked particular games or styles of play with the child's phase-specific developmental needs. Nor, in contrast to Progressive Era play organizers, did they believe that structured play experiences could effect changes in the child's psycho-physiological inheritance. Prewar Americans, in short, did not approach children's play from the perspective of evolutionary theory.[5]

This is not to say prewar America was a land without play. Americans in those years were, however, clearly ambivalent about play in general and children's play in particular. While Americans seldom passed up opportunities to watch boxing and wrestling matches, horse and boat races, or to participate in games of bowling and shuffleboard, these activities were more akin to recreation than play, especially when they were pursued casually. They were diversions, forms of relaxation for the overworked or, less charitably, underworked adult. No doubt games like football, baseball, and bowling provided antebellum youths and adults with healthy exercise, but exercise per se had little to do with the way Baker and other play advocates approached play. For play organizers, play was a scientifically structured experience characterized by a wide variety of forms that corresponded to distinct phases of the life cycle. Infant games must not simply amuse the child; rather they should be used to prepare his mental and physical faculties for the next developmental phase. This view of play would have had little meaning to many antebellum Americans.[6]

Indeed, some evidence suggests that prewar Americans were inclined to passively witness, and actively wager on, boxing matches and horse races, rather than to participate in strenuous games or other forms of exercise. One historian has observed that most eighteenth- and early nineteenth-century Americans thought exercise "unfashionable"—"Neither in east nor west did Americans esteem the human body."[7] Henry Adams went so far as to say that in the Boston of his youth, "sport as a pursuit was unknown."[8] Oliver Wendell Holmes was more caustic. City youths in particular, he observed, were a "set of black-coated, stiff-jointed, soft-muscled, paste-complexioned" beings. He found it exceedingly difficult to believe such creatures "sprang from Anglo-Saxon loins."[9] In 1856 the editor of *Harper's* was more succinct: "the rocking chair is an American invention, and is expressive of the physical inaction of the people."[10] As late as 1859 an English observer painted a gloomy picture of the physical condition of Boston youths. "A Boston boy is a picture of prematurity. It can almost be said that every man is born middle aged in the Union. . . . Athletic games and the bolder field sports being unknown, all that is left is chewing, smoking and drinking."[11]

If Baker's view of play would have puzzled prewar Americans, his belief in its moral utility would have shocked them. One attitude toward children's play in that period was summed up in the school master's axiom: "Those who play when they are young will play when they are old."[12] Play was the antithesis of work. Perhaps this belief was a legacy of Puritanism. After all, in 1647 the General Court of Massachusetts outlawed bowling because "much pcious [sic] time is spent unfruitfully" in its pursuit.[13] Seventeenth-century Calvinists agonized over the social and moral degeneracy spawned by card playing, gambling, and cock fights.[14] Or perhaps the notion that play was morally harmful stemmed from the need to tame a wilderness and push back the frontier. Seventeenth- and eighteenth-century Americans had precious little time or energy to expend on rigorous games.[15] By the middle of the nineteenth century the United States was a burgeoning industrial society committed to the proposition that personal industriousness was the key to social and individual prosperity. This attitude was hardly compatible with a positive view of play.

It would be misleading, however, to assume that Americans ignored the significance of physical fitness prior to 1860. If some Americans resisted the temptation to play or prohibited their children from playing, others viewed play as vital for physical health and as essential to the moral well-being of youngsters. A number of New Englanders who had studied in German universities before 1860 were exposed to the physical fitness philosophy of Friedrich Jahn. Jahn, a fervent German nationalist, believed the heroic qualities needed to unify Germany could be instilled in young people through rigorous physical discipline and gymnastics. Jahn's American disciples founded a number of gymnasiums in Massachusetts during the 1820s and 1830s. The first attempt to incorporate physical education into the school curriculum, at the Round Hill School in Northampton, Massachusetts, in the 1820s, was inspired by Jahn's philosophy. At Round Hill teachers emphasized the relation of exercise to the pupil's moral and physical well-being. The school's cofounder, the historian George Bancroft, noted that gymnastics promoted moral purity by occupying students during hours when they were neither in class nor studying. Bancroft's notion of "moral purity" was one-dimensional by the Darwinian standards of the Progressive Era: it was not particularly child-centered or phase-specific, but applied equally to all ages. According to Bancroft the main function of gymnastics was "to keep watch over health."[16] One proponent of physical fitness in that period observed that exercise checked "indolence and listlessness" in the young,[17] while another noted that exercise injected a needed dosage of "savage life" into the overly civilized "soul" of the city dweller.[18]

Thus, while some Americans saw play and exercise as fostering "indolence," others viewed it as an invaluable antidote to laziness. In either case, however, many Americans in this period were not inclined to view play as an integral part of the life cycle or as useful for the political socialization of the youth. Mid-century Americans who thought about play largely approached it in negative terms: play and exercise prevented physical atrophy and moral "indolence." What, if anything, play promoted in young people besides physical vigor and a static notion of "moral purity" was not often investigated.

Attitudes of intellectuals toward play and exercise were equally ambivalent. On one level, the philosophical idealism common to many prewar thinkers often compelled them to scorn physicality. Physicality at best distorted, and at worst corrupted, the absolute realms of spirit and beauty. Some prewar intellectuals believed physical inaction a condition for meaningful intellectual activity.[19] Among idealists this attitude was modified after 1860 by Friedrich Froebel's kindergarten pedagogy, which emphasized the relationship between intellectual development and children's play. But even American disciples of Froebel thought children's play significant mainly for what it revealed about their intellectual processes rather than their bodies. What was important was the "Idea" realized by play activities, not the physical acts themselves.[20]

There were exceptions. As Roberta Park has recently pointed out, some noteworthy proponents of idealism, Emerson and Thoreau among them, were keenly interested in physical fitness. According to Park, these intellectuals believed physical vigor and mental rigor went hand in hand as essential ingredients for optimal human development.[21] This attitude was a genuine precursor of Progressive Era notions about play.

This rare positive attitude toward play was not shared, however, by most park planners. Frederick Law Olmsted's monumental work on New York City's Central Park before the Civil War and his creation of Boston's park system after the war exemplify mid-century ambivalence toward play and physicality. Olmsted designed his parks to foster what Geoffrey Blodgett aptly called "a highly contemplative sort of recreation." In Olmsted's view, the intrusion of rural beauty and idyllic calm into the "urban wilderness" would help soothe the battered nerves and senses of factory workers and their harried employers. The idea of setting aside space in his parks for rough and tumble athletic games horrified him.[22]

Before and after the war some college administrators actively promoted intercollegiate athletics. Between 1826 and 1831 gymnasiums were built at Harvard, Princeton, Yale, and Amherst.[23] The emphasis at these institutions, as at Round Hill, was on individual gymnastic exercise rather than on group games. After the war, team games became favorite collegiate pastimes. Football in particular was played with fanatical intensity—and without protective padding—in many colleges. But even in the 1880s some college officials were dismayed by the popularity of these games. President James McCosh of Princeton was disturbed by what he saw as the immoral influence of competitive games upon students.[24]

Because mid-century Americans were ambivalent about play, sport, and recreation, it is dangerous to categorize their attitudes one way or the other. Regardless of their opinions about children's play, however, prewar Americans did not systematically link the social issue of children's play to the psycho-physiological problems of child development. Nor is this failure surprising, since they lacked a Darwinian perspective of ontogenesis.

Sport, as distinct from children's play, did have a major role within certain mid-century ethnic and status communities. Unassimilated ethnic groups, especially Scots and Germans in the 1850s, organized sport clubs. Scottish Caledonian clubs and German Turner societies provided concrete links with old-country traditions and offered members psychological shelter from the indifference or hostility of native Americans. For these ethnic communities, sport clubs created a sense of common identity and ideological cohesiveness.[25]

Ironically, sport clubs also became popular with certain native elite groups. In the burgeoning urban-industrial world of mid-century America, nothing seemed certain except the inevitability of change and the inexorability of democratization. Elite groups, wary of the democratic threat to both their status and their version of "gentility," organized exclusive social clubs. Some clubs sponsored athletic and sporting events, emphasizing golf, tennis, and yachting, which their organizers felt promoted a genteel, respectable style of life and manners. It was through the activities of these clubs that such sports became associated with elites.[26]

Finally, a word is in order about the rise in the popularity of sport in the late nineteenth century and its relation to the play movement. By the 1880s the sporting craze was sweeping the country. Baseball had begun to arouse the passionate spectator interest that would soon make it the national pastime. Scores of amateur and professional baseball teams were organized and attracted tens of thousands of fans yearly. Cycling became a national passion, as auto racing was later to become.[27] Equally significant, Americans wanted to read about sporting events and figures almost as much as they wanted to watch races and to play games. In the 1870s and 1880s magazines as different in their readership as the *Police Gazette* and *Scribner's* published numerous articles on sports. With James Gordon Bennett's *New York Herald* leading the way, most major newspapers established separate sports departments.[28]

Scholars have offered a number of reasons for the postbellum rise of sports. Americans had more leisure time and, therefore, greater opportunity to play games and watch others play. The mass production of sporting goods made equipment available to the majority of people at reasonable prices. Intellectuals who wanted Americans to retain the physical valor, sense of purpose, and national identity of the war years, saw the cooperation, uncritical loyalty, and physical rough and tumble of team games as moral and social "equivalents of war."[29]

On the whole these developments were of relatively marginal significance to the play movement. While the sporting craze made it easier for play organizers to persuade the public of the importance of children's play, the roots of the two phenomena were distinct. Play organizers discouraged spectatorship, for example, because they thought it was morally hazardous. "Rooting" encouraged players to strive for victory at all costs; it was therefore inimical to the development of sportsmanship and respect for rules and order. The rise of sports was to some degree a response to a craving for recreation among those with increased leisure time, while the play movement had little to do with recreation. Play organizers did not want children to relax, or nonchalantly pass the time of day on playgrounds. Organized play was a means of shaping mental and moral faculties: it had little in common with the escapism of either sport or casual recreation. Organized play, as play advocates were fond of pointing out, was educational, not recreational: it was related to physical and psychological development as well as to political socialization. The rise of sport was also a multifaceted phenomenon. Its proponents hailed from all classes, ethnic groups, and regions. By contrast, the play movement was directed almost exclusively toward working-class youngsters dwelling in urban ethnic ghettos. Most play advocates were middle class, Anglo-Saxon, and Protestant. While the rise of sport and the movement to organize children's play coincided in time—and no doubt reenforced one another to some degree—they were far apart in motivations, leadership, and goals.

THE BEGINNING OF ORGANIZED PLAY: SAND GARDENS, VACATION SCHOOLS, AND SCHOOL PLAYGROUNDS

A modest initial attempt to organize the play of city children was made in Boston in 1886. Someone suggested that the city establish and maintain a European innovation called "sand gardens" for preschool youngsters who lived in heavily trafficked slum wards. This proposal was significant for two reasons. First, it was addressed to social conditions Progressive Era reformers would cite as the reasons for the play movement's existence: poverty, congestion, filthy slums, and inadequate parental supervision of children. Second, the proposal was made by a medical professional, Dr. Marie Zakrzewska, who related city children's physical health and moral well-being to their social, economic, and aesthetic environments. In a letter to the Massachusetts Emergency and Hygiene Association, Dr. Zakrzewska excoriated the effects of slum conditions on children of the poor, and urged the association to assist in alleviating these conditions by establishing sand gardens. These devices, which Zakrzewska had observed on a recent trip to Berlin, were simply piles of sand bordered by wooden squares large enough to accommodate five or six children. Zakrzewska hoped they might keep unsupervised small children from playing in congested, foul, and dangerous streets.[30]

The following year Boston officials approved construction of ten sand gardens in the city's poorest districts. Sand gardens were usually supervised by kindergarten teachers. By 1895 they were common features in most school yards and in settlement houses like Chicago's Hull House and New York City's Henry Street Settlement.[31]

Sand gardens were hardly a solution to the staggering problems of child welfare. They accommodated only a small fraction of a city's young and were irrelevant to the problem of adolescent play. Their establishment was, however, an initial attempt to deal with the inadequacies of public recreational facilities and parental supervision.[32]

The first significant attempt to organize the leisure time of the urban young was the establishment of vacation schools. These schools, like sand gardens, first appeared in Boston in 1885 and then spread rapidly to New York City, Cleveland, Chicago, and Pittsburgh. Vacation schools were organized by philanthropic groups to keep the children of the poor out of mischief during the summer months and to provide them with vocational training. Through excursions into the country, vacation schools also gave city youngsters a respite from the "artificiality" of city life.[33] The schools were funded by private organizations, including the Association for the Improvement of the Poor in New York, the Civic Club in Pittsburgh, the Playground League in Rochester, and the Massachusetts Civic League in Boston. By the late 1880s, however, most vacation schools were administered by boards of education and staffed with professional educators.

Usually vacation schools were located in public school facilities and conducted four- to six-week programs. Curricula varied from school to school and city to city. Each of Boston's five vacation schools emphasized training in a different industrial occupation, ranging from carpentry and iron work for boys to various branches of "domestic science" for girls. By contrast, the Chicago vacation school curriculum, developed by John Dewey, offered young people a wide variety of activities including gymnastics, musical training, and nature study, as well as the industrial "arts."[34] Regardless of curriculum, the main objectives of the vacation school were to organize the activities of city children during the summer and expose them to vocational and domestic studies. They were also seen as ideal media of "Americanization." For example, in a vacation school run by the Pittsburgh Playground Association, children sang patriotic songs before going to classes. As a New York City district school superintendent pointed out, vacation schools Americanized foreign-born parents as well as their children, because youngsters inevitably brought home social skills and "manners" learned in school.

> The immediate results are apparent in betterment of conditions in the tenements. Table cloths have been introduced where none were used, and families have gathered around the board and eaten a well-cooked dinner when our little housekeepers have from chaotic disorder evolved something akin to comfort. This means a great step toward civilization.[35]

The use of public school buildings for vacation schools paved the way for philanthropists to demand the construction of summer play facilities on school grounds. By the mid-1890s civic groups and settlement workers were requesting that school boards furnish funds and personnel needed for summer school playgrounds. The most conspicuous victory in this campaign was won by Jacob Riis in 1895 when he persuaded the New York City Council to approve a bill mandating that new schools have open-air playgrounds on their premises.[36]

By 1895, it was clear that sand gardens, vacation schools, and summer school playgrounds were inadequate for meeting the recreational and social needs of city children. According to one play organizer, these facilities could not accommodate adolescents, and it was foolhardy to exclude adolescents from structured play activities, for as soon as young children outgrow small playgrounds and vacation schools they "find their way into the Juvenile Court."[37] Reformers wanted spacious, year-round supervised play facilities capable of accommodating children of all ages. Moreover, it was essential to staff play facilities with social workers who understood children and who also understood the significance of what reformers called the "play instinct," that is, the child's biologically conditioned impulse to play. As this phase of the movement to organize children's play gathered momentum during the mid-1890s, many vacation schools were either closed—so all effort and funds could be devoted to playground development—or moved onto playground sites.[38]

THE PLAYGROUND MOVEMENT: LOCAL INITIATIVES, 1887–1906

What was a playground? First and foremost, it was an organized alternative to unsupervised street play. Street games like stick ball, prisoner's base, tops, and marbles were dangerous not only because they were played in busy streets, thereby posing a danger to both players and passersby, but also because they were unsupervised by adults. They were controlled by a more or less autonomous street culture, where might often made right and where bullies flouted game rules at will. Play organizers argued that the moral and social lessons implicit in these games were lost if left to the vagaries and "anarchy" of the street. In short, they felt that children's play was too important to be left to children.

While all play organizers frowned upon street culture, they were not always in agreement about the functions or appearance of an ideal playground. The noted city planner Charles M. Robinson, for example, viewed the playground in much the same way Frederick Law Olmsted viewed the city park, as a sylvan sanctuary from the pressures of city life. "To my mind," wrote Robinson, the whole playground conception has heretofore been wrong. We have taken as our ideal a bare city lot equipped with paraphernalia for children's exercise. The truer ideal would be an acre or so of natural looking country, which we should create if necessary and where a chance for the city child to know the delights of a real outdoors, of a place where in the night there might be fairies, as there never would be in the ordinary city playground.[39]

While Robinson's idyllic playground might attract fairies, it would be unlikely to attract the slum children the reformers wanted to reach. Most play organizers wanted supervised playgrounds built in a city's most congested immigrant "colonies." If space permitted, the playground might be "embellished with plants and shrubbery."[40] After 1903, however, most playgrounds were constructed in small vacant lots in the city's poorest wards. Limitations of space and money in these areas compelled play organizers to settle for something less than "natural looking country."

The typical urban playground was likely to be bounded on three sides by the drab, prison-like stone or wooden background provided by

Children on a New York City playground, ca. 1908. (Library of Congress)

dilapidated tenements, and on the fourth side by a noisy, congested street. The largest portion of the facility was reserved for team games, particularly football and baseball. The remaining space was filled with paraphernalia for smaller children's games: slides, seesaws (which cultivated both a "sense of balance" and "a certain feeling of responsibility"), sand gardens, and perhaps horizontal bars. As one play organizer pointed out, such a playground was hardly redolent of Coney Island, but then the point of organized play was not to amuse the child but to coordinate his psychological and physical "apparatus as efficiently as possible."[41]

The drive for municipally owned playgrounds where youngsters could play games supervised by social workers did not become part of the urban reform movement until the late 1880s. The movement was strongest in the industrial Northeast and in Chicago and was led primarily by social settlement workers.[42]

In New York City the movement to organize children's play began in 1887, when the city passed a law written by the noted settlement leader Charles Stover. The law permitted the city to spend up to one million dollars a year for the establishment of small parks and play-

The "Poverty Gap" playground in New York City, photographed by Jacob Riis in 1889. (Library of Congress)

grounds. But members of the city council were reluctant to spend these funds, and the law became a dead letter. Not one cent of the earmarked funds was spent by the city until 1901.[43]

Stover was incensed by the council's myopia. This gifted graduate of Union Theological Seminary suffered grave doubts about the relevance of traditional Christian dogma to contemporary social realities. In the mid-1880s he gave up his ministry and joined Stanton Coits's Neighborhood Guild (later called the University Settlement) on the Lower East Side. Stover was shocked by the absence of play facilities in that part of the city and by what he termed the public's "dense ignorance" of the needs and problems of its children. He believed that organized, sustained lobbying efforts by concerned citizens might persuade lawmakers to spend funds allocated by the 1887 law. With the aid of Jacob Riis and Mayor Abram Hewitt, Stover launched the New York Society for Parks and Playgrounds in 1891. The society's efforts had little effect upon City Council members, most of whom were dubious about the necessity of organizing children's play and about the right of the government to do so. Although the society was instrumental in persuading city officials to level the infamous Mulberry Bend slum on the Lower East Side and erect a park in its place, the funds for the creation of a network of fully equipped, supervised playgrounds in the city's ghettos remained unused.[44]

In 1898, Stover created another organization aimed at mobilizing the city's moral and financial resources in support of playgrounds. With the help of Lillian Wald of the Henry Street Settlement (who argued that the power to influence slum children was "given to those who play with, rather than to those who only teach, them"),[45] Riis, Ethical Culture Society director Felix Adler, and J. G. Phelps Stokes, Stover launched the Outdoor Recreation League. The league was financed by the city's Social Reform Club and the Athletic Association of New York. At its own expense, the league opened the city's first outdoor playground in Hudsonbank Park, later named DeWitt Clinton Park, in 1898. The following year, the league organized a large playground on the site of municipally owned Seward Park. According to Riis, the experimental playground in Seward Park on the Lower East Side succeeded in a way that would have pleased Olmsted and Robinson.

> The sight of these little ones swarming over a sand heap until scarcely an inch of it was in sight, and gazing in rapt admiration at the poor show of a dozen geraniums and English ivy plants on the window-sill of the overseer's cottage, was pathetic in the ex-

treme. They stood for ten minutes at a time, resting their eyes upon them. In the crowd were aged women and bearded men with the inevitable sabbath silk hat, who it seemed could never get enough of it. They move slowly, when crowded out, looking back many times at the enchanted spot, as long as it was in sight.[46]

These and other playgrounds started by the league were operated, staffed, and maintained at its own expense until 1902. In that year, Stover finally persuaded the city to assume fiscal and legal responsibility for them.[47]

The Outdoor Recreation League's major contribution to the play movement was its success in persuading the city to assume ownership of playgrounds. From 1887 to 1900 New York City spent none of the earmarked playground funds, but between 1900 and 1915 it spent over 17 million dollars.[48] With the league's lobbying mission successfully completed, and with Stover installed as commissioner of city parks, the league was disbanded in 1910, leaving the field to the recently organized Playground Association of America and to the city's bureau of recreation.[49]

In Chicago, social settlement workers also led the way. Graham Taylor's Chicago Commons was one of the first settlements in the country to rent vacant lots in slums, equip them with play facilities, and hire directors to supervise children's play. Taylor eventually persuaded city officials to assume responsibility for the operation of these playgrounds.[50]

Hull House was not far behind the Commons in recognizing the importance of supervised play. In the early 1890s Jane Addams ordered the construction of a sand garden and small playground on the settlement's grounds. Space was scarce at Hull House, and residents were compelled to experiment with games requiring less space than football and baseball. The settlement's residents invented a game called "indoor baseball," which required only one-third the area needed for regular baseball. This game became very popular with other settlements hard pressed for space. Addams was immensely pleased with the playground experiments at Hull House. She was convinced that organized sports "will be the only agency powerful enough" to break the cycle of crime and poverty in slum wards.[51]

Taylor and Addams, along with Charles Zueblin of the Northwestern University Settlement, led the Chicago play movement in the 1890s. They urged lawmakers to create a network of playgrounds in the city's immigrant wards because they believed supervised play, especially team games, to be an effective agent of Americanization. "We are," said Zueblin, "welding the people together as in a great melting pot on the playgrounds of Chicago."[52] The efforts of Chicago's settlement leaders were spectacularly answered in 1903 when construction of the massive, innovative South Park System began.

This system consisted of ten parks, the majority of which were located in the most congested, impoverished immigrant wards. Each park had an athletic field for adolescent team games, a small playground for young children, indoor gyms for men and women, a track, an outdoor pool, and—the crowning glory—a field house which included a library, lecture hall, and club rooms. During its early years the system accommodated about five million South Side residents annually.[53]

No other city built recreational facilities comparable to the vast South Side System, but the progression from initial agitation and experimentation by private groups to municipal ownership of playgrounds was common to most major cities. In Boston the Massachusetts Civic League, under the dynamic leadership of the philanthropist Joseph Lee, organized experimental playgrounds and lobbied for municipal ownership. In 1900 the league started a "model" playground in North End Park that catered exclusively to adolescents, most of whom were children of immigrants. They played supervised team games that, according to Lee, impressed upon them "the essential qualifications of the citizen." The city eventually assumed the expense of maintaining the playground.[54]

The pattern of movement from private experimentation to public ownership was the same in other cities. In Philadelphia the Culture Extension League began the agitation for municipal playgrounds in 1893. In Rochester it was the Children's Playground League; in Baltimore the United Women of Maryland; and in Detroit the Department of Philanthropy and Reform of the Twentieth Century Club.[55]

The distinctive feature of this initial phase of the play movement, with the notable exception of Chicago, was its relatively short-lived success. Although play advocates persuaded some public officials that organized play was vital to the moral well-being of city children and that its provision should be a government responsibility, they did not succeed in equating organized play with public schooling as a responsibility of government. The movement for compulsory mass education resulted in a dramatic increase in taxation, and city officials were loath to ask citizens to support playground construction, supervision, and maintenance. During the last years of the nineteenth century municipally owned playgrounds deteriorated, and in some cases came "to such a condition as to be known as public assignation places."[56] City governments failed to retain skilled play directors and to repair or replace damaged equipment. There were a number of reasons for this.

Most organizations that agitated for playgrounds were concerned with other aspects of urban reform as well, and had neither time nor money to follow up their initial successes in the play area. If the city did not provide adequately trained play directors or pay them enough, there was little a settlement or an associated charity could do to remedy the situation. Indeed, although most of the organizations that lobbied for playgrounds demanded expert supervision, they offered few concrete ideas about how personnel might be recruited and trained. Consequently most playgrounds, especially those catering to adolescents, were ill-equipped and inadequately supervised.[57]

In addition, although some play organizers believed that properly directed play activities promoted Americanization and were deterrents against juvenile crime, there did not yet exist a body of thought that systematically portrayed the role of play in ontogenesis and socialization. It was one thing to state, as did one play organizer, that "a playground built to-day saves the building of a jail to-morrow," but quite another to demonstrate why this was so. Even so eminent and popular a play advocate as Ben Lindsey, the "children's judge," found it hard to convince frugal taxpayers and wary elected officials that supervised playgrounds more than paid for themselves because they reduced juvenile crime. With neither the resources to sustain organized lobbying efforts nor a compelling theory of the meaning of play, the movement to organize children's play began to lose momentum by 1905.[58]

Finally, the early phase of the playground movement lacked ideological consistency. Some play organizers, for example, wanted responsibility for supervising play activities placed squarely on the shoulders of public school teachers. Other play organizers were loath to entrust this responsibility to educators, whom they thought to be ignorant of the child's nature and incapable of understanding the moral and intellectual significance of physical activity.*

By 1905 the movement to organize children's play was floundering. It had alerted the public to the moral dangers of the "street," and had persuaded some city governments to construct and maintain play facilities in slum districts. The movement had not, however, been able to sustain itself within individual cities or move beyond local roots to establish a national organization. Nor had play organizers been able to persuade citizens to support year-round play facilities. While the play

*Play organizers' opinions about the public school and public school teachers are discussed in chapter 3.

movement had appeared to be gaining momentum in the mid-1890s, by 1905 only twenty-four cities in the United States operated a total of eighty-seven playgrounds, and most of these were open only during the summer.[59]

Some reformers argued that the play movement would languish unless an adequately funded national organization was created to mobilize support for publicly financed playgrounds. In their view, it was foolhardy to advocate the organization of children's play without knowing how many children in which cities lacked adequate parental supervision and neighborhood play facilities. These reformers needed reliable data about the social composition, recreational needs, and financial resources of every American city. A national playground association was also needed to lobby for government financing of play facilities and to tap the economic resources of wealthy individuals and corporations.

In 1906, under the leadership of Henry Curtis, Joseph Lee, Jane Addams, Jacob Riis, and Luther Gulick, and with the financial backing of the Russell Sage Foundation, such an organization was created.

THE PLAYGROUND ASSOCIATION
OF AMERICA, 1906–1920

The idea of organizing a national playground association originated with Henry S. Curtis, a student of the eminent psychologist G. Stanley Hall. After earning a Ph.D. in child psychology from Clark University in 1898, Curtis was appointed director of New York City's playground system. During his three-year tenure in this post, Curtis, with the help of Dr. Luther H. Gulick, the director of the city's public school physical education program, supervised playground programs in the city's poorest wards. In 1902 Curtis studied recreation administration in England and Germany, where he developed a distaste for what he called the "individualistic and militaristic" implications of gymnastics. He believed team games were more "social" and democratic than gymnastics and should become the focus of the play movement in America. Upon his return to the United States in 1905, he was named director of the Washington, D.C., playground system. By then he thought the time was ripe for the creation of a national playground association, and he asked Gulick to join him in the venture.[60]

The choice of Gulick was a wise one. No American in 1905 was more knowledgeable about the problems and prospects of physical education and children's play. Gulick was born in 1865 in Honolulu. His father, the Reverend Luther H. Gulick, Sr., had been sent there by the American Bible Society to convert the "natives." After spending his formative years in missionary outposts in Honolulu, Japan, and Italy, Gulick attended Oberlin College intermittently between 1880 and 1885. The Oberlin years were troubled ones for him. He was incessantly haunted by doubts about his "calling" to the ministry, and depressed by his inability to follow in his father's footsteps. Plagued by intense migraine headaches, which often forced him to miss classes, Gulick stumbled through these years, uncertain of the strength of his commitment to the ministry and unable to secure a foothold in an alternative career.[61]

His situation changed dramatically one Sunday afternoon in 1885. Gulick and a roommate were sitting beside a rail fence on the Oberlin campus discussing their common inability to choose careers when it suddenly occurred to Gulick that organized physical education was every bit as useful in the modern world as organized religion. Indeed, the friends wondered whether physical education might have the same "uplifting" relation to the body as religious education had to the soul. Was it possible, Gulick wondered, that "good bodies and good morals" went hand in hand? Was there a relationship between physical discipline and moral rectitude? Could the physical discipline inherent in

Luther H. Gulick, Jr. (1865–1918). First president of the Playground Association of America and perhaps the play movement's most sophisticated theoretician. (Library of Congress)

team games effect "direct spiritual results?" Gulick answered these questions in the affirmative. "That day," he said in retrospect, "that hour, was a turning point."[62]

In 1886 Gulick became director of the Young Men's Christian Association's Gymnasium in Jackson, Michigan, the beginning of his long association with the YMCA. Between 1886 and 1898 he was director of the association's physical education department at Springfield College in Massachusetts. His major goal as a physical educator was to shift the emphasis away from "Germanic" gymnastics and exercise for the individual and toward a program of physical discipline stressing the "social" aspects of recreation. This meant a shift toward team sports. Using the psychological theories developed by his friend G. Stanley Hall, Gulick explicitly linked the moral lessons and "technical" skills learned by the "team player" to the attitudes and aptitudes necessary for the citizen's adaptation to modern society. Among other things, his experiments with team games at Springfield College were directly responsible for the invention of that quintessential team game, basketball, whose invention is generally credited to one of Gulick's students, James Naismith.[63]

Perhaps Gulick's commitment to investigating the relationship between physical discipline and moral rectitude was most aptly illustrated by his decision to study medicine. He believed that the scientific study of the body might divulge a nexus between physicality, control

Henry Curtis: a founder and first secretary of the Playground Association of America. (National Recreation and Parks Association)

of the emotions, and morality. In 1889 he graduated from New York University's Medical College.[64]

Between 1889 and 1905 Gulick had refined his ideas about the moral relevance of physical training, and he readily agreed to Curtis's invitation to join him in creating a national playground association. Gulick was convinced that the play movement had floundered in the 1890s because it lacked a systematic theory to describe the role of play in the child's moral and physical development. Gulick had such a theory, and he felt that a national organization would give him a forum to promote his ideas and put them into practice.

Gulick and Curtis invited Joseph Lee, the wealthy Boston philanthropist and founder of the Massachusetts Civic League, to become president of the proposed association. Lee's efforts on behalf of urban children, especially his administration of experimental playgrounds in Boston and his collaboration with Louis Brandeis in a successful campaign for a juvenile court system in Massachusetts, had made him a nationally known expert on the plight of city youngsters.[65] Curtis and Gulick were disturbed by Lee's involvement with the Immigrant Restriction League, but they were convinced that although Lee wanted to limit the right of southern and eastern Europeans to come to the United States, he was equally intent on both "Americanizing" them and fostering their welfare once they became citizens. Since they shared these latter sentiments, Gulick and Curtis hoped Lee would join

Joseph Lee (1862–1937). Second president of the Playground Association of America and one of the play movement's leading theoreticians. (Library of Congress)

them. Lee declined, however, and suggested instead that Gulick and Curtis join the recently formed American Civic Association of St. Louis, which was also interested in launching a national playground association.[66]

Gulick and Curtis preferred their own path. They contacted reformers, mostly settlement workers interested in children's play, including Lillian Wald, Jane Addams, Graham Taylor, Mary McDowell, and Jacob Riis. All of these reformers agreed to join them. In the spring of 1906 an organizational congress was held in Washington, D.C., and the participants agreed to call their organization the Playground Association of America (PAA). The association received the imprimatur of Theodore Roosevelt at a well-publicized White House ceremony.

The following year PAA delegates gathered in Chicago to work out the details of organizing a national playground movement and elect officials.[67] Roosevelt was named honorary president, Riis honorary vice-president, Gulick president, Curtis secretary, and Addams a vice-president. Lee, who had been persuaded by his friend Jane Addams to join the PAA, was also named a vice-president.[68]

The Chicago delegates declared that the purpose of the PAA was

Four members of the Washington, D.C., Playground Association attending the Playground Association of America's national convention in New York City, September 1908. (Library of Congress)

to secure for urban children "their natural birthright—play," under the auspices of "elevating leadership." The author of this statement of purpose, probably Curtis, was quick to point out that securing play facilities for urban children meant more than simply keeping youngsters off the street. The organization of children's play was an integral part of the urban reform movement and an essential tool in the struggle against poverty, vice, and political corruption. The scope of the PAA, then, was "as broad as the impulse to play is universal."[69]

Just how broad its scope should be was spelled out by Gulick a few years later in an amendment to the PAA's "statement of purpose." The movement to organize children's play was relevant to the solution of the most abrasive social problems confronting the United States.

> Dependency is reduced by giving men more for which to live. Delinquency is reduced by providing a wholesome outlet for youthful energy. Industrial efficiency is increased by giving individuals a play life which will develop greater resourcefulness and adaptability. Good citizenship is promoted by forming habits of co-operation in play. People who play together find it easier to live together and are more loyal as well as more efficient citizens. Democracy rests on the most firm basis when a community has formed the habit of playing together.[70]

Despite its lofty purposes and its influential founders, the PAA would not have been viable without the financial support of the Russell Sage Foundation of New York City. An observer attended the Chicago congress and sent an optimistic report of the PAA's prospects to foundation president John M. Glenn. Gulick was singled out as the outstanding leader and most acute theoretician of the play movement. Glenn invited Gulick to become director of the foundation's education and recreation department. Gulick countered by suggesting that the Sage Foundation create a "playground extension committee," with himself as chairman, to act as a liaison between the foundation and the PAA. Glenn consented, and Gulick became head of both the PAA and the extension committee. The Sage Foundation paid his salaries for both posts. The purpose of the playground extension committee was to funnel money from the foundation to the PAA to pay for publicity campaigns, lobbying efforts, and staff salaries.[71]

The PAA was organized as a federation. Autonomous playground associations were established in major cities, mostly in the industrial Northeast. These local associations were represented by delegates on the PAA's board of directors. The de facto policy-making body of the

PAA, however, was the New York City branch of the board's executive committee. The New York branch was headed by Gulick and included Wald, Lee, Curtis, and Mary Simkhovitch. Gulick divided board members into three committees, each of which was asked to "scientifically" analyze a specific aspect of play and playground organization. These aspects included the creation of standards of "optimal" physical fitness for specific age groups, methods for training playground directors in normal schools, and the organization of lobbying efforts.[72]

In Gulick's opinion, the PAA had to convince Americans that "the organization of leisure is just as important and technical a matter as the organization of industry."[73] Play organizers should make the local playground "a sort of public settlement"—a "melting pot of the races" —where "Jews and Greeks, and Italians and Slavs" might develop what Curtis called "that sense of trust and affection which is essential to highly organized and frequent play."[74] Finally, urban surveys had to be made in order to determine the recreational needs of every city, and pressure had to be put on boards of education to make physical education compulsory in public schools.[75] The responsibility for achieving these goals fell for the most part on the shoulders of the PAA's field secretaries and playground directors.

The Field Secretary and the Urban Survey
In 1907 Gulick appointed Lee Hanmer, former director of Maine's Charity Organization Society, chief field secretary of the PAA. Hanmer's duties included collecting data about the status of public and private recreation facilities in cities with populations exceeding five thousand, and helping cities that requested the association's aid in launching a playground system.[76] Three years later Gulick appointed a field secretary for each of three regions: the Northeast, Midwest, and West Coast. At the same time, he notified officials of every city in the nation of the existence and availability of field secretaries.[77]

The field secretary's duties were outlined by Gulick in 1909. The efficient organization of recreation required two processes. First, it was necessary to make a citywide survey to ascertain how the inhabitants used their leisure time. The field secretary was to take a district census, dividing inhabitants into ethnic, class, and occupational categories and tabulating the number of people using private recreation facilities, such as dance halls, billiard parlors, and taverns. Through this method the PAA would discover who was using which facility during what hours. Once they had this information, it would be relatively easy for field secretaries to decide which types of "wholesome" public recreation facilities were needed to direct people away from "immoral" private forms of recreation.[78]

Second, the field secretary had to formulate a comprehensive, economically viable recreation plan for the entire city. He had to present recommendations to city officials and persuade them to hire experts to administer the new program.

> Not only must municipalities and philanthropic associations coordinate their efforts in some harmonious scheme, but the whole plan must be administered by experts with definite goals in view. It is not enough to give everyone the chance to play. We must also direct that play to specific as well as attractive ends.[79]

Gulick's guidelines for making urban surveys became the focus of the field secretary's work. In 1911 Rowland Haynes, field secretary for the Midwest and perhaps the PAA's most successful field worker, applied Gulick's theories in Milwaukee. The results were so successful they became the model for PAA urban surveys.

The first thing Haynes did in Milwaukee was obtain data about the city's most congested immigrant districts, or "foreign colonies" as he called them, including the number of children who lived there. He got this information from settlements and associated charities. He then made a survey of how primary and secondary school children used their spare time. While these data were being tabulated, Haynes plotted the amount of street space available for play in comparison with the number of people living on the most populous blocks. He investigated commercial recreation establishments and made a survey of the number, ages, ethnic origins, and occupations of their patrons.[80]

> There are three standards for judging the quality of recreation. First is the purely recreative standard. Does the given form of recreation make the persons using it more or less fit for their regular working life? A second standard is the educational standard, for both physical and mental education. Does the given form of recreation bring about development along with the pleasure obtained? On the side of mental development, does the given form of recreation build up habits of quick thinking, of initiative in dealing with new situations, of self control, of ability to work with others in the give and take of group activities. Third and most important is the moral standard.[81]

After his data had been collated and analyzed according to these standards, Haynes found the recreation facilities in Milwaukee to be

both immoral and inadequate. The city's inhabitants collectively enjoyed 10 million hours of leisure per week. Yet they spent most of this
time in activities unrelated to educational development and moral
"uplift." For instance, the vaudeville, burlesque, and legitimate theaters played to a weekly audience of nearly 350,000, out of a total population of 400,000.[82] Haynes was outraged by the popularity of the legitimate theater, as were most other play organizers. Haynes's friend Jane
Addams incisively portrayed the theater's influence on the young people of Chicago:

> . . . while many young people go to the theatre if only to see
> represented, and to hear discussed, the themes which seem to them
> so tragically important . . . there is no doubt that what they hear
> there, flimsy and poor as it often is, easily becomes their actual
> moral guide. In moments of moral crisis they turn to the sayings
> of the hero who found himself in a similar plight.[83]

Another disturbing situation brought to light by the Milwaukee
survey was that the majority of children in the "foreign colonies"
played in the street. Since street play was illegal, the majority of the
city's young people were breaking the law and getting away with it.[84]
This was hardly the best way to teach respect for American laws to
children of the foreign born.[85]

Haynes recommended that city officials authorize a massive program of playground and social center construction in slum districts. He
also suggested that twice as much money be spent on supervision (including the salaries of play directors) as on equipment. Finally, Haynes
asked the city fathers to create a politically nonpartisan recreation
commission of experts to oversee the operation of the city's play facilities. City officials agreed to all of these suggestions and hired Haynes
to supervise the construction of Milwaukee's new playground system.[86]

Field secretaries were purveyors of the play movement's ideology.
They were responsible for making the PAA a genuinely national organization with a network of influence reaching into nearly every section
of the nation. Through their urban surveys, the field secretaries provided the association with knowledge of the political, social, and ethnic
contours of American cities that few public or private agencies could
equal.

The Play Director
Because "a playground left to itself stands for little but fresh air,"[87]
leaders of the PAA expended a good deal of energy and funds to recruit

and train play directors. Actually, the designation "play director" was a catchall term for a person entrusted with a wide variety of administrative and supervisory responsibilities. On a small playground, for example, the play director might be responsible for safeguarding and repairing swings and seesaws, organizing team games, and serving as umpire or referee. By contrast, on a large playground, such as one of those in Chicago's South Park System, directorship duties might be divided among three persons: a supervisor of the playground plant, a director of play activities, and a playground assistant, who officiated at games and took care of equipment.[88]

The most important and complex task assigned to a play director was the supervision of the young patrons. As the supervisor of the South Park System put it, play directors had to be "chemists of human desires" and "interpreters of child and adolescent life."[89] They also had to be martinets. Oakland's superintendent of recreation suggested that the ideal play director should have the same qualities as the "efficient" corporate manager or army officer.[90] An Ohio play director was more explicit: the playground was not an amusement park, but a "play factory" that must run on "schedule time" and "turn out the maximum product of happiness."[91] Indeed, the following description of the beginning of a "typical" day at a New York City playground operated by the board of education evokes images of a company town or boot camp: "It is one o'clock. The pianist has struck the welcome chord, and all the children assembled fall in line for the grand march. At a signal, the flag is saluted; then two or three patriotic songs are heartily sung, after which the order is given to 'break ranks.' "[92]

But the play director had to be more than a drill sergeant. Clark Hetherington, professor of education at the University of Wisconsin and special consultant to the PAA on playground organization, created a normal school training course for play directors. Hetherington's course, which was adopted by a number of normal schools, emphasized the biological, social, and psychological sciences rather than physical education. Physical education might be "the missing link in the present struggle for efficiency in education," but unless the playground director or school play supervisor understood the meanings of childhood and play he might retard the child's development.[93] As Hetherington put it:

He needs social psychology and sociology in order to put himself in the place of those whose spontaneous and instinctive activity he is to lead. In a country with the diversity of interests, mixture of national traditions, and variety of social conditions which this democracy has, the student of play needs to be a student of society, for we are coming to understand that play is one of the means, perhaps the most important means, by which society functions.[94]

PAA officials wanted the play director to have the same status as a social worker, just as the playground itself was to be a sort of outdoor social settlement. Like the college-trained social worker, the aspiring play director should be required to demonstrate his ability before he was certified as an "engineer of the big muscle activities of childhood and youth."[95] Henry Curtis designed a written civil service test for play directors, and the PAA persuaded a number of cities to adopt it and hire only those applicants who received training approved by the association. By 1915 there were 744 full-time and 5,000 part-time directors in the United States, most of them recruited from normal schools, settlements, and kindergartens.[96]

The play director had numerous duties. In order to provide a suitable model for children, he had to possess an "unsoiled" moral character. Play organizers assumed, moreover, that the proficient, skillful, successful, much admired director would provide a counter-model for

Supervised team games on Manhattan's Carnegie Playground.
(Library of Congress)

children whose immigrant fathers were neither especially successful nor much admired in their new country.[97]

The play director's other responsibilities were the development of a playground curriculum and the oversight and coordination of various special events, particularly play festivals and patriotic pageants. While director of the New York City and Washington, D.C., playground systems, Curtis developed a model playground curriculum that PAA officials encouraged play directors to emulate. For adolescents, Curtis designed the following after-school weekly schedule:

1:30–2:00, patriotic songs
2:00–2:30, supervised "free play": tugs-of-war, marbles, etc.
2:30–3:00, track and field events
3:30–5:00, team games, vocational training, and folk dancing.

Curtis emphasized that teams should be permanent in order to enable youths to develop a cohesive, stable sense of loyalty to peers. The director should also try to integrate playground and community by exhorting parents to attend weekly exhibitions of their children's activities.[98]

Play directors also supervised the "class athletics" and "badge tests." Class athletics were used by directors to promote group cooperation and deemphasize competition between individuals. Whether youths played team games or engaged in track and field events, play directors told them that they were competing as a "class," or team, rather than as individuals. The score compiled by a "class" of boys during a broad jump meet was computed by adding the individual records and dividing by the number of boys in the class. Directors hoped that this method of competition would encourage the less gifted athletes to participate and at the same time discourage "antisocial" forms of competition.[99]

On the other hand, "badge tests" encouraged competition, albeit of a unique variety. Badges of merit were awarded to boys who demonstrated "evidence of athletic prowess," but in this case "prowess" was defined as the attainment of a "prescribed standard of personal efficiency." The badges were given not as symbols of victory or of superior talent, but as evidence that the individual had "gotten the most out of himself," and exploited his abilities, however limited, to the fullest.[100]

The most common special events supervised by play directors were festivals and pageants celebrating patriotic holidays and stressing themes of national unity. The purpose of festivals was to instill "civic pride" in children and spectators. In New York City, for example, the Metropolitan Museum of Art, the Civil Service Commission, the De-

partment of Parks, and the PAA sponsored a Fourth of July festival in
1909 whose highlight was a parade of patriotic floats, built by the
children, depicting important events in American history. Some festivals had overt reform messages, such as the one held in Pittsburgh in
1911 in which fifteen thousand children, watched by thirty thousand
adults, enacted the "Pied Piper of Hamelin" in Forbes Field. According
to the festival's organizers, the point of the play was to demonstrate to
children and spectators that the "suffering of the village was brought
about by the greed and corruption of the council and the people of
Hamelin."[101]

The most common theme of play festivals was the dire need, as
Jane Addams put it, to generate a feeling "of companionship and solidarity" between immigrant groups.[102] In 1908 the director of the Philadelphia affiliate of the PAA described how play festivals promoted
national unity:

> German and Italian, Slav and Hebrew played side by side. The day
> was a prophetic glimpse of the social spirit which will one day
> permeate the commingled nationalities which in the modern in-

New York City youngsters learning patriotism on a New York City
playground, ca. 1908. (Library of Congress)

dustrial city now crowd and jostle each other. Field Day and playgrounds are weighty units in the mass into which a solid republic
is being welded, hammered into one rich alloy from many diverse
races and nationalities. The first annual Field Day of the Playground Association, with its five thousand six hundred participants, is only a beginning.[103]

Play directors and field secretaries were the neurons that transmitted the ideology of the play movement across the nation. The spectacular success of the movement to organize children's play after 1906,
the growing conviction of Americans that play was indeed the definitive characteristic of childhood, and the enormous increase in organized play facilities across the country were perhaps due more to the
daily toil of field secretaries in strange cities and playground directors
in equally strange "foreign colonies" than to the influence and visions
of the play movement's theoreticians.

ORGANIZING CHILDREN'S PLAY, 1906–1920

The first decade of the PAA was the golden age of the play movement.
While statistics often conceal more than they reveal, the spectacular
growth of municipal and private play facilities during these years cannot be denied. In the ten years ending in 1909 American cities spent
over 55 million dollars on play facilities, most of it after the founding
of the PAA in 1906. In 1905 24 cities operated a total of 87 playgrounds.
After the PAA's first year of existence the same 24 operated 169 playgrounds. More important, nearly two-thirds of the 200 cities with playgrounds in 1908 supported such facilities exclusively with public funds.
Between 1906 and 1916, PAA affiliates increased from 189 members to
5,000, and its yearly income increased from $2,164 to $115,455.[104]

Between 1910 and 1920 the increase in the number of organized
playgrounds was even more spectacular. The PAA collected data on the
annual growth rate of supervised playgrounds, and a comparison of
"playground progress" in two of the years between 1910 and 1920 provides an interesting perspective on the success of the play movement.
In 1911, 257 cities informed the PAA that they possessed 1,543 organized
playgrounds and employed 4,132 full- and part-time play directors. Of
the 257 cities, 83 had privately funded playgrounds, 88 were publicly
supported, and 86 combined public and private funding. In 1917, 481
cities operated 3,940 playgrounds and employed 8,748 directors, the
majority of whom obtained their jobs through civil service examina-
tions approved by the PAA. Of the 481 cities, 253 owned and maintained

playgrounds with public funds and spent a total of 6.5 million dollars for play directors' salaries and playground equipment.[105]

On the surface, the movement to organize children's play appeared to be a remarkable success story. Yet by 1917 there were signs of stagnation. While the movement appeared to be gaining support on the West Coast and in the Midwest, it never really transcended its New York City–Chicago–Boston axis. Of the 55 million dollars allocated for playground development between 1898 and 1909, nearly 35 million dollars was spent by these three cities.[106] The enthusiasm for organized play, while not confined to the urban Northeast, was less than overflowing in the West and totally dormant in the South, which had fewer large cities and fewer immigrants than the industrial Northeast.

Even in the urban Northeast and Chicago, play organizers found it hard to attract a substantial following from the youth group that was the primary target of playground socialization, the children of immigrants. Although accurate figures are difficult to obtain, it is unlikely that more than 10 to 20 percent of the children in "foreign colonies" attended organized playgrounds with regularity and became members of permanent teams.[107] Play organizers' reactions to this relatively small turnout were typical of their attitudes toward immigrants. Charles Zueblin placed the blame squarely on the immigrants. The Polish children of Chicago seemed "utterly unused to organization." Even those who attended organized playgrounds lacked "initiative," and were "ignorant" of the social and moral significance of team games. Yet Zueblin himself cited figures on park and playground construction in Chicago which help account for the relatively low rate of attendance and the lack of interest on the part of immigrant youngsters. In the city's eleven most affluent wards, there was one acre of park and playground area for 234 residents; in its poorest twenty-three wards, there were 4,720 people per park and playground acre.[108]

Zueblin's observations were made in 1898, five years before the construction of the South Park System and eight years prior to the founding of the PAA. Nonetheless, while play organizers lobbied, often with success, for playground construction in ethnic ghettos and slum wards, the attendance rate for both native and immigrant poor does not appear to have increased appreciably after 1903.[109] Some youngsters were not interested in organized games and sports; others were kept from playgrounds by parents who wanted their children to work or study after school, on weekends, and during the summer. Some immigrant parents equated play with idleness, playgrounds and parks with sexual licentiousness, and play organizers' intentions with "American" condescension.[110] But even if all the children of a city had wished to use organized playgrounds, there was not enough land available, particularly in crowded slum wards, to accommodate them. Nor, for that matter, were there sufficient funds to build and equip the number of playgrounds needed.

Thus, as early as 1910 Gulick lamented that playgrounds alone "can never be made to provide for the needs of all the children of the city." In 1917 Curtis observed that playgrounds were "not adequately realizing the ideals" of the play movement despite the significant increase in the number of organized playgrounds during the preceding decade.[111]

PAA leaders responded to the problem in two ways. In 1911 they changed the name of the association to the Playground and Recreation Association of America in an attempt to broaden its appeal. Some play leaders tried to extend their influence by promoting indoor recreation, especially within social centers.[112] However, though some play organizers believed club meetings, debating societies, and lectures were useful and uplifting, many doubted that social centers could provide the discipline and control associated with playground activities. In terms of moral and cognitive training, social centers were never more than adjuncts to organized playgrounds.

Play organizers were also ambivalent about using the public school to solve their problems. PAA policy makers, particularly Curtis and Gulick, believed the "only solution of the play problem" was the incorporation of the play movement into the school curriculum through physical education courses and extracurricular sports. The public school seemed an ideal solution to the two most vexing problems confronting the PAA: lack of funds and poor attendance. Compulsory school attendance laws would solve the latter, and the enormous increase in spending for public schools during the Progressive Era, especially for high schools, would eliminate the financial problem.[113]

To many play organizers, however, this solution was less than ideal. They argued that public schools, even those permeated with the values of progressive educators, were innately competitive institutions that could never convey to youngsters the moral importance of "team work." Competition for grades in the classroom would inevitably influence patterns of interaction within, and between, school teams. Since only a fraction of students possessed the ability to play on varsity teams, the problem of how to control the rest of them after school remained. Finally, by encouraging students to attend interschool sport contests and "root" for their school team, schools consigned most students to the status of spectators. Play organizers felt that moral values and cognitive skills instilled by team games were imparted to participants, not to spectators for whom the team experience had no meaning.[114]

The public school did nevertheless become the focus of organized play after 1920.* With the American entry into World War I most of the PAA's funds and nearly all the energies of its members were geared to the war-related activities of War Camp Community Service. By 1920 voluntary play organizations like the PAA had clearly passed the boom stage, and were overshadowed by the public school.[115]

In effect, this is what play organizers had sought all along. From the beginning of the movement, play organizers saw themselves as pioneers whose task was to explore, experiment, and then hand over the gains to the state. They wanted the government to be responsible for children's play, and by 1920 reformers had succeeded in making organized play a concern of public policymakers.

More important, play organizers had convinced some influential Americans—especially those holding the purse strings of municipal governments—that organized play had moral and political implications. These Americans were now persuaded that play was a vital medium of cultural transmission, and that team games were essential for promoting ethnic harmony, physical vigor, moral direction, psychological stability, and specific social skills in urban young people.

The organizational phase of the movement to organize children's play, then, was successful. We need to know, however, why this was so.

*This development meant in part that the approach to children's play would become far more diverse than it had been on playgrounds operated by voluntary play organizations inspired by a more or less consistent ideological perspective. Unlike the voluntary organized playground, the public school was subject to pressures from a wide variety of political and parental groups, each of which possessed its own conception of education and of the educational and social value of physical education and interscholastic competition. In short, the history of organized play changed dramatically once voluntary organizations like the PAA were overshadowed by the public school.

There is a sense in which all good conduct and morality might be defined as right muscle habits.—G. Stanley Hall

2

Child Psychology, Physicalism, and the Origins of the Play Movement

The movement to organize children's play was part of a general upheaval in attitudes toward childhood. In the quarter-century between 1885 and 1910, Americans redefined the social and moral implications of traditional child-rearing practices. In a sense, they rediscovered the child during these years, for the psychological and biological characteristics of this "new" child were radically different from those of his mid-nineteenth-century predecessor.

One of the most significant consequences of this upheaval was the emergence of theories of child psychology grounded in the biological and environmental assumptions of Darwinism. These theories, particularly those of James Mark Baldwin, Edward L. Thorndike, G. Stanley Hall, and John Dewey, had a profound impact on the processes of redefining childhood. Before the Civil War, the child was defined mainly in terms of his moral predispositions and social roles. Although he may have been seen as different from the adult in physical and mental capacity, his behavior was measured with the same moral yardstick. Both child and adult possessed an innate, God-given moral kernel, or soul, which made them human and distinguished them from brute nature. Both had the potential to develop moral autonomy and to withstand the materialistic and sensual lures of society. Thus, while for practical purposes the child was perceived as distinct from the adult, the difference was quantitative rather than qualitative: the adult was simply older and therefore more competent than the child.

49

Child and adult occupied different places on the same moral yardstick.

By contrast, post-Darwinian theories of psychology presented the child as an organism whose physiological qualities were as important as his spiritual and psychological ones. The child's psycho-physiological maturation was dependent upon his successful passage through distinct ontogenetic stages. Like his ancestors, the child had to evolve from one stage to the next: ontogenesis, like phylogenesis, was a struggle to create a delicate, if relatively short-lived, balance between the organism and his physical and social environments. The child's physical environment, like that of his forebears, had a bearing on the success of his maturation. Thus, according to the new psychologists, maturation was segmental and problematical, not linear and inevitable as many pre–Civil War thinkers had believed. Each stage of development had its own peculiarities, mandates, and "laws." As he reached each stage, therefore, the child's needs and behavior were utterly distinct from those of other stages, including adulthood. Child and adult could thus not be judged with the same moral yardstick.

Not only were the social-training techniques used on organized playgrounds rooted in the Darwinian assumptions of the new theories of child psychology, but the play movement's very existence was inseparable from the upheaval in child training mandated by these theories. The new theories focused on the significance of the child's material environment and the importance of his physical, as well as intellectual and psychological, development. It was this physicalistic dimension of the new theories that permitted play organizers to assume that supervised physical conditioning could determine what a child valued and how he thought.

PHYSICALISM AND TRADITIONAL CHILD REARING

Physicalism had two distinct but related implications for child training. First, it was a method of moral training. Play organizers linked the muscular coordination and "efficiency" acquired through careful physical conditioning to moral development and control. In fact, they argued that it was possible to determine both the content and strength of the child's moral faculty by means of prescribed, and repetitive, physical drills. The major purpose of organized play was to instill desirable moral habits through vigorous physical exertion.

Physicalism also had implications for cognitive training. Play organizers were obsessed with a desire to control their physical environment. The city in particular seemed to them a threatening hotbed of chaotic, truncated sensations. The sights, sounds, and smells of the city merged into an indistinct, unanalyzable, and overpowering assault upon the senses. According to Luther Gulick, the force and immediacy of urban stimuli threatened to overwhelm the child's delicate senses and permanently impede his capacity to sift through, isolate, and analyze the significant aspects of external reality.[1] By contrast, according to G. Stanley Hall, the rural youth could calmly cultivate an inner "garden" of subjective perception because he lived in a world where objects were more or less "at rest." The slow pace of rural life allowed the child to study objects at his leisure instead of being overwhelmed by them. The child rather than the object controlled the learning process in the country, whereas "the subjects which occupy the city child are mainly in motion and therefore transient." Cognition in the city was a truncated process: objects momentarily impinged upon the senses, then disappeared. Consequently, the child often succumbed to what Hall called "brain strain and over-stimulation." Traditional educational techniques, most of them based upon rural models of learning, would prove fruitless in the city.[2] In order to adapt to and control his environment the city youngster had to be trained to respond quickly and decisively to unanticipated events. He should be taught to pay careful attention to the physical qualities of his environment—to the stimuli that peppered his senses—and learn to analyze them objectively. Play advocates were convinced that supervised play activities could instill this capacity in city youngsters.

Physicalism was a radical departure from traditional approaches to child nurture. Through most of the nineteenth century Americans had assumed that mind and body occupied distinct spheres and that the mind was the superior faculty. The child, of course, could be socialized, but his soul, the essence that defined him as human, transcended the material world and constituted his link to God. Play organizers, on the other hand, argued that mind, body, and emotions were not distinct, separate "faculties" but existed instead on a fluid continuum, interpenetrating each other. They believed that muscular conditioning could influence the content and quality of mental and moral processes. Advocates of physicalism believed that external conditioning could transform the child's inner world, and alter his "essence."

An overview of eighteenth- and nineteenth-century perceptions of child nurture should clarify these differences. Child-rearing practices in these centuries were influenced by three views of the child's nature. The "conservative" Calvinist perspective was that the child was an innately depraved vessel of original sin whose asocial "will" and desires had to be broken or repressed in the interests of both social order and personal salvation. At the other extreme, a "radical" Protestant view, often associated with Transcendentalism, became popular with the educated middle class during the 1830s and 1840s. While the child might be a congery of wayward appetites, radicals felt that he also possessed a divine spark of innocence and an impulse for moral perfection. If not encumbered by undue external restraint or exposed at an early age to materialism and corruption, the child's innate capacity for spiritual perfection might attain fruition. A third, compromise view of the child's nature became popular after the publication of Horace Bushnell's *Christian Nurture* in 1847. Bushnell, a liberal theologian, saw the child as a bundle of contrapuntal tendencies that were neither good nor evil in themselves, but were capable of becoming socially manifest as good or evil. To a great extent, according to Bushnell, whether the child eventually came down on the side of God or the devil depended upon the quality of nurture that he received from his parents. They should encourage his good qualities and repress, though not with undue harshness, his negative ones.[3]

None of these views ever held exclusive sway over child nurture practices. Indeed, while the conservative notion of innate depravity was clearly on the wane by the 1830s, all three perspectives survived in one form or another, and found adherents in different social classes at different times. Perhaps this was because they possessed a vital element in common: the belief that the child was divinely endowed with a permanent spiritual nature. For good or ill, he embodied God's purpose. While external training might repress or cultivate specific behavioral expressions of his nature, it could neither destroy that nature nor transform it. In short, the child's essence or "soul" was more or less static.

This belief accounts for the moral individualism that dominated child-training practices prior to 1880. The conservative Calvinist might argue that the most efficacious means of placing the wayward youngster on the path to salvation was through a generous use of the rod, while the Transcendentalist protested that careful nurture permeated by love and understanding was more effective. But both camps agreed that external threats and importunities availed little unless the child, spiritually speaking, pulled himself up by his own moral bootstraps and used his God-given inner resources to control himself.

Thus, in mid-nineteenth-century orphan asylums and reformatories a common method of punishing the recalcitrant child was to put him in solitary confinement "so he could reflect on his vices."[4] Educators of the period continually emphasized the dangers of emulation. The welfare of both the child and society depended upon his capacity to march to his own inner moral tune, as God intended he should.[5] The emphasis on moral individualism was not simply an ideological reflection of economic individualism. Even proponents of the kindergarten, who scorned selfishness and economic individualism, organized their curriculum around the objective of instilling a relentless moral autonomy in the child. Only a "self-realized" individual was capable of mobilizing the moral fortitude necessary to establish a "spiritual union of all mankind."[6] These notions of the child as a moral island were based on a belief that each individual possessed an irreducible, indivisible spiritual essence that could, in one way or another, transcend worldly enticement.

Although Americans might argue about whether God was thinking of a devil or an angel when he created the child, no one doubted that the child was indeed one of God's creatures. On this basic level they knew who and what the child was. This certainty ebbed during the last third of the nineteenth century. A series of events drastically altered both the role of children in American society and the concept of childhood. By 1890 some of the country's ablest educators and psychologists, along with thousands of parents, felt the need to participate in a national "child study movement" in order to rediscover how their children functioned and why they behaved as they did.

What had happened? First, the theory of evolution cut down two vital props of traditional ideas about childhood. The very idea that mankind had evolved from "lower" creatures subverted the idea that each person was made in the image of God and embodied a preordained divine purpose. More significantly, the theory of evolution suggested that the initiative for both human development and social change came from environmental pressures rather than from divine or human intelligence. The purpose of life, which proponents of evolution blithely defined as "progress," was achieved by the adaptation of organisms to changes in the external environment. As John Dewey put it, Darwinism implied a shift away from "an intelligence that shaped things once for all to the particular intelligences *which things are even now shaping*" [italics added].[7] In other words, mind, soul, spirit, or whatever one chose to call man's irreducible "inner" divine reality, was the result rather than the cause of history. Whatever man was, he was less a purveyor of a divine purpose than an evolving *physical* organism whose destiny was determined by his ability to adapt to what Dewey aptly described as "things."

None of the traditional conceptions of the child's nature could survive this aspect of Darwinism because all of them adhered to the idea that the child possessed a spiritual dimension that transcended environmental conditions and pressures. It would be incorrect to assume that all Americans suddenly discarded their preconceptions about childhood in the wake of the Darwinian revolution. Nonetheless, by the 1890s, Americans had begun to reconsider fundamental propositions about the meaning of childhood. The child study movement, progressive education, and the play movement, all of which were grounded in Darwinism, provided evidence of this reconsideration.

Reasons other than Darwinism compelled them to take another look at the older propositions. As Joseph Kett has shown, the Industrial Revolution generated economic and demographic changes that prolonged both the duration of childhood and the dependency of young people. An increasingly productive economy created new opportunities for economic and social mobility. But the new economy was complex as well as productive, and in order for young people to take advantage of it they had to prolong their period of schooling. Therefore, "youth," which had been thought of as a rather broad, ill-defined period of time between leaving home and making a mark in the world, began to be equated with the period of schooling and of preparation for adapting to the vagaries of an ever-changing social economy. By 1880, particularly for the middle class, youth had become associated with dependence upon, rather than independence from, parental and school authority.[8]

Prolongation of dependency made youth both more conspicuous and more problematical. On one level, the young person was both child and adult. Dependence made him a child, while intellectual and sexual development made him physically, at least, an adult. At the same time, however, he was neither a child nor an adult, for he was not allowed to assume social roles peculiar to either stage. The result was a pervasive sense of confusion and maladjustment on the youth's part, and a failure to provide him with a defined social role on society's part. By 1900 it was common for Americans to call this period of preparation and uncertainty "adolescence." Whatever they called it, this period of life created problems that compelled Americans to rethink or discard many traditional notions about the nature and social meanings of childhood and youth.

As Americans during the Progressive Era redefined childhood and youth, their principal tools included not only evolution-based psychological theories but also a commitment to careful, "scientific" observation of children. As the progressive educator Michael V. O'Shea noted, study of children before 1880 "had been principally of an incidental or intuitive kind, just as before the time of Bacon nature was studied intuitively." The Darwinian revolution overthrew "formalistic metaphysical and religious" assumptions about how the child's mind worked, and caused Americans "to make scientific what has heretofore been only intuitive."[9]

Among the educators and psychologists who tried to make the study of childhood "scientific," John Dewey, G. Stanley Hall, James Mark Baldwin, and Edward L. Thorndike are especially relevant to an understanding of why Progressive Era Americans sought to organize children's play. These educators disagreed with each other, sometimes vehemently, on many fundamental issues,[10] and not all of them had documentable influences on the ideas and behavior of play organizers. Baldwin's theory of imitation, for example, will be discussed not because play organizers explicitly subscribed to it, but because their playground social-training techniques emphasized the centrality of emulation in the child's development. On the other hand, Hall's and Dewey's influences on the play movement were more direct. Henry Curtis and George Johnson, two of the play movement's most important spokesmen, earned doctorates under Hall's tutelage at Clark University. Luther Gulick and Hall were close friends and frequently discussed the moral and social implications of organized play. At the same time Dewey had a profound influence on Gulick. When asked to define his philosophical perspective, Gulick said he considered himself a Deweyan pragmatist. Jane Addams's relationship with Dewey, particularly during the early years at Hull House, is well documented.[11] But what is important is not how each child psychologist influenced particular play organizers, but how the social-training methods employed on playgrounds were directly or indirectly related to the diverse and sometimes contradictory currents of thought about children during the Progressive Era.

G. STANLEY HALL

Hall was born in 1844 and grew up in the small farming community of Ashfield, Massachusetts. At eighteen he entered Williams College, and after graduation attended Union Theological Seminary in New York City. But Hall found the empiricism of modern psychology more compelling than the metaphysics of old time religion. After studying in Germany for three years, he earned a Ph.D. in psychology at Harvard in 1878. Three years later he was named professor of psychology at Johns Hopkins University. But it was not until his appointment as president of Clark University in 1889 that Hall established a reputation as the country's most learned and controversial authority on child development.[12]

Hall was known to a generation of concerned parents and educators as the father of the child study movement. During the 1890s he brought to Clark some of the brightest young psychologists in the country, including Lewis Terman, Edgar Swift, William Burnham, and Frederic Burke. Under Hall's dynamic and often imperious leadership, his students attempted to discover, or rediscover, who and what the child was. In the words of Hall's able assistant Sarah Wiltse:

> Previous to 1880 practically no scientific observations of child life had been undertaken in America. There were no data for comparing feeble-minded and normal children on entering school, and one searched libraries in vain to find what the average child could either know or do at a given age.[13]

Most of the "scientific" analyses of child life made by Hall and his students were based upon questionnaires they designed and distributed to parents, educators, and child study groups across the country. The questionnaires supposedly measured how children and adolescents thought, felt, and behaved in specific social situations. For example, when one of Hall's students wanted to know the "relative importance of city and country in shaping character," he designed a questionnaire and sent it to nearly two thousand educators in rural and urban school districts. His questionnaire measured the "relative" degrees of altruism, selfishness, and "imitativeness" among urban and rural youngsters. After observing and questioning their students, the teachers completed the forms and returned them to Clark University, where they were tabulated. Presumably, the results charted the interaction between environment and character formation.[14]

Questionnaires were devised to measure children's feelings about punishment, property, leadership, pity, and disobedience. Between 1890 and 1910, hundreds of thousands of completed forms were collated and analyzed by Hall and his students. Their conclusions were published in the *Pedagogical Seminary* (later the *Journal of Genetic Psychology*) and the *American Journal of Psychology*, both of which Hall founded and edited.[15]

Hall's critics questioned both the statistical methods and scientific validity of his version of child study; they even more gravely doubted the theory that Hall had used in designing and interpreting the questionnaires. Hall believed the child's physiological and psychological development "recapitulated" what he called "racial history." Each ontogenetic stage re-created specific psychological and physiological events experienced by the child's forebears untold ages ago. Hall argued that the adaptive behavior that allowed primitive man to survive created habits that were eventually somatically ingrained as instincts. The instincts, transmitted across generations, existed in what Hall called hierarchical "zones" or "strata" of the psyche. As the child passed through the stages of life, the psychological attitudes and physical postures ensconced in specific psychic "zones" made themselves felt. Thus, the ten- or eleven-year-old betrayed a restlessness and desire for adventure corresponding to the nomadic period of "racial" social organization. On the other hand, the adolescent's peer-group orientation and clannishness were redolent of tribal psychology. As Hall put it, the "child is father of the man in a new sense" because "his qualities are indefinitely older and existed well compacted untold ages before the more distinctly human attributes were developed." More succinctly, the child was the adult's "half-anthropoid ancestor."[16]

Hall claimed that his version of the recapitulation theory was solidly grounded in evolutionary theory. In fact, both Charles Darwin and Herbert Spencer had implied that evidence of species mutation was implicit in ontogenesis. Darwin assumed that the child's emotional development corresponded to the historical evolution of affect in the "race," and Spencer had based his tentative notions of biological recapitulation on studies conducted by German embryologists. Following Spencer's lead, Hall pounced upon "evidence" of the embryo's cold-bloodedness and rudimentary gill slits as proof of biological recapitulation. Thus, the infant's "wonderful power to cling and support itself for a minute or two during the first few weeks after birth" was interpreted as a recapitulation of mankind's "arboreal" past.[17] Although he never produced solid evidence to substantiate his theory, Hall argued that, psychologically and biologically, ontogeny recapitulated phylogeny, and that biological and psychological recapitulation were correlated processes.[18]

What emerged from these ruminations was a confusing, and at times contradictory, genetic psychological theory concocted from a potpourri of Darwinism, neo-Lamarckianism, primitivism, and geneticism. To Hall's satisfaction at least, the application of genetic psychology to the studies of child development undertaken at Clark "proved" that the child's ontogenetic development was homologous to specific historical phases of human social and presocial organization.[19]

The recapitulation theory's standing within the scientific community during the Progressive Era was dubious to say the least. Nonetheless, it was the ideological heart of a child study movement that attracted thousands of people to its banners between 1890 and 1910.[20] The theory was successful because it replaced what Darwinism had destroyed. The recapitulation theory once again made the child and his behavior comprehensible to adults. It was true that Hall's theory substituted a precivilized "wild animal," our "half-anthropoid ancestor," for the empyrean innocent of the mid-century Transcendentalists. Still, the child was an ancestor, half-anthropoid or otherwise. Hall's primitivism located the child in space and time by tracing his untamed instincts and often asocial behavior to ancestral roots, and by suggesting that his behavior had evolutionary logic: it was necessary for the survival of the species as well as for his personal development.

Primitivism was the cornerstone of the recapitulation theory. According to Hall, primitives did with their muscles and instincts what modern men did with their minds or with mechanical devices. The same held true for differences between children and adults. The modern adult was primarily a thinker. But the child was a throwback to a mental and moral universe predating the ages of rationalism, science, and industrialism. Like his nomadic and tribal ancestors, who seldom survived if they experienced significant gaps between knowing and doing, the child thought and moralized with his muscles, senses, and instincts. For both primitives and children, muscular conditioning was the key to mental and moral efficiency. In Hall's words:

> The muscles are nearly half the body-weight. They are the organs of the will . . . and if they are kept at concert pitch the chasm between knowing and doing, which is often so fatal, is in a measure closed. There is no better way of strengthening all that class of activities which we ascribe to the will than by cultivating muscle.[21]

Hall contended that the adult and the child lived in distinct moral universes. In terms of civilized manners and morals "children are more or less morally blind."[22] It was fruitless for parents and educators to use didactic moral tales to instill "right conduct" in youngsters. It was equally meaningless to cite a rising juvenile crime rate as proof that young people's morals were in a state of decay. Because children were "all instinct," morality for them was action. That is, their morality was encoded in an instinctual apparatus programmed to react instantaneously and decisively to appropriate environmental signals. Rather than consisting of abstract and rational, or civilized, ethical imperatives like adult morality, the child's "values," like his other faculties, were peculiarly action-oriented.[23]

Hall's psychology was relevant to social training because of his insistence that the child's action-oriented, muscular morality had great value in modern society. True, the precivilized roots of the child's behavior created disciplinary problems at home, in school, and on the street. His instinctive, normal quests for adventure were often interpreted as mischievous or delinquent behavior by ignorant adults. However, modern man had much to learn from the child's moral style. Hall interpreted modern life as a "disease."[24] From crib to classroom desk to work bench and office desk, modern man led a sedentary life. Life in the modern city was both unhealthy and overstimulating. Living in a sedentary, polluted environment threatened not only physical health, but moral vitality as well. Morality was originally forged when men lived in a hostile, primitive world, where survival demanded constant vigilance and incessant physical activity and no boundaries separated the musculature from cognitive and moral faculties, for survival depended upon synchronization of perception and reaction, or knowing and doing. This explained the peculiarly physical or muscular quality of primitive man's, and the modern child's, moral life. Modern urban life, however, led to muscular atrophy, which for Hall was synonymous with moral decay. Indeed, he equated morality with "right muscle habits," and warned that flabby muscles inevitably fostered flabby morals.[25]

For Hall, modern man's morality was nothing if not flabby. The primeval nexus between muscles and morals had been shattered by modern living conditions and by the increasingly abstract nature of mental life. Proof of this lay in the moral decay Hall saw around him. The adolescent's inclination to masturbate, the capitalist's "public-be-damned" attitude, and the striker's "lawlessness" all signified that modern man's life had become abstract, rational, and separated from his physical existence.

> The trouble is that few realize what physical vigor is in man or woman, or how dangerously near weakness often is to wickedness, how impossible healthful energy of will is without strong muscles, or how endurance and self-control, no less than great achievements depend on muscle-habits. Good moral and physical development are more than analogous; and where intelligence is separated from action the former becomes mystic, abstract, and desiccated, and the latter formal routine.[26]

The implication of these ideas was clear: strength of character in young people could not be achieved through intellectual training in the classroom; it had to be instilled by rigorous physical drill and conditioning. Morality had to be stamped into the youngster's "very nerve-cells and fibres" through repeated physical drill until "right conduct" became habitual. The city youth was exposed every day to a plethora of temptations and dangers. He might succumb to them unless his senses and muscles were habituated to instantly react to, and, if necessary, to resist, the endless stream of immoral urban stimuli. This is what Hall meant when he said "all good conduct might be defined as right muscle habits."[27] One of Hall's disciples aptly summarized the relationship between physiology and morality.

> We are coming to appreciate more clearly than we have in the past that conduct is an expression of the life as a whole, and not merely of the will in a narrow sense. Physiological conditions exert an important influence upon behavior. Students of juvenile crime have shown that the majority of those who are sent to reform schools are below par physiologically. They are often depleted nervously, so that their inhibiting power is reduced, and they yield readily to temptation.[28]

Hall's primitivism and theory of recapitulation were warnings to Americans that their civilized manners and work routines were detrimental to moral vigor. Modern Americans lacked the stern and certain conviction of right and wrong that Hall believed had characterized men in preindustrial society. Rather than force children to go against their instinctual grain and act "civilized," Americans should promote the specific elements in their "primitive" psyches that were linked to pre-civilized morality. Americans must allow children to express their primitive promptings on playgrounds, where physical activity and moral rigor went hand in hand. Indeed, according to Hall, there was no better means of preserving what was morally valuable in our primitive heritage than through play. Play was a "rehearsing of racial history," the principal medium through which "the motor habits and spirit of the past" persist in the present. The child's intellect should be trained in school, but his moral and instinctual equipment could only be organized and controlled during play, "the best of all methods of organizing instincts":[29]

> running and dodging with speed and endurance, and hitting with a club were . . . basal to hunting and fighting. Now that the need of these is less urgent for utilitarian purposes, they are still necessary for perfecting the organism. This makes, for instance, baseball racially familiar, because it represents activities that were once and for a long time necessary for survival.[30]

JAMES MARK BALDWIN

No psychologist influenced play organizers more than Hall, because he, more than anyone else, located the genesis of morality in the flexing and conditioning of muscles. Other authors of psychological theories of moral genesis also contributed to the discovery of children's play and the development of playground social training, however. One of these was James Mark Baldwin's psychology of imitation. Baldwin adhered to a modified version of the recapitulation theory, but his concept of imitation was based neither on that theory nor on the muscular morality and primitivism of Hall's psychology.

Baldwin was interested in the psychological implications of personal morality and social cohesion. How, he asked, was social order possible? What kept individuals from destroying each other in the struggle for survival? Those questions were on the minds of many Americans in the 1890s, a decade characterized by social unrest, economic depression, and political assassination. Baldwin was professor of psychology at Princeton during that decade and wrote two books, *Mental Development in the Child and the Race* and *Social and Ethical Interpretations in Mental Development,* in which he argued that social order and personal morality were securely founded upon the individual's innate need to imitate significant environmental figures.

According to Baldwin, the child's penchant for imitation was the catalyst for the development of his most distinctly human qualities. At birth, for instance, the human being did not possess a memory faculty as such, but rather the neurocortical potential for one. As he began to mimic physical stimuli impinging upon his senses, especially the facial expressions, tone of voice, and physical movements of parents, the child's unrefined neurocortical apparatus gradually became a memory bank. Memory was simply "copy for imitation taken over from the world into consciousness." In other words, unless the infant was attentive to physical nuances such as facial expressions and hand movements, his capacity for memory would go unorganized or at best remain primitive. Even his capacity for self-awareness remained dormant in the absence of external "copy." The child's subjective awareness was a reflection, an echo, of his perception of "other selves."[31]

Basic human qualities were structuralized during ontogenesis because of the child's imitation of, and sensitivity to, physical stimuli. The youngster was an empty vessel, or at most a congery of unorganized potential, until he received psychic organization and social direction from the physical environment. The "instinct" to imitate made him readily accessible to social control.

Baldwin assumed that the infant's capacity to imitate took on social significance around the eighth month of life. From that point on, the infant was able not only to imitate but also to make novel adaptations, or what Baldwin called "accommodations," to the environment. For example, the infant would perceive that kicking during a diaper change brought a frown to his mother's face, while passivity caused her to smile or at least express approval. Her happiness over his behavior was "copied" by him, and became his joy. Repetition of this pleasurable experience caused it to be registered in his nervous system as a habitual response to a specific environmental cue.[32]

Baldwin defined habit as a child's tendency to repeat adaptive, pleasurable responses to stimuli. A habit was formed for good when "copy for imitation" gave him a surplus of pleasurable over painful feelings. Once the habit was established, the child did not have to consciously react to stimuli: he responded automatically and unreflectively.[33]

If for one reason or another environmental conditions providing copy were altered, or responding to them on the basis of old accommodations engendered pain, a new accommodation developed in the same way as the old one—by imitation of external copy. Imitation was the internalized reproduction of external copy, and, therefore, the new accommodation, "by the very reaction which accommodates, hands over its gains immediately to the rule of habit." As the child developed, this circular process continued ad infinitum: simpler habits were continuously replaced by new, more complex accommodations. Through the "habit-accommodation dialectic" the child learned what to expect from his environment and what it expected from him.[34]

This "dialectic" explained significant aspects of the infant's physical relationship to the environment, especially his incorporation of the techniques of social competence. He learned how to manipulate objects and people by imitation. Habit and accommodation, however, could not account for the development of morality. Habitual behavior did not help the child cope with new social and personal problems or pressures. Habit simply reinforced old moral accommodations. Nor could the accommodation process, which was simply a reaction to a novel situation, define what *ought* to be done in a given situation.[35] Morality transcended the habit-accommodation series.

Through careful observations of his children, Baldwin located the genesis of morality in a dramatic change in the infant's perceptual apparatus. Around the seventh month of life, he evinced a noticeable inability to distinguish the "boundaries" separating his body from those of significant providers. The boundaries became fluid and permeable, creating an osmotic process Baldwin defined as a "return dialectic." In effect, the attributes of significant external bodies, especially parents, became "projected" onto the infant as his sense of self. His subjective self-awareness was reduced to his perception of other, external selves. At the same time, he "ejected" his subjective selfhood back onto the external selves. Thus, "other people's bodies, says the child to himself, have experiences in them such as mine has. They are also me's."[36]

From here on, self and other, personal desire and social accommodation, became what Baldwin called "ego and alter." Ego and alter were bound together by incessant imitation, which allowed the child to internalize the characteristics of his "projects," that is, his significant others. Concomitantly, he "ejected" his own physical and affective states onto others.

> This process of taking in elements from the social world by imitation and giving them out again by a reverse process of invention never stops. . . . We never outgrow imitation, nor our social obligation to it. Our sense of self is constantly growing richer and fuller as we understand others better—as we get into social cooperation with them.[37]

Baldwin called interactions between ego and alter the "socius." The socius was a kind of psychic arena where the ego's desire for pleasure and self-aggrandizement met, and sometimes conflicted with, the alter's demand for social accommodation and cooperation. Inevitably, according to Baldwin, the all-powerful need to imitate guaranteed alter's, that is, society's, triumph over the ego.

> Your example is powerful to me intrinsically; not because it is absolutely good or evil, but because it represents a part of myself, inasmuch as I have become what I am in part through my sympathy with you. So your injunctions to me bring out a difference of motor attitude between what is socially responsive in me, in a sense public, and that which is relatively me alone, my private self.[38]

Around the fourth year of life the ego-alter bipolarity coalesced into a structural part of the psyche that Baldwin called conscience. Conscience was the child's "ideal self." In the early years of childhood, conscience was simply an idealized image of parents, internalized as alter, whose behavioral mandates the child tried to emulate. As he matured and became a student, church member, and citizen, the individual abandoned parental ideals and followed the imperatives of powerful social institutions. Church, state, school, and peers each provided him with ideals, defined his social roles and identity, and outlined his relation to authority. Gradually, these imperatives became internalized as an ideal self, which he strove to become. Thus, for Baldwin conscience was an internal "presence," incorporated through the process of imitation, which symbolized "in general the lawgiving personality." The attributes of this "personality" were "projected" into the individual as an ideal self, in much the same way as the parental alter had been internalized during childhood. The individual, in turn, "ejected" his consigned social roles and values back onto society. Thus, individual and society existed in a state of reciprocity as ego and alter: the individual realized that "in his greater part" he was "someone else."[39]

The concept of imitation, at least as Baldwin used it, provided an answer to the most compelling philosophical, ethical, and political question of the Progressive Era: how could the needs of the individual and society be balanced and brought into harmony? Baldwin argued that the dynamic imitative relationship between ego and alter generated a creative, viable balance between the drive for personal gratification and the requirements of social order. "As the socius expands in the mind of the child," he wrote, "there is the constant tendency to make it real—to eject it—in some concrete form in the social group."[40]

According to Baldwin, children's play was a perfect example of ego-alter mutuality. Play was an important social phenomenon because, like the socius, it preserved "some degree of balance" between the interests of child and society. Play activities allowed the child to explore the outer boundaries of his skills and limitations. "He finds out how fast he can run, how much he can lift, how dextrous he is in dodging." Play not only honed individual skills, but, in the case of competitive team games like basketball and baseball, allowed the youngster to compare his skills with those of peers. Play thus served as "the education of the individual for his life-work," because it compelled him to confront both his abilities and his liabilities.[41]

The primary value of team games, however, was their role in teaching the child that he must conform to the values and aspirations of his social group. Baldwin contended that a group game was one of the most effective tools for cultivating the "instinct of imitation." For instance, baseball engendered a "spirit of union" among the players, a desire for each to be like all. If the youngster wanted to be accepted as a valued member of the team, he had to acquire "the habit of suspension of private utilities for the larger social good."[42] In sports, society's values, mores, and techniques of social competence were "projected" into the child. The individual learned that his abilities and desires were meaningless outside the context of communal approval. In play:

> A premium is put upon united action just by the fact of united knowledge. To exhibit what I can do alone, is to exhibit my importance as an ally. The sense of my weakness in myself is a revelation to me of my need of you as my ally. . . . And the victory which we win over the stronger by the alliance is both a confirmation to us of the utility of social co-operation and a convincing proof that society is stronger than the individual.[43]

Baldwin wanted Americans to promote children's play because it gave greater scope to the instinct to imitate than did most social activities. Unlike Hall, Baldwin was not interested in the flexing and conditioning of muscles. Imitation, not muscularity, generated morality. During play, as in few other activities, the child, or ego, became "a new self, a socius," which "grows grandly on the playground of every school."[44]

Like the game of baseball, the game of life "balanced" ego and alter by giving alter, in the guise of parents, peers, and social institutions, the upper hand. In Baldwin's psychology the individual was essentially a passive recipient of societal values. While he recognized the importance of individual genius, Baldwin left little room for moral autonomy. The child's "insides" were internalized echoes of externally imposed values. Baldwin balanced individualism and social order, but his scale, regardless of intent, was decidedly weighted in society's favor.

JOHN DEWEY

Like Hall and Baldwin, John Dewey viewed play as a mediator between the child and society, but not for the same reasons. Neither Hall's muscular primitivism nor Baldwin's exclusive emphasis on imitation appealed to Dewey. For him, play, like education, was a means of focusing the child's multifaceted instincts and diverse interests on his culture's important environmental objects, activities, and social roles. Play juxtaposed the child's innate capacities and desires with society's artifacts and values.[45]

Significantly, Dewey argued that play must "not be identified with anything which the child externally does." Play signified a "mental attitude" in which the child's interests and instincts were mobilized to attain specific personal and social ends.[46] In other words, play was serious business. Educators should not use it to placate or amuse the child, for play was the means of securing the "normal estate of effective learning, namely, that knowledge-getting be an outgrowth of activities having their own end, instead of a school task."[47]

> It is the business of the school to set up an environment in which play and work shall be conducted with reference to facilitating desirable mental and moral growth. It is not enough to introduce plays and games, hand work and manual exercises. Everything depends upon the way in which they are employed.[48]

Dewey's ideas about how play should be "employed" in the classroom were inseparable from his theory of how knowledge was acquired and used by the child. Dewey maintained that most traditional psychological and pedagogical theories of knowledge assumed that children obtained knowledge about objects through the medium of sense impressions. He disagreed: while objects existed independently of perception they could not, simply by impinging upon the senses, lead to knowledge. "Genuine" knowledge involved the pupil's understanding of the social functions of objects and awareness of their cultural meanings. In short, acquiring knowledge was not a one-way street in which the student passively absorbed sense impressions that somehow evolved into ideas. Knowledge derived, rather, from an active, social encounter between pupil, object, and the social uses to which the object was put.[49]

Learning, then, was inseparable from use. Use, however, inevitably transformed objects from brute facts into "instrumentalities" that the pupil used to attain his ends. One learned the meaning of an object by using it. "Action" upon objects was therefore the only valid "test of comprehension" and the most efficacious means of acquiring knowledge.[50]

Dewey's instrumental theory of knowledge portrayed learning as a peculiarly social process that had little in common with visions of the solitary scholar communing with abstract ideas. If knowledge was inseparable from use, it was imperative that the individual be able to link the antecedent social conditions and the results of his actions upon objects. One had to tie past and anticipated experiences to current problems and prospects. Dewey reasoned that if learning involved understanding both the physical properties of objects and the social conditions in which they were used, intellect itself was simply the capacity to analyze and anticipate the potential consequences of those uses.

Mind was the capacity to mobilize purposeful action on the basis of correct perception and analysis of social reality.[51]

In effect, Dewey argued that learning, like evolution, was a continuing process, an interaction between mind and object, rather than a once and for all intuitive or intellectual grasp of what the object meant. Insofar as the historical and cultural meanings of the object changed, its uses were altered, and its meaning changed as well. Truth, therefore, was a process rather than an eternal, unchanging verity. Acquiring knowledge implied an active, social experience on the part of the pupil in which he had to pay careful attention to the nuances of his physical environment.

Dewey's theory of knowledge influenced both his famous concept of the classroom as a "miniature community" and his opinion about the role of play within the school community. Because pupils acquired knowledge by studying the social uses and values of objects, it followed that the most effective method of teaching was to have students "act out" in plays and games the actual uses to which objects and social roles were put in society. In other words, Dewey wanted students to assume on a miniature scale the social roles and activities of adult society during their play activities.

> To do this means to make each one of our schools an embryonic community life, active with types of occupations that reflect the life of the larger society and permeated throughout with the spirit of art, history, and science. When the school introduces and trains each child of society into membership within such a little community, saturating him with the spirit of service, and providing him with the instruments of effective self-direction, we shall have the deepest and best guaranty of a larger society which is worthy, lovely, and harmonious.[52]

Play was an integral feature of this miniature community. In contrast to the fruitless inculcation of abstract ideas through reading and lectures, play allowed younger students to act out an idea until it became real to them. Play compelled the pupil to "learn through doing."[53] Because pupils enjoyed playing, it was an effective method for instructors to get a "hold of the child's natural impulses and instincts, and to utilize them so that the child is carried to a higher plane of perception and judgment, and equipped with more efficient habits." Finally, since play sparked the pupil's interest, it allowed him to freely exercise his cognitive and physical faculties, to gain greater control over them, and to obtain insight into his abilities and limitations.[54] Of course, all this occurred within a cooperative, social context where pupils worked together to achieve the goals of the miniature community. In kindergarten games:

> the child's interest naturally develops to the needs of a family and then of a whole community. With paper dolls and boxes, the children make and furnish dolls' houses for themselves, until all together they produce an entire village. . . . This construction work not only fills the children with interest and enthusiasm they always show for any good game, but teaches them the use of work. In supplying the needs of the dolls and their own games, they are supplying in miniature the needs of society, and are acquiring control over the tools that society actually uses in meeting these wants.[55]

In his theories of knowledge, play, and the miniature community, Dewey did not clearly distinguish between social or intellectual knowledge and moral knowledge. He assumed that the pupil acquired moral precepts in the same way he learned about the social values of objects —by an "instrumental" inquiry into the social implications of his behavior. If the pupil knew the antecedent conditions and potential consequences of his desires, and if he analyzed and understood how his wishes affected himself and his community, his analysis became normative. As Dewey put it, "the moral and social qualities of conduct are, in the last analysis, identical with each other."[56]

As Morton White has pointed out, Dewey's concept of moral knowledge equated the normative and the factual, the "is" of an objective social analysis with the "ought" of moral evaluation.[57] The importance of Dewey's thoughts about moral knowledge for our study of the movement to organize children's play, however, transcends the philosophical issues that concerned both him and White. In their social-training practices, play organizers like Gulick, Lee, and Addams translated Dewey's philosophical concept of moral knowledge into a psychologically concrete method of moral socialization. It behooves us, therefore, to take a brief look at the philosophical rationale Dewey employed to justify his theory.

In 1903 he outlined his theory of how moral judgments should be made in a pamphlet aptly entitled "Logical Conditions of a Scientific Treatment of Morality."[58] At the outset, Dewey claimed he was not attempting to "reduce the statement of matters of conduct to forms comparable with those of physical science."[59] He then proceeded to do precisely that by describing the affinity between the processes of making moral and scientific judgments.

The empirical origin, the experimental test, and the practical use of the statements of science are enough of themselves to indicate the impossibility of holding to any fixed logical division of judgments into universal as scientific, and individual as practical [that is, moral]. It suggests that what we term science is just the forging of instrumentalities for dealing with individual cases of experience —cases which, if individual, are just as unique and irreplaceable as are those of moral life.[60]

In other words, the mental operations leading to universally applicable scientific judgments were the same as those generating individual moral evaluations. Both were "instrumentalities and methods of controlling judgments." In effect, Dewey argued that a rigorous cognitive analysis of the objective social situation in which we find ourselves compelled to make a moral evaluation was itself normative. That is, once we make our desires and ideals "objective" by analyzing their social implications and consequences, and once we place them "in sequence with other similar attitudes," we have a psychological or ethical law that "can be employed as a tool of analysis upon concrete moral experience." Such a law has "exactly the same validity that is possessed by any 'physical law.'"[61]

Dewey claimed that the affinity between scientific and moral judgments was not adventitious, but a result of the pervasive influence of the scientific method in modern society. He believed modern man, consciously or otherwise, was incorporating the elements of the scientific method into many areas of his daily life. By 1900 the scientific method, which Dewey defined as "command of an apparatus which may be used to control the formation of judgments," was being used by corporations and governments to organize and bureaucratize their spheres of interest.[62]

To Dewey this was a promising development, for it indicated that Americans were thinking more rigorously, critically, and scientifically about themselves, their environment, and, most of all, their behavior. It also signified that they were developing a style of thinking about everyday issues and problems that promised to make their social interactions less volatile and confusing, and their reactions to social stimuli more decisive and effective. "Gradually," he wrote, the use of scientific judgment:

becomes more and more habitual. The "theory" becomes a part of our total apparatus. The *social situation takes on a certain form or organization.* It is pre-classified as of a certain sort, as of a certain genus and even species of this sort; the only question which remains is discrimination of the particular variety. Again, we get into the habit of taking into account certain sources of error in our own dispositions as these affect our judgments of behavior, and thereby bring them sufficiently under control so that the need of conscious reference to them in intellectual formulation diminishes. [Italics added.][63]

The relevance of Dewey's concepts of science and morality to the play movement will become evident in the discussion of the adolescent team experience in chapters 4 and 5. For now it should be noted that play organizers used the structure of team games to teach adolescents how to base moral judgments on objective analyses of game situations. As a technique of moral socialization, Dewey's theory of morality did more than confound, in White's philosophical terms, the social "is" and the ethical "ought." Dewey also diminished the psychological distinction between cognitive and moral operations by elevating cognitive analyses of social phenomena to the status of moral evaluations. In a sense, the focus of moral valuation shifted from the child's "insides" to his public environment, just as in the theory of evolution the catalyst of human development had shifted from an interior "soul" or mind to environmental changes.

WILLIAM JAMES AND EDWARD L. THORNDIKE

The theory of habit formation was another aspect of Progressive Era child psychology important to the rise of the play movement. Essentially, a habit was a psychological or physical predisposition instilled in the child through repeated physical drill; it was a nonvolitional response automatically triggered by appropriate environmental stimuli. Proponents of habit training believed it to be an efficient mode of social training that equipped young people to deal effectively with the stresses, ambiguities, and uncertainties of city life.

The physiology of habit training was simple enough. William James, who popularized the concept in the late 1880s and early 1890s, theorized that the senses were linked to muscular and glandular organs through "nerve-currents" flowing along the nervous system's "reflex paths." The nervous system was a sort of switching station that used reflex paths to relay incoming sensory impressions to muscles and glands. It was, then, a relatively simple matter to "drill" into young children a predisposition to respond to appropriate stimuli in a programmed manner, because their nervous systems were new and plastic. Repetitive physical drill caused nerve currents to "shoot through" the nervous system, thereby forging new paths between senses and muscles. If the new paths were "traversed repeatedly" a new habit was formed, that is, the muscles became predisposed to react instantly and involuntarily to appropriate stimuli.[64]

Habit training had obvious relevance to the socialization of city children. A habitual response, as James pointed out, did not require "conscious attention." On the contrary, "sensation is a sufficient guide" for the mobilization of habitual responses.[65] In other words, the child equipped with adaptive habits was programmed to respond decisively to dangerous city sensations. Habit was a kind of psychic antenna that removed, or at least mitigated, the element of surprise in daily life. It was a weapon in the battle against the uncertainties and contingencies of the city.

James never thought of habit as a substitute for moral and intellectual autonomy. Habit was a kind of psycho-physiological janitor who did menial mental chores and liberated "our higher powers of mind . . . for their own proper work."[66] But Edward L. Thorndike of Columbia Teachers College, whose stimulus-response approach to habit training was popular among many Progressive Era educators and play organizers, argued that most important moral and intellectual functions could be made habitual. "What we call intellect, character, and skill," he declared, "is, in the case of any man, the sum of the man's tendencies to respond to situations."[67]

Thorndike believed the "sum" of a child's tendencies could be "stamped" into his nervous system through a stimulus-response, habit-formation series. Significantly, Thorndike called the key element in an S-R series the "law of exercise." By this he meant that "desirable" habits, such as obedience to parents, could be inscribed in the nervous system by repeated physical exercise. Eventually, the child would "learn" to respond automatically and unreflectively to the stimulus.[68]

It is not surprising that Thorndike and other proponents of the S-R method favored rigorous physical exercise and play.[69] Thorndike's theory of habit formation became the focal point of curriculum organization for progressive kindergarten teachers. In 1919 a subcommittee of the International Kindergarten Union issued a report on curriculum reorganization. The report, written by progressive educators, decried the abstract, intellectual nature of traditional kindergarten play and games, and recommended that these activities be supplemented by more physical games, especially those that "cultivate desirable habits and attitudes,"[70] designed in accordance with Thorndike's S-R theory of habit formation. But play organizers took a back seat to no other group of Progressive Era child savers in their enthusiasm for habit formation training.

CONCLUSION

Hall, Dewey, Baldwin, Thorndike, and James disagreed with one another on many significant issues. While Dewey and Thorndike opposed Hall's notion of recapitulation, Baldwin's theory of imitation had little in common with Hall's emphasis on muscularity and was only marginally related to Thorndike's S-R series.[71] For our purposes, however, what is significant about these diverse child psychologies is that each of them emphasized a mode of child training that could effectively be practiced by rigorous physical drill and games on organized playgrounds. In chapters 3 and 4 we will see how emphasis on peer pressure during adolescent team games closely resembled Dewey's theory of the moral relevance of miniature community experiences. The definitions of play made by important play organizers, especially Gulick, Curtis, Johnson, and Addams, were drawn explicitly from Hall's recapitulation theory. Other play advocates, Joseph Lee for one, believed that the tendency to emulate was cultivated by group games and was essential to the child's moral development. In fashioning their social-training techniques, play organizers drew selectively from all these theories.

The fibre of the man will depend on the spirit of the game.—Joseph Lee

3
Play and Socialization: Infancy to Adolescence

The child-training techniques championed by play organizers were as diverse as their political and philosophical perspectives. Joseph Lee, the Boston philanthropist who succeeded Gulick as president of the Playground Association of America, believed that voluntary philanthropic organizations were the most effective and democratic agents of social reform. Lee distrusted government bureaucracy and felt ill at ease with the bureaucratic jargon of scientific management that permeated Gulick's ideas about playground organization. While Lee favored municipal ownership of playgrounds, he saw public ownership as an economic necessity rather than a political ideal. The ideal playground system, he felt, would be owned and maintained by the government, but managed by expert play directors who received their inspiration and ideas, if not their salaries, from neighborhood philanthropic organizations, particularly social settlements and reform clubs like the Massachusetts Civic League, which Lee founded.[1]

In fact, Lee viewed the playground as a promoter of decentralization and localism: it should be a catalyst of neighborhood revival, a boon to civic pride, and an instrument for reestablishing local control over individual behavior. Lee saw cities as dirty, noisy, overstimulating ethnic fortresses where cultural fragmentation and moral anonymity went hand in hand with the destruction of democratic ideals and republican principles.[2] The role of the organized playground was to reverse these trends.

73

In order to accomplish these rather monumental goals, playground social training had to emphasize social unity, social order, and ethnic assimilation. The focal points of Lee's philosophy of play were the themes of social organicism and ethnic assimilation. Like his former Harvard professor and lifelong friend Josiah Royce, Lee believed that physical training fostered "that spirit of loyalty to loyalty" needed to "bring to pass the spiritual union of all mankind." Organized play, especially the experience of "pulling together" during team games, lured immigrant children away from particularistic ethnic traditions and helped them internalize American values. Lee's suggestions for playground social training consequently stressed Baldwin's concepts of imitation and accommodation: the child's "innate" impulse to imitate and to assimilate new "copy" should be exercised in games that emphasized peer-group direction and "American" ideals of democracy, equality, and cooperation. As a political institution, the playground recreated in the twentieth-century urban neighborhood Lee's version of the early nineteenth-century idyllic village community, where supposedly everyone knew what everyone else was doing. As an institution for socializing city youngsters, the playground should provide the ideological and emotional unity needed to counteract the fragmentation generated by ethnic diversity and moral "individualism."[3]

On the other hand, Gulick was an "organizational" progressive and the play movement's most articulate proponent of scientific management and bureaucratic planning. Economic prosperity, social order, and individual stability were inseparable from industrial and social efficiency. "Efficiency is the ideal," he wrote, "the end rather than the means of a prosperous, meaningful, orderly life." Big government was not a threat to personal liberty if it was efficient. Gulick perceived American society as a theater of interdependent but distinct interests and values that should be managed rather than "merged." Centralized, efficient government planning by experts, rather than "unrealistic" visions of social organicism, was the most effective tool for the establishment of social order. It is hardly surprising that Gulick saw organized play as a means of instilling desirable and efficient habits in young people.[4]

The differences between Lee and Gulick highlighted the political and ideological diversity of the movement to organize children's play. All play organizers shared important assumptions about the social and moral implications of children's play, however. They insisted that childhood was not only a distinct stage of life—hardly a new discovery—but also a period distinguished by unique and evanescent needs, desires, impulses, and instincts. The child was not merely distinct from the adult. He was a totally different being with qualitatively different behavior, motives, and morality.

Play organizers subsumed the notion of qualitative adult-child difference under the superordinate category of play. The biological and cultural implications of the child's behavior were most lucidly revealed during his play, for play was his most distinctively "childish" activity. Indeed, the child should be defined as "a playing animal."[5] Play was the medium through which he expressed his "animal," precivilized and preadult, desires. Organized, structured play was the arena in which the imperatives of civilized society clashed head-on with his untamed animal needs. Play was the most effective character builder, the medium through which the child incorporated the attitudes and aptitudes appropriate to his culture.[6]

Regardless of their political perspectives, most play organizers used Hall's theory of recapitulation to analyze the meanings of childhood and play. Some, like Henry Curtis, were doctrinaire Hallians, while others, including Jane Addams, wedded a sort of sociological poetry to Hall's physiological psychology. In Addams's words:

> Each boy comes from our ancestral past not in "entire forgetfulness," and quite as he unconsciously uses ancient war-cries in his street play, so he longs to reproduce and to see set before him the valors and vengeances of a society embodying a much more primitive state of morality than the one in which he finds himself. . . . To set his feet in the worn path of civilization is not an easy task, but it may give us a clue for the undertaking to trace his misdeeds to the unrecognized and primitive spirit of the adventure corresponding to the old activity of the hunt, of warfare, and of discovery.[7]

If the youth was a bundle of irrepressible, untamed energies bequeathed by humanity's savage past, what safer outlet could modern society provide for the expression of those energies than organized play? As Lillian Wald put it, the "young offender's presence in the courts may be traced to a play-impulse for which there was no safe outlet."[8]

If the recapitulation theory explained the causes of the young "animal's" behavior, it did not prescribe a cure for it. This was the organized playground's task. Play directors, or "social engineers" as Gulick called them, had to provide safe outlets for young people's instincts. At the same time, directors had to channel the instincts into forms of play that were both appropriate to the youngster's stage of life and useful for adapting him to social imperatives. In short, the organized urban playground was a social interface where the barbarism of the past confronted the exigencies of urban-industrial civilization.[9]

PLAY AND RECAPITULATION

According to Henry Curtis, it was impossible to understand either the historical role of play in human evolution or its contemporary social significance without reference to the recapitulation theory. On the surface, play appeared to be "a useless bit of poetry strayed in the bitter prose of the actual." On the basis of Hall's theory, however, Curtis reasoned that the desire to play survived the evolutionary process because it re-created important psychological and physiological processes that had been useful to men and women living in primitive environments. The modern boy's desire to hurl objects toward a target or to run aimlessly from one city block to another were "instinctual" re-creations of ancient social activities. These instincts played important roles in the child's physical and intellectual development. In other words, play was "the instinct to pursue the activities of our forefathers." Play guaranteed that primitive but useful adaptations to environmental stimuli developed in the primordial past would be preserved. Put another way, "play represents almost exactly those conditions and activities through which the human brain was developed."[10]

Luther Gulick, George Johnson, and Joseph Lee each made sophisticated longitudinal studies of the interactions between play and recapitulation. For the most part all three approached the problem in a similar fashion, and it would be redundant to discuss all of them at length. I will concentrate on Lee's study because it was the most acclaimed both within and outside the ranks of the play movement. That most avid student of the dynamics of "social control" during the Progressive Era, the sociologist Edward A. Ross, hailed Lee's book *Play in Education* as the most perceptive, incisive, and "wonderful" description of child development he had read.[11]

Lee thought that play was important because the style of play dominant during a specific stage of development was the medium through which the child received the biological and intellectual "equipment" peculiar to that stage. During each stage of ontogenesis one form of play dominated. The role of this play style was to promote expression of instincts and "ideals" rooted in a specific historical epoch, which were vital for the child's optimal phase-specific development. At a particular stage of ontogenesis only one of the numerous instincts Lee believed essential for mankind's survival and progress—hunting, fighting, social solidarity, personal initiative, curiosity, or nurture—dominated the child's style of play. If, for example, hunting was the "historical force" recapitulated between eight and twelve years of age, it would determine the form taken by the child's play.[12]

Lee isolated four major ontogenetic stages and associated a specific play style with each of them. The first, "babyhood," lasted from birth to three; the "dramatic age" lasted through the sixth year; the third period, the "Big Injun" or self-assertive stage, terminated around the eleventh year; finally, adolescence, "the age of loyalty," extended into the mid twenties.[13]

During "babyhood" the infant was motivated by two desires: to cling to his mother and to possess, by means of oral incorporation if necessary, valued objects. Not surprisingly, the most significant activity of this period was the child's use of his hands to manipulate objects. At first he used his hands only to cling to his mother, but Lee perceived ambivalence in this "reaching out." The hands could be used to manipulate as well as cling to loved ones. Thus, even in his earliest years, the child exhibited the primeval human desire to own and control valued objects and to beguile those who had the power to thwart his desires.[14]

The need to grasp was important for a number of reasons. Grasping enhanced the child's ability to understand the composition and social utility of objects. Through manipulation the child learned the relationship between touch, utility, and knowledge. According to Lee, this technique was the basis for man's designation as the tool-using animal.[15]

Manipulation was also vital for the development of "mastery," that is, the desire to own property. Lee was convinced that this "instinct," essential to primitive man's survival, was the biological fuel for the urge to acquire private property. But if this aspect of the clinging, manipulative impulse overwhelmed the loving, sympathetic paradigm established, ideally, in the early weeks of mothering, the desire to own material objects might dominate the individual's behavior in later years. Unless early grasping patterns were mitigated by benign mothering, the child, like the "public be damned capitalist," would develop asocial, selfish tendencies.[16]

The play style of this stage was manipulation of sand and mud. Somehow children were "infused" with memories of the species' primordial amphibious origins, "when our seaborn ancestors first made good their footing on the beach, and recognized their ancient playmate"—sand. The manipulation of sand—making mud pies, construct-

ing models of people and things, hoarding it in containers—was a play
style fundamental to "all constructive works of man," including the
creation of religious images and the institution of private property.[17]
Notwithstanding the paradigm of "social unity" represented in the
early mother-child relationship, babyhood, according to Lee, was the
recapitulation of the manipulative, individualistic designs evident in
sand games.

By contrast, the craving for social unity dominated the dramatic
stage. From three through six, the child's most compelling desire was
to grasp "by one sheer leap of intuition" the personalities of his significant "others" and to imitate them:

> the practice of impersonating during these three impressionable
> years creates a power to impersonate,—a power to put yourself in
> another person's place . . . to see people as they really are; it is the
> intuitive sympathy that sees with another's eyes, feels with his
> nerves, that can realize him not merely as a phenomenon of sense
> —a thing, an obstacle, a convenience—but also as a feeling, strug-
> gling, human being, embodying a purpose, commanded by ideals.[18]

The three-year-old's primitive capacity to imitate and empathize was
the basis of personal morality and social order. The "impulse" to imitate was not simply a desire to think about or care for others; it was
the expression of a "racially" rooted "belonging instinct," which compelled the child to "feel as the social body of which you and they are
parts."[19]

The impulse first appeared within the family circle, especially in
the mother-child relationship. Once the child was exposed to peer-
group activities at play and in school, however, the "belonging instinct," which was the somatic residue of mankind's earliest social
formations, prescribed the style assumed by the child's play. Ring
games like ring-around-the-rosy dominated this period. These games
encouraged the development of what Lee described as the "sixth
sense," the desire for social unity, and taught elementary lessons in the
importance of belonging to, and being governed by, a "corporate personality." Through them the child learned that the "mark of all morality is subordination." In contrast to individualistic play with sand, ring
games were social exercises in which success depended upon the subordination of personal interests to the goals of the group. "It is when you
lose yourself in the game," Lee wrote, "give yourself to the cause, begin
to feel that the work is bigger than you are, that full life possesses you."
Ring games instilled such feelings.[20]

A pulsating, biologically conditioned force, which Lee called "rhythm," was the unifying element in ring games. Rhythmic songs and movements fused separate individuals into a corporate body that thought, felt, and acted as one person. Lee believed he saw this "corporate unity" in action on his model playgrounds in Boston when children of diverse ethnic backgrounds played ring-around-the-rosy. He campaigned successfully to have ring games incorporated into the city's public school curriculum. He believed "these infant commonwealths" provided children with invaluable training in what it meant to be an American.[21]

Rhythm was also a medium used by children to compel peers to play the game according to the rules. The "teasing rhymes" of childhood forced the rebellious, "individualistic" youngster to abide by the opinions of peers through the threat of ostracism.

Rhythm is the social alchemist, who can fuse individual minds and temperaments into one substance by his spell. When people sing or march or dance together, each knows with accuracy, as in the ring games, what all the rest are doing and are going to do and

Supervised ring game: the sign on the left warns youngsters on New York's Carnegie Playground to play only when adult "play leaders are present." (Library of Congress)

in great part how they feel about it; each knows that the other knows—and so on; to the depth that the song or the movement goes the mutual understanding is complete. And it goes deeper as the rhythmic influence continues, and, until the whole emotional being of each member of the company swings to the same pulsation like a tidal wave.[22]

This primitive form of social order and solidarity was over-whelmed, however, by the rampaging, anarchistic urges that possessed the child when he entered the "Big Injun" stage. This period, a recapitulation of humanity's nomadic level of social organization, gen-erated a resurgence of individualistic, asocial urges. The child was solicitous about his own needs but ignored both the rules of the game and the welfare of his peers. Above all he sought adventure and the chance to participate in the real world of adults. The "instinct" of curiosity compelled the youngster to question rules and authority. His games, such as riding in railroad cars, running away from home, and truancy, were tantamount to law breaking. Lee was quick to point out that these pranks were both inevitable and inexorable: they were rooted in "racial" urges and must not be perceived as criminal. These activities were echoes of an impulse that, in a less complex age, was a virtue—the desire for unhindered self-assertion.[23]

Nevertheless, the individualism of the Big Injun years temporarily disrupted the development of the child's "sixth sense" of social solidar-ity. A resurgence of the desire for "social fusion" which characterized the imitative stage was needed to offset the antisocial individualism of the Big Injun. Adolescence, which Lee called the "age of loyalty," accomplished this by reconstructing the peer group world of moral and social unity destroyed by the nomadism of the preceding stage.[24] This crucial reconstruction is discussed in the following chapter.

Play organizers drew a number of conclusions from the longitudi-nal studies undertaken by Lee and others. They were convinced not only that the person was "incomplete" at birth, but also that he passed through a series of stages, each of which provided him with unique and vital biological and existential "assets." In other words, human devel-opment was epigenetic. They believed the most efficient way to analyze the meaning of ontogenesis and recapitulation was to study the child while he played. As Gulick put it:

It appears to be not only true that the body rehearses the life of the race; it appears to be true that the mind must do so also, and that the plays of children are the rehearsal of the activities of the race during forgotten ages—not necessarily the selfsame activities, but activities involving the same bodily and mental qualities. Putting it exactly, play is the ontogenetic rehearsal of the phylogenetic series.[25]

Organized play was also the best way of directing the youngster's "impulses" toward specific social and moral ends. And it was the physicalistic quality of play that made it an ideal medium of social reform and value change.

MUSCLES AND MORALS

In one of the most significant sentences written by a play organizer, Gulick wrote: "Muscular contraction appears to be closely related to the genesis of all forms of psychic activity."[26] The human organism, he contended, was not a triadic structure divisible into more or less distinct spheres of mind, body, and emotions; on the contrary, "our cue to the control of emotions" comes from the fact that the health and disposition of the *muscles* determine emotional health and moral predispositions.[27]

Emotions were "body-states" whose meaning and expression depended upon muscular contractions. The most distinct aspect of an emotion was its "queer physical qualities," such as rapid heartbeat, trembling knees, and "the hard-to-define disturbances in the abdomen." Gulick was not maintaining that these physical reactions were "external" evocations of "inner" affective states; rather, the quality of the affect was inseparable from muscularity: "where the muscular expression can be inhibited, the feeling itself is not the same."[28]

This was also true of mental states. Thinking was both truncated and directionless apart from "muscular contraction."

Muscular contraction appears to be closely related to the genesis of all forms of psychic activity. Not only do the vaso-motor and muscular systems express the thinking, feeling and willing of the individual, but the muscular apparatus itself appears to be a fundamental part of the apparatus for these psychical states. Without the muscular system, material for psychic activity can not be secured. All three of these processes—thinking, feeling, willing—are more or less remotely connected with a rehearsal in the body, both neural and muscular, of the acts by which the original material for the mental processes came in.[29]

Along with Hall and Thorndike, Gulick insisted that it was possible to determine the quality and social implications of affects and motives by exposing the child to specific and repetitive muscular drills. While the social-training implications of this idea are discussed in subsequent chapters, it should be pointed out that Gulick's notions of physicality systematically devalued the child's "inner" world and reduced his motives and values to their "objective" social expressions. In fact, in his view there was no such thing as an inner motive apart from social experience. Gulick was not saying that motives were useless apart from their expression in overt behavior, but that organized motives and affects *did not exist* apart from muscular contraction. In the absence of muscularity, they were "vague and irresponsible" tendencies.[30]

This was why reformers thought play was important for socializing the young. Specific play activities, like ring games, compelled youngsters to use phase-specific "instincts" like imitation to achieve the game's social ends. Organized play isolated and selected those recapitulated instincts that play organizers thought appropriate in the modern world. Thus, in ring games individual development took a back seat to the more social "belonging instinct." As Lee put it, play exercised a "selecting power" over instincts: organized games cultivated certain phase-specific impulses and preserved them in a dormant state when the child entered the next life stage. Ring-around-the-rosy and playing on a seesaw encouraged the four-year-old to express, in an organized fashion, his otherwise innately aimless, instinctual penchant for imitation. But incessant repetition of rhythmic physical exercises during these games made imitation and "other-direction" habitual. They might be temporarily overshadowed by the individualism of the Big Injun stage, but they could not be destroyed. They would simply remain dormant until his "new birth" at adolescence revived them and gave them a new social meaning.[31]

The key to this process was the power of repetitive physical activities to instill habits in children. George Johnson, a Hall student who used William James's notion of habit formation to analyze children's play, assumed that carefully supervised games "filtered out" socially maladaptive aspects of an instinct while they simultaneously selected its socially useful aspects. Incessant repetition of this process caused the undesirable elements to wither through disuse while the desirable elements "grew" because they were "exercised."[32] In the words of play organizer Frank Nagley:

When a child, who is always full of impulses, forms his habits he subordinates a certain line of impulses to a fixed system, while the opposing ones are neglected. When he wishes to break the habit he has found that the impulses which were originally on the opposite side have been either lost or become inactive through disuse. Since young children form most of their self-expressive habits on the playground, we can see the self-evident opportunities lying open to make good men and women by directing the play activities of children while they are forming their life habits.[33]

In short, habit was destiny, and organized play was an ideal method of instilling desirable social habits.[34]

Prior to joining the Harvard faculty as professor of education, Johnson was director of the Pittsburgh chapter of the Playground Association of America. During his tenure as leader of the Pittsburgh play movement, he wrote an article entitled "Play as a Moral Equivalent of War," in which he analyzed how organized play selected and refined the child's instincts. According to Johnson, most instincts were echoes of the "historic activities of the race." Because most "racial" history consisted of incessant struggle and warfare between groups, the child's instinctual inheritance was dominated by antisocial, warlike impulses. "How often," he wrote, "the enraged infant smites with his chubby hand the smiling face of the mother who would woo him back to good nature with her kisses."[35]

It would be foolhardy, insisted Johnson, to repress the child's "natural" pugnacity: American society needed the "spunk," tenacity, self-interest, and initiative that sprang from it. Instead, the child's pugnacity needed "to be directed and consecrated to some ideal," which would both preserve the spirit of the instinct and repress its destructive, antisocial qualities. Because supervised play "holds the biological vantage ground to morality," the organized playground was the most appropriate institution for transforming innately destructive instincts into valuable social sentiments.[36] The youngster inherited the instincts for throwing and running. In the absence of concerted efforts to direct them into desirable channels, the city youth "will inevitably end up" in juvenile court. By repeated exposure to the physical discipline of supervised team games, on the other hand, the youth's instincts could be controlled by his musculature and directed toward morally "uplifting" ends.

It is quite in keeping with the beneficent and refining process of nature that the very joy of exercising powers or instincts should swallow up in good nature the inherited memory of ill will and destruction. Play preserves, purifies, perpetuates the martial capacities, while it diminishes the belligerent spirit.[37]

The social role of organized play was to educate the child's muscles. A finely honed and efficient musculature was essential to the child's moral and physical well-being. The muscles were the entering wedge into the child's "inner" world of ancient instincts and hidden emotions. To ignore the role of the muscles in his education was, in Curtis's words, "likely to bring disaster."[38]

EDUCATING THE BODY: THE ROLE OF THE PUBLIC SCHOOL

As was noted above, play organizers were ambivalent about the role of the public school in the play movement. Some saw the school, with its economic resources and captive audience, as the movement's logical successor. Luther Gulick, as director of physical training for the New York City school system, attempted to link playground and school in 1903 by founding the Public Schools Athletic League (PSAL) to organize athletic contests between schools. Similar attempts to forge links between playground and school were made in Chicago and Detroit.[39]

Many play organizers believed, however, that radical changes were needed in the philosophy of American educators before the public school could serve as a purveyor of their muscles-and-morals approach to child training. Like their fellow reformers in the progressive education movement, play organizers sharply criticized the ineffectuality of public education in the United States. What distinguished play organizers' critique of public schools from that of progressive educators was the former's insistence that the school was incapable, even if reformed, of educating the whole child. In school, they claimed, the child's health was endangered, his body misunderstood and despised, and his mind and morals corrupted by an undemocratic struggle for grades and status. Play organizers believed that some of these problems, particularly the health factor, could be remedied, but that others were inherent in the nature of formal education.

This was particularly true, they said, of educators' attitudes toward the pupil's body. According to play advocates, teachers had a "profound contempt for the body," and despised it as much as "any flagellant or ascetic." They approached the child as if he were a disembodied mind and were ignorant of the role played by muscle training in moral development and intellectual growth. In the classroom the "animal" child was forced to be a scholar, and therefore his true nature was "hermetically sealed" and immune to even the most sophisticated pedagogical techniques.[40]

By ignoring his body, the school endangered the pupil's physical health. Students sat immobile at desks for five or six hours at a time in classrooms that were both inadequately ventilated and ugly. Congested tenements, dirty streets, and parents all too often ignorant of the fundamentals of hygiene made city life perilous enough for children. An unhealthful school environment compounded the danger.[41]

As head of the child hygiene department of the Russell Sage Foundation, Gulick was probably the nation's best-known advocate of medical inspection programs in schools. He especially urged municipal governments to institute such programs in city wards with large foreign-born populations, on the theory that most of the alleged intellectual defects of foreign-born and native poor children were caused by lack of physical vigor, nutritional deprivation, and hearing or vision impairment. Since "the whole man is built fundamentally on what he is physically," it was essential, said Gulick, to have nurses and doctors periodically inspect students.[42]

But even with medical inspection and proper ventilation, the school was still considered by some play organizers to be a hopelessly inadequate agent of moral acculturation. Instead of fostering cooperation between individuals and groups, the school encouraged competition, using the lure of success to tempt pupils to "stand apart" from their peers. Moreover, most teachers assumed that the role of education in modern society was to "make scholars." According to Curtis, this was a dangerously myopic view of the needs of modern American society. The object of education should be to make "men of loyalty in civic affairs, and men of efficiency in business affairs."[43] The school fostered individualism instead of loyalty, favored the native child over the immigrant, and the rich student over the poor one. By contrast:

> On the playground there is no rich or poor, high or low. You have to deliver the goods if you stay on the baseball team, though your father is a millionaire. There is always an almost complete equality between those who play together. The playground is far more democratic than the school.[44]

Even if the school could be transformed into a cooperative, democratic utopia, it would still be less than ideal as an agent of moral transmission. Although compulsory education laws provided teachers with a truly captive audience, there were two significant checks on their ability to influence the moral development of pupils. First, the student often perceived himself as a captive; many pupils disliked school and had little respect for teachers.[45] In the view of play organizers, the fact that students were legally compelled to obey teachers limited the educators' moral influence. Teachers could, of course, force the pupil to behave, but coerced morality was superficial: it was binding only in the classroom and had little influence beyond the school grounds. The school, as Jacob Riis put it, did not "build character," for character was based upon respect for authority, as well as on a willingness to submit oneself to another's "will." According to play organizers, many students neither respected their teachers nor attended school voluntarily.[46]

If conclusive evidence were needed to support these claims, play organizers could point to the "fact" that crime increased nearly 50 percent in poor city wards after the end of the school day. From their perspective it was obvious that moral ideals promoted in the sedate, intellectualized atmosphere of the classroom failed to take hold. But in those same wards, they asserted, the juvenile crime rate fell off to the "normal amount" as soon as supervised playgrounds were constructed. The implication was clear: character was a product of emotionally charged physical activity and had no relation to the mental gymnastics of the classroom.[47]

Nor would the introduction of physical education courses and extracurricular athletic events make the school a more effective transmitter of values. Physical education courses would inevitably be tainted, they claimed, by the competitive spirit permeating the classroom: competition, the desire to win at any cost, and a gross ignorance of the social and moral meanings of play characterized most physical education programs and extracurricular athletic events. "If we look at the social results of [school] athletics," wrote Curtis, "there has not been much more to say. The athletics have been under the domination of coaches who have been hired to win games. They have not been looking for social or educational results but for victories."[48]

To be sure, the PAA lobbied vigorously to persuade boards of education to make physical education a mandatory part of the curriculum. Most play organizers, however, viewed physical education courses as boons to the students' health rather than to their moral development. Gym classes temporarily rescued pupils from ill-lit, enervating classrooms, but they were hardly considered attractive alternatives to the moral curriculum of the organized playground. In addition, extracurricular athletics catered to the few gifted student athletes and left the vast majority to roam the streets after school in search of cheap thrills.

Their commitments to the recapitulation theory and to moral physicalism led most play organizers to promote supervised urban playgrounds rather than to look to the school or the family as the primary transmitters of moral values. Only on organized playgrounds was it possible to develop "a better balanced system of child culture that will take the child as he is and our complex civilization as it is, and harmonize the two in a humane, scientific manner."[49] And the child "as he is" was neither a thinker nor a docile, innocent son eager to obey his parents' commands. He was an untamed specter from the precivilized past. As was true of humanity during its historical childhood, the modern child incorporated enduring moral values and learned useful social skills while exercising his motor impulses. At no time in his life was this more true than in adolescence, and it was during this period that the social-training techniques developed by play organizers reached fruition.

If you were to ask me the goal we are striving after, where we shall
be quite safe, where the slum cannot come, I should lay before you
a map of the City of New York and put my finger upon the islands
that lie in the East River. And I should tell you that on the day when
we shall have grown civic sense and spirit robust enough to set them
apart as the people's playground forever, on that day shall we be
beyond the reach of the slum and of slum politics for good and
all.—Jacob Riis

4
Taming the Wild Animal:
Adolescence, Team Games, and Social
Reform

The movement to organize young people's play was in part an attempt
to harness and transform the experience of adolescence. The need to
control adolescence symbolized the desire of reformers to understand
the problems, conflicts, and prospects of American life in the twentieth
century. To a certain extent, the youth's psychosexual instability, volatile mood swings, and apparent disdain for adult authority justified
play organizers' interpretations of adolescence as a "new birth" and
the adolescent as a "wild animal," but it would be a mistake to assume
that their perceptions of adolescence were rooted solely in objective
analyses of this difficult, transitional phase of life.

For play advocates, adolescence in fact symbolized the transitional
status of American society. *Fin de siècle* America, like the troubled,
"maladjusted" youth, seemed bereft of a stable identity. Just as the
adolescent had difficulty applying childhood ideals to his present realities, the American people, according to play organizers, appeared unable to harmonize traditional rural ideals with current urban realities.

And like the adolescent who was individualistically rebellious and assertive one moment and militantly group-oriented the next, Americans could not easily blend entrepreneurial aggressiveness with the quests for social order and commonality of interests. Finally, like the youth whose personality seemed to be a mosaic of incongruous character traits, Americans were confused about how to harmonize the lifestyles of the new immigrants with traditional perceptions of national unity and identity.

To an extent, then, adolescence was a symbol of a general social problem for play organizers, and their prescriptions for helping young people transcended the issue of child saving. These prescriptions were implicitly aimed at resolving a more general social malaise. The ideal team player was their blueprint for the ideal American citizen.

Reformers' perceptions of adolescence were strikingly modern. They believed that physiological and psychological maturation generated moral instability and "identity" confusion. The youth's sexual and intellectual development disturbed, and sometimes subverted altogether, his commitment to parental values. He was susceptible to conscious and unconscious anxieties caused by the discontinuity between a past of nearly total dependence upon parental authority and protection and the social demand that he should now transcend that dependence. One consequence of this situation was that ethical ties to the

Jacob Riis (1849–1914). Best known for his exposés of slum conditions in New York City, Riis, a journalist, was a leader of the playground movement in New York. (Library of Congress)

past, especially those anchored by idealized images of his parents, were incapable of containing and synthesizing his burgeoning intellectual and sexual powers. Since parental ideals represented a past the youth had to transcend, he often found himself seeking new moral values and guidelines.[1]

Moral instability was the most obvious and socially volatile result of this situation.

> A year ago this wild animal was a well behaved, studious boy, a model in the school and at home; now we don't know what to call him. All the emotions of manhood are stirring and budding within the veins of this irresponsible boy. Before, he was a member of the family thinking what they thought was law; now he must find out for himself.[2]

But adolescence was more than sexual stress and alienation from parental values. The inadequacy of parental values, as well as specific impulses created by the recapitulation process, impelled the youth to make a new social and moral commitment: loyalty to his peer group. Following Hall's lead, play organizers emphasized the peer orientation of youths: they referred to adolescence as the "age of loyalty." The youth compensated for the loss of parental ties by identifying with the wishes and goals of his peers. He yearned to become part of a group in order to find companionship, moral direction, and a new source for self-esteem.[3]

Peer-group formations, such as the adolescent urban gang, were created because of a so-called belonging instinct, a physiological remnant of tribalism—the historical stage of human development that adolescence recapitulated—according to Hall's followers. The need to belong forced the youngster to conform to the tastes, ideals, and aspirations of the gang. This fact, along with his desire for male companionship and willingness to pugnaciously defend the good name and territory of the gang, "proved" that adolescent peer groups were "modern counterparts of the tribe." To be a member in good standing of his gang, the youth had to become "social" and renounce the childhood models and ideals that had generated egoism and individualism, just as his tribal forebears had renounced savagery and submitted themselves to the dictates of family and tribe. As Gulick put it:

> Those early fighters who had not the gang instinct were so effectively eliminated, and the qualities of those with the more social natures were so thoroughly stamped upon the human race through

the action of selection, that now the normal boy demands associates of his own kind as naturally as the baby cries, or the bird builds its nest. The gang is a masculine unit. It is the modern counterpart of the tribe. It is the germ out of which the club, the society, the corporation—every effective organization—develops. The instinct is the chief formative element in the character of most boys, because the opinion of the gang is for them the strongest opinion that exists.[4]

Play organizers assumed that loyalty to the gang was uncritical during adolescence. The youth's identification with the group's "mind" and his desire to relinquish self-interest in deference to its goals were recapitulatory urges and therefore unconscious. The adolescent surrendered himself to the imperatives of group life, even if it resulted in antisocial behavior such as juvenile delinquency or the transgression of parental values that had been the moral touchstones of his childhood.[5]

At the same time, gangs and clubs were viewed by play organizers as invaluable ways of gaining the urban youth's allegiance to social

A boy's gang in Cleveland. (Library of Congress)

order and democracy. Although the unsupervised gang often committed delinquent acts, it was nonetheless the "very source from which all laws are sprung," because it compelled the youth to transcend his "natural" egoism. In order to be accepted by the group he had to renounce his right to act and think as an "individual." The adolescent "belonging instinct" recapitulated ancient psychosocial impulses which gave primacy to the rights and welfare of the group.[6]

Play organizers tried to cultivate this impulse toward group direction because it fostered ideals and behavior they deemed essential for orderly, democratic interaction: cooperation, social service, loyalty, and obedience to group dictates. Rather than destroy adolescent group gangs, play organizers wished to structure their activities by channeling them through the supervised play experience.[7] Specifically, they wanted to harness peer-group dynamics to the structure of team games in order to control and direct the social activities and moral values of urban young people. They assumed that a properly controlled "belonging instinct" would not fade once its recapitulatory force was spent at the end of adolescence. The playground team experience would transform an otherwise evanescent tribalism into a habitual, lifelong moral posture.[8]

THE TEAM GAME AND
TEAM EXPERIENCE

What was a team? According to play organizers, it was a form of association rooted in the cultural traditions of the Anglo-Saxon "race." Other groups had engaged in team sports, but the history and culture of ancient Anglo-Saxon tribes were believed to have been uniquely shaped by activities that fostered group consciousness, such as team sports.[9]

Teamwork blended individual competition and group cooperation, with emphasis upon the latter. For a team to function efficiently, each player had to "merge" his sense of self and body control "into a new unity, and play the game as a unit for common victory." The competent and respected team player was one who saw himself as a mere cell "in the race brain"; his role was to secure the goals of the "organism" and to embody its "will." A team was an "organic" phenomenon greater than the sum of its parts.[10]

Teamwork required both obedience to the rules of the game and specific attitudes on the part of the players. The player should obey the rules, but he must also be loyal to teammates, willingly sacrifice personal glory to the common cause, graciously accept defeat, perceive victory as a group rather than an individual achievement, and obey the team captain.[11] Of course, the game itself was structured: it had rules and explicit imperatives for undertaking specific types of social action at specific moments. The team game had definable goals attainable through tangible means.

Because team games were supposed to make "racial" traditions and ideals relevant to modern society, they were to be organized by play experts and conducted on scientifically designed and well-equipped playgrounds. In unsupervised street games physical force might triumph over fairness and obedience to rules, as reformers thought was often the case with laissez faire capitalism. In street games —and in unregulated big business—moral "anarchy" and unhindered individualism held sway. By contrast, in supervised playground games flouting of rules and untoward forms of competitive individualism were unlikely. According to Curtis, youths organized in permanent teams imbibed respect for law, order, and justice:

> There are now three new factors that tend toward a closer regard for the rules. They are the reputation of the team, the decisions of the umpire, and a growing consciousness that breaking the rules is unsportsmanlike. This is a fundamental training in obedience to law which is needed by every child, for the lack of it leads to many excesses of lawlessness and delinquency in our cities.[12]

Individual subordination and conformity to peers was the core of the play movement's ideology. We must not assume, however, that reformers wanted to obliterate the youngster's individuality. Individual competition was integral to team games, and play organizers wanted it to survive. Play organizers thought regulated competition essential for success in American social and economic life. The team experience was an attempt to create an equilibrium, a creative balance, between individuality and group direction.[13] Society, wrote George Johnson, consisted of atoms and molecules; both were necessary for creative, orderly, and efficient social interaction.[14] Not mindless conformity, but a new concept of freedom was implicit in the team experience. "We are only beginning," wrote Gulick,

> to learn what freedom means. It is not the privilege of doing, irrespective of everybody else, what one wants to do. That would make the tramp the ideally free man. Freedom lies in the recognition and joyful acceptance of relationships. In organized play,

where every child is a unit on a larger, mutually responsible whole, all reach a higher and more significant stage of individual freedom than is possible on the unorganized, free-for-all playground.[15]

The hallmark of this "joyful acceptance of relationships" was the voluntary subordination of the player to the goals of the team and the rules of the game. The youth had to acquire a conscience "larger than the conscience" that recognized and esteemed only individual goals. Genuine subordination to the group prescribed cognitive and affective recognition that the social "unit" was more important than the personal one, and that "the most perfect self-realization is won by the most perfect sinking of one's self in the welfare of the larger unit—the team."[16]

Significantly, play organizers thought that subordination and self-sacrifice transcended utilitarian motives like the desire for victory. The team player had to be taught that peer judgment of his behavior depended as much on his cooperative attitude and unstinting loyalty to the team as it did on his contributions to victory. The spirit with which he played the game was as important to the group as were his physical abilities.

> A long hit or a daring run may not be what is needed. The judgment on his play is a *social* judgment. It is estimated not on the basis of its individual excellence, but by its effect on the success of the team. The boy must come out and practice when he wants to go fishing. He must bat out in order that the man on third may run in. Many a time he must sacrifice himself to the team. This type of loyalty is the same thing we call good citizenship as applied to the city, that we call patriotism as applied to the country. The team game is undoubtedly the best training school for these civic virtues. [Italics added.][17]

The team experience was not supposed to instill a "rational" or conscious awareness of peer-group dependence. The team experience generated what Lee called an unreflective or unconscious "expansion to a larger personality." Games like football and baseball demanded rhythmic muscular movements that created an almost mystical sense of oneness among the players, an unconscious state of "losing his own individuality in a larger whole."[18] In fact, the organized team resembled the nervous system: the actions and reactions of each "cell" were meaningless without reference to the functions of the entire organism. The basketball team's tempo and rhythm were generated by a fusion of each player's reflexes into a unit whose skills were qualitatively distinct from those of each player. At this level of organization, the spirit of team unity dominated the youth, "vibrating in his nerves and tingling to the ends of his fingertips."[19]

The Playground Association of America created team game sporting meets in which competition between individuals took a back seat to competition between groups. The purpose of the meets was to make victory and defeat group, social experiences rather than individual, personal experiences. George Johnson supervised a typical PAA experiment in "team competition" in Pittsburgh in 1912. One hundred boys were divided into four teams for participation in an assortment of team contests, including the broad jump, tugs of war, and the five-mile relay. The idea of the meet was to demonstrate that competition between groups could diminish the intensity, and personal joy and disappointment, of individual competition. Johnson was pleased with the results:

> I am inclined to believe that the spirit displayed by both the victors and the vanquished after the meet was the finest that we had ever seen at one of our meets, as though the success of the team enlarged the satisfaction of winning in the heart of each boy and as though the bitterness of personal defeat were lost in the feeling that all had done what they could and had stood together.[20]

The relationship between the team experience and the genesis of group loyalty was vividly described by the philosopher Josiah Royce in a speech to the Boston Physical Education Association in 1908. Royce, who was Joseph Lee's instructor at Harvard during the 1880s and his friend and intellectual mentor in later years, told his audience that loyalty was more than mechanical allegiance to group causes. Genuine loyalty issued from a "cause" transcendent to the individual's self-interest, a cause that monopolized his consciousness and influenced his moral judgments. The truly loyal person was so devoted to his cause that his "psycho-motor" apparatus functioned as if it were aware of the moral distinction between private interests and public causes. The group cause was something "vast, dignified, imposing, compelling, objective."[21] The loyal person

> always views persons in their deeper relations to something that seems larger than any mere collection of persons can be. The cause is not only other than his private self. His private self is its willing instrument. The cause inspires him, acts through him. Loyalty is a sort of possession. It has a demonic force which controls the

wayward private self. The cause takes hold of the man, and his organism is no longer his own, so long as the loyal inspiration is upon him.[22]

According to Royce, group loyalty was the moral fulcrum of personal morality and social order, and few activities were more effective in imbuing the young with this sense of loyalty than team games. Royce told his audience that calling oneself loyal was meaningless unless the "muscles somehow express this loyalty." Membership in a supervised athletic team offered one of the best hopes for the development of a generation of "loyal" young people because team games combined motor discipline with a commitment to communal control of the individual. In a team game, loyalty was expressed through physical activity, and muscular discipline was the most efficacious means of instilling morality:[23]

> When the apostle compared the moral work of the saints to the running of a race, his metaphors were therefore well chosen because of this perfectly definite analogy between the devotion of the trained organism to its physical task and the devotion of the moral self to its cause. In both classes of cases, in loyal devotion and in skilful and strenuous physical exercise, similar mental problems have to be solved. One has to keep the self in sight in order to surrender it anew, through each deed, to the task at hand.[24]

While few play organizers subscribed to Royce's philosophical idealism, all of them shared his view about the moral relevance of physical exercise. The rhythmic, disciplined texture of the organized team game created affective as well as physical synchronization. It united peer-group judgment and obedience to rules with the drama, elation, and excitement of the athletic contest.

Nonetheless, the game itself could guarantee neither the player's adherence to team goals on the playground, nor his commitment to group aspirations outside the playground. The team experience therefore included sanctions for the enforcement of the cooperative ideals inherent in teamwork within, and beyond, the confines of the playground.

THE TEAM EXPERIENCE AND PEER-GROUP MORALITY

The peer-group team embodied the moral values learned on the playground. Not only did the team's goals and ideals define what the individual should value, but peer judgment of his behavior was the sole sanctioning force on organized playgrounds. The team's reaction to his behavior and attitudes was supposed to be the source of the youth's moral self-evaluation. Play organizers spent a good deal of time trying to make this ideal a reality.

E. B. DeGroot, a friend of Jane Addams and a Hull House resident before he became director of Chicago's South Park System, developed innovative methods for establishing peer-group morality on the playground. DeGroot tried to decrease the authority of adult game officials; he wanted the team itself to compel the player to comply with the rules. For example, he altered the personal foul rules in basketball, believing that a player who was selfishly competitive or a bully would not be deterred by the threat of personal fouls. The team, rather than the player, was penalized by allowing the opposing team points for the infraction. "Team" fouls had "a better relation to the concrete problems of good citizenship" because the adolescent knew that if he violated a rule his teammates would stand together in "keen and silent" judgment of his behavior. The player would realize that unsportsmanlike or self-aggrandizing behavior threatened the team's prospects, and that the team, not he alone, would suffer the consequences. Fear of arousing his teammates' ire would compel him to act like a "team player."[25]

DeGroot also suggested that adult officials be eliminated wherever feasible as a means of diminishing the baneful effects of competition. He wanted "free" throws eliminated in basketball, lest players think that they should profit because of another's wrongdoing. In baseball he wanted the catcher to call balls and strikes on opposing hitters to elevate honesty and fair play over competitiveness.[26]

In the South Park System, DeGroot developed a team game "rating" system to institutionalize his ideas. Winning a team game was determined by three criteria: the ability to cooperate (35 percent); fair play and honesty (25 percent); and outscoring the opposing team (40 percent). It was thus possible for a team to outscore its opponent and lose the game because of moral lapses. Presumably Chicago's adolescents learned that cooperation with one's group was more important than either personal aggrandizement or competition between groups.[27]

The wish to embody moral authority in the team was the core of playground "socialization." On playgrounds in Boston, New York City, and Chicago, systems of player self-government were instituted. Playground "citizens" elected mayors, chiefs of police, judges, and juries. These officials judged the playground conduct of their peers and carried out "sentences" against those who violated rules, vandalized playground property, or refused to subordinate themselves to the team. The ultimate penalty was banishment from the team or playground. The purpose of the peer police system was to make the adolescent peer group, rather than adult playground directors and game officials, responsible for moral compliance. Curtis thought the peer system effective because adolescents "dislike a punishment that is inflicted by their peers more than they do one that is imposed by the director."[28]

The idea behind peer-group sanctions was to recreate within the playground, and by implication within the modern city, the ambiance of the "village community," which Lee called the "crucible of the race." The player had to be made aware not only that his behavior affected the well-being of his playground neighbors, but that he was incessantly observed by them as well. On the playground, if not on the street or in the tenement, a form of community opinion existed that limited the youth's freedom of action.

This pervasive system of observation was designed as a substitute for parental authority. In the opinions of play organizers, neither parents nor the general community were capable of supervising urban youngsters, who were exceedingly adept at losing themselves in the urban maze of alleys, streets, vacant lots, abandoned buildings, dark hallways, and darker cellars. The "urban wilderness" freed adolescents from adult authority and often created an atmosphere conducive to juvenile lawlessness. Worse still, it created a citywide atmosphere of social anarchy and anomie. "The danger," wrote Lee,

> often realized, is that the city dweller may have no neighbors, or at least no neighborhood—no group of any sort in which he feels a membership—no immediate social atmosphere, no standard which holds him up and which he feels it his business to uphold. . . . the greatest injury to the individual from the atrophy of the neighborhood in modern life is through the loss of its reflex effect upon his own morality. The people of his own street need know nothing of his life. There is nobody to whom he must give an account of himself or present a definite and comprehensible personality, no public opinion to which he is effectively amenable.[29]

Supposedly, the playground would help remedy this situation. Peer pressure made the adolescent "effectively amenable" to law and order by "squeezing" him into "the desired pattern" of behavior.[30] Peer pressure during the team game helped fill the urban moral void by making his group the youth's "village community." The team was supposed to incessantly observe and approve or censure his behavior. It was de-

signed to become the arbiter of his ideals and personal tastes. Ultimately, the gratification he derived from exercising his cognitive and
motor skills was tied to his teammates' estimation of his behavior and
attitudes.

The ultimate weapon used by peers against the habitually recalcitrant youth was the one play organizers assumed he feared most: ostracism. Gulick was convinced that urban work conditions and residential
patterns created conditions conducive to what we call a "youth culture." Young people were supposedly free of parental supervision and
reveling in a street life where social order depended upon the power of
the peer group to harness the youth's behavior. If peer values were in
fact the major source of the youth's ideals, it followed that peer sanctions had a greater impact on his conscience and behavior than "parental authority or reason." Fear of peer ostracism was the only sanction
powerful enough to compel the city youth to toe the moral line.[31] "A
participant in team play," Lee wrote,

> feels to the marrow of his bones how each loyal member contrib-
> utes to the salvation of the rest by holding the conception of the
> whole so firmly in his mind as to enable them to hold it also, and
> how the team in turn builds up their spirit. And he so perceives
> the effect of the disloyal member, the one who refuses adherence
> to the going conception of the team, usually one in whom the power
> of membership is weak, the chronic objector.[32]

The team as "one great community mind" shaped and legitimized
the player's behavior and values. It also placed specific limits upon his
right to behave in a "competitive" or "individualistic" manner.[33] The
rhythmic, synchronized movement of a basketball team as it roamed
up and down the court forced players to see, feel, think, and act as a
unit rather than as individuals. The physical discipline and rhythm of
the game produced an overarching muscular orchestration, an athletic
symphony that, ideally, melded the players into an undifferentiated
unit. An official of the Playground Association of America succinctly
described the process: "First the feet begin to keep time, then the whole
body catches the rhythm, then the individual forgets his dignity, his
pride, becomes as a little child and has entered the kingdom of heaven,
has joined the dance and has become a part of the team."[34]

Because the team experience forged social unity out of individuals
from diverse ethnic, class, and religious backgrounds, play organizers
viewed it as an antidote to the alienation, violence, and loneliness
seemingly inherent in urban society. Team membership provided each

player with a specific role, an assigned task to perform within the context of communal goals and control. A football game forced the individual to "lose" himself in the task at hand until he was no longer conscious of whether he was "carrying the ball or merely the one at the bottom of the heap so long as the ball is pushed across the line."[35] Such examples of social unity and its benefits were bound to have a salutary affect on city life, and to neutralize the painfully lonely condition of the urbanite. During the baseball game, Jane Addams wrote, players and spectators alike

> are lifted out of their individual affairs and so fused together that a man cannot tell whether it is his own shout or another's that fills his ears; whether it is his own coat or another's that he is wildly waving to celebrate a victory. Does not this contain a suggestion of the undoubted powers of public recreation to bring together all classes of a community in the modern city unhappily so full of devices for keeping men apart.[36]

The team experience also cultivated the youth's empathic faculty and helped him to understand "reality" from the other person's point of view. Team games transformed the youth into what Curtis called "a ganglion cell in the brain of humanity." The ideal team player perceived reality from "a common soul and consciousness."[37] Organized teams often consisted of youths from diverse ethnic backgrounds, and the team player's ability to empathize with his fellows mitigated ethnic tensions. Players were imbued with a commitment to fair play and equal justice for all.[38]

Another facet of team morality was its creation of what play organizers called a "corporate conscience." Participation on a team made the adolescent a member of an organization that transcended his finite individuality. The sensation of being a member of the team, of being the "eye, the hand, the foot," of a powerful organization, was essential to the youth's psychological and social stability during the troubled years of adolescence.[39] But the importance of the "corporate conscience" went beyond its usefulness for decreasing adolescent instability. The team player's self-esteem was inseparable from his efficiency as a team member. The team experience was supposed to compel the player to realize that his role and behavior had no meaning apart from communally defined goals and values. In other words, team membership was an ideal tool for teaching young people what it meant to be a loyal member of an efficient organization. The adolescent team experience thus instilled cognitive skills and moral values appropriate for

success in an organizational, bureaucratized society. The ideal team
player not only identified with his team, but could not distinguish its
goals from his desires. Lee aptly described the relationship between the
adolescent team experience and the adult "corporate conscience":

> The point is not in making money but in making good, in holding
> down the part assigned to you in the economy of the social whole
> to which you may belong, as the boy in the school team holds down
> third base. It is only as he thrills and vibrates to the structure of
> the whole, as the life of the social organism flows through him and
> compels him to his task and his place, that the full life of the
> individual comes forth.[40]

Play organizers' ideas about the necessity of peer-group moral sanctions were based as much on their sociological analysis of urban society
as on their assumptions about the crisis of adolescence. They were
convinced that the adolescent peer group was one of the few viable
agencies of moral transmission remaining in American cities. The economic and physical configurations of the modern city eliminated the
family as an effective transmitter of morality. At least one parent spent
most of the day working and commuting to and from the work place.
Even if the mother did not work outside the home, she might contribute
to the family's income by engaging in "domestic industry" within it.[41]
Tenement living made it unlikely that parents could supervise their
children's street activities or even know where they were at any given
moment. According to Gulick, the city family could neither control its
children nor transmit moral values because the social and economic
activities "out of which morals arose" in rural societies were altered or
destroyed in the city. The family's moral impotence meant that the
"community," in the form of organizations like the PAA and the public
school, had to assume responsibility for the child's moral acculturation.[42]

Play organizers were of the opinion that moral compliance was not
secured through "rational" methods, and that paternal authority did
not rest upon the child's cognitive appreciation of the father's practical
importance as family breadwinner. It was not sufficient to organize
children's play or restructure the school curriculum along "progressive" lines, they felt, because moral compliance depended upon fear of
sanctions and respect for authority, neither of which was necessarily
a rational or conscious attitude. Addams implied as much when she
wrote that organized recreation generated emotions that were stronger

than those generated by vice.[43] Team players did not incorporate meaningful moral values when they learned to subordinate self-interest for the good of the team as a means of achieving victory. On the contrary, getting along with teammates from different ethnic and class backgrounds and adherence to the rules of the game became morally meaningful only when they were linked to fear of peer ostracism and to what DeGroot called the "keen and silent" judgment of teammates. In short, play organizers believed that the motivations behind moral compliance were often emotional and unreflective rather than conscious and cognitive.[44]

That is why they emphasized the affective qualities of muscular activity and discipline. Team games did not simply elicit emotion; they tied emotional expression to muscular and cognitive responses. The team experience melded physical discipline, perception of the action and choices involved in the game, and moral compliance to the game's rules and the team's ideals into what play organizers perceived as a unified flow of action. The focus of that activity was the omnipresent peer group, and the youth's dread of alienating its affections. Ideally, adult play directors simply set the team experience in motion. Play organizers thought that the organized play experience was so refined and "scientific," and its physical and moral effects on youth so inevitable, that it was merely necessary to set it in motion and leave the rest to biology and the peer group.

Obviously, radical changes in ideas about morality and the meaning of adolescence were inherent in this conception of peer-group autonomy. (These changes are discussed in Part Two.) The optimism—one is tempted to say complacency—with which play organizers viewed their prospects is noteworthy. They were convinced that if enough urban young people were exposed to the team experience—either on organized playgrounds or on school teams—and became peer-directed, American society would inevitably be changed for the better. Most assumed, for example, that class antagonism and industrial strife were caused by unregulated economic competition and lack of understanding between social classes. Many play organizers were "reform Darwinists," staunchly opposed to the notion that society could be organized around the ideals of rugged individualism and the survival of the fittest. Most favored industrial concentration as a means of minimizing the inefficiency and waste of competition and mitigating economic exploitation. The PAA viewed the corporation as an ideal laboratory for testing their ideas about the relationship between team sports and social cooperation. The association's field secretaries encouraged corporations to build athletic facilities near their plants and to sponsor team contests in which workers and supervisors played on the same team. The assumption was that "teamwork" on the playing field would carry over into the workshop. "Pulling together" for a common goal on the playing field would create a common allegiance between workers and employers: they would develop loyalty to the company and put their particularistic interests aside. The association did more than exhort. It supervised construction of play facilities for large corporations like the Johnson and Johnson Company.[45] Joseph Lee hoped that worker-supervisor cooperation on the athletic field would generate a spirit of camaraderie between these groups. "The worker," Lee wrote,

> must feel that the work is his work; that what the company achieves he achieves; that he holds a worthy and responsible place in the great organization whose wares are known in the markets of the world. He is to be dealt with, not as a parcel of hired muscles, but as a partner, an associate, a member of the team.[46]

The modern work process, however, not only exacerbated class conflict; it was alienating and boring as well. What if, Addams wondered, the modern worker approached his or her industrial task in the same spirit of playfulness, adventure, and cooperation that inspired the ideal team player? Would not the work process be less boring and alienating, regardless of how enervating it might appear at first glance?

> It takes thirty-nine people to make a coat in a modern tailoring establishment, yet those same thirty-nine people might produce a coat in a spirit of "team work" which would make the entire process as much more exhilarating than the work of the old solitary tailor, as playing in a baseball nine gives more pleasure to a boy than that afforded by a solitary game of hand ball.[47]

It was equally important to instill these values in future workers during the morally impressionable adolescent years. Play organizers assumed the peer-group moral paradigm of the adolescent team experience carried over into adulthood. A population of group-directed adults would make city life less frightening and more humane. The playground values of cooperation and mutual observation would infiltrate neighborhoods. In other words, the playground was to the modern city what "the church, the cathedral and the town square" were to the medieval town: a symbol of social unity and security.[48] Those who played the organized team game as adolescents were likely to understand the necessity of reviving local control over individual behavior. Indeed, group direction would restore the social cohesion damaged by urban mobility and anonymity. In Addams's view, the ideal of pulling together for the general good, which typified the organized team, would help neutralize the centrifugal effects of social and geographical mobility and ethnic exclusivity.[49]

The tendency of ethnic groups to isolate themselves and their children in urban ghettos was particularly alarming to play organizers. If the urban family in general was an ineffectual socializing agency, the immigrant family was infinitely worse.[50] Play organizers believed that the team—that is, the peer group—obtained the youth's moral compliance far more effectively than the working, and often "ill-adjusted," immigrant father. The promise of adventure and comaraderie offered by the playground kept the youth off the street and out of trouble more effectively than the prospect of spending hot summer evenings in a crowded tenement. The skills learned through participation in organized sports prepared children of immigrants to adapt to the "rules of the game" played by American society more effectively than their alien parents could.[51] Children of both native and immigrant parents, according to Lee, exposed to the team experience "became fused as parts of one another in a way which crosses the limits of race and caste and economic class."[52] As Graham Taylor pointed out, organized play was a most efficacious way of generating ideological and social unity from ethnic and class diversity.[53] No one summed up the aspirations of the play movement in the area of immigrant acculturation more accurately than Henry Curtis, who was director of the New York City playground system before he organized the PAA. Curtis had firsthand knowledge of the ethnic tensions and diversity of that city:

> For a long time on the East Side of New York there was a faction between the Jews and the Italians, and nearly every afternoon they used to get out on the streets and chase each other up and down with sticks and stones and banana peelings. This would go on until the police would come out and stop it. Finally, a playground was opened on the border line between the two sections. The children came into the playground, but the Jews stayed on one side and the Italians on the other. Then we began to organize games . . . that required a large number of players on a side, and little by little the children fell in and played with us. After six weeks, they did not know whether they were Jews or Italians.[54]

Curtis's naiveté may be hard to comprehend, but his point is well taken: peer direction on organized playgrounds was supposed not only to replace parental authority, but to subvert the youth's allegiance to the cultural traditions embodied in that authority; the peer group, in short, was an instrument of "Americanization."

Finally, play organizers believed that organized play deterred juvenile crime. They saw juvenile crime as rooted to some extent in social conditions that the playground either controlled or ameliorated: ethnic antagonism, moral anonymity, and lack of parental supervision. Reformers like Riis, Addams, Frederic Howe, Judge Ben Lindsey, and Allen Burns, head of the Chicago School of Civics and Philanthropy, were quick to point out that on Chicago's South Side juvenile crime decreased an average of 44 percent in wards with supervised playgrounds, and that in Cincinnati youthful offenses decreased by more than 50 percent one year after the city funded a playground system. Similar figures were reported for other major cities. These statistics were often misleading, but they nonetheless created a broad base of support for the construction of publicly financed playgrounds in slum wards.[55]

Obviously, play organizers' assumptions about the impact of urban-industrial life on the family, particularly the immigrant family, were among the central tenets of their ideology and key reasons for the existence of the play movement. It is noteworthy, therefore, that play organizers' perceptions of the immigrant family in an urban-industrial setting were at best inadequate, and at worst erroneous.

Play organizers held the questionable belief, echoed in later years by such eminent scholars as Oscar Handlin and S. N. Eisenstadt, that southern and eastern European immigrant families were ill-equipped to withstand the rigors of urban life and therefore were incapable of preparing their children for the stresses, challenges, and prospects of the New World.[56] Children of immigrants were seen as refugees roaming aimlessly in a cultural no man's land between maladaptive parental values and confusing, though alluring, American values.

This was a tragically myopic perception of the immigrant family. The cohesiveness of southern and eastern European families may have been somewhat loosened by American social conditions, but they were hardly shattered. In fact, evidence amassed by scholars over the past decade indicates that Old World patterns of family authority and organization not only survived in America, but strongly influenced the values and aspirations of the second generation, and that immigrant families, far from passively fitting into the mold dictated by industrial work rhythms and economic imperatives, often used industrial work patterns to sustain traditional ideals of family authority and solidarity.[57]

Play organizers and other child savers competed for, rather than dominated, the allegiances of immigrant youngsters. It is inconceivable, for example, that the team experience functioned in reality as it did in play organizers' flights of fancy. While visions of merging and fusing "units" of team players danced in the heads of play organizers as they witnessed a team game, most youths probably had a good time playing what, after all, was only a game—at least to them. This does not mean, of course, that playground social-training techniques were entirely ineffectual: their effectiveness is impossible to gauge. But the playground was only one of many, often conflicting, influences on urban immigrant youngsters. Even in the realm of playgrounds, as Roy Rosenzweig has recently pointed out, immigrant children probably had their own ideas about what games to play and how to play them.[58]

To a great extent, therefore, the reactions of play organizers toward children of immigrants were forged from a combination of wish fulfillment and myopia. They were fighting for control of those children, and they knew it. Perhaps that is why Curtis's description of allegedly delinquent Jewish and Italian youths becoming Americans "after six weeks" of exposure to the team experience smacks more of hysterical paralysis than historical analysis.[59]

I am concerned less, however, with the accuracy of play organizers' sociological analyses than with their motivations, intentions, goals, and the sources of their social-training methods. To understand these methods, we must analyze the psychosocial dynamics of the peer-group morality that they created on organized playgrounds. To comprehend their tendency to view childhood and adolescence through the lens of the recapitulation theory, we must uncover the social and intellectual reasons for the theory's attractiveness to Progressive Era reformers. Finally, to understand their belief in the moral relevance of physical exercise, we must try to uncover the links between their ideas about social and moral reform and their perceptions of physicality.

PART TWO

Interpretations: The Playground and Cultural Change

A boy who does not play a great deal with his fellows can not develop a broad ethical character. In association with adults only he is not brought into a wide range of vital situations in which he may learn that in the measure that he gives in that measure will he receive.

MICHAEL V. O'SHEA

Play is far more important than mere muscular activity. It is the most potent expression of the child's personality. The future lies in it.—Luther Gulick

---

5
The Anatomy of Moral Change: Organized Play and Moral Reform

When thinking about the organization of children's play, the structural aspects of the play movement most readily come to mind. This structural dimension includes the "scientific" study of play made by reformers, the development and deployment of playground equipment, and the training of play directors. There was, however, another, and far more important, dimension of playground organization: the psychological organization of the playing youth. The ideal adolescent team player was supposed to think and behave in a specific and highly integrated manner. In other words, he was a distinct personality type.

It is important to analyze his personality, because the ideal team player's moral, emotional, and cognitive makeup reflected the kind of adult—and the kind of social relationships—that play organizers hoped would infiltrate American society from the organized urban playground. To a significant degree, the personality of the ideal team player represents the moral legacy of Progressive Era reformers who participated in the play movement.

To be sure, play organizers were a diverse group. Every major tendency and paradox of progressivism was represented in their ranks. Thus, Joseph Lee and Robert Woods viewed organized play as a way of asserting society's control over adolescents and "Americanizing" the children of immigrants. On the other hand, reformers like Jane Addams and Lillian Wald believed in the ideal of ethnic pluralism and perceived the team game as a symbol of diversified unity. The "rules of the game" represented the consensus to which all players adhered so that the game could be played. At the same time, the idiosyncratic talents each player brought to the field or the court symbolized the unique contributions each ethnic group, profession, or craft could make to the strengthening and diversification of American culture. For them, the team game represented what John Higham has called the social ideal of early twentieth-century pluralism—"an aggregate that has several components."[1] Luther Gulick's emphasis on the merging of moral judgments and physical activity during the team game had important implications for a society enchanted with the social and economic benefits that could be derived from the scientific management and bureaucratic organization of people and things. Gulick's ideas represented the play movement's contribution to the creation of values, attitudes, and skills necessary to reap the promise of an efficient, orderly, and organized American life.

None of these reform tendencies dominated the ideal team player's personality. Each, however, made significant contributions to it because, translated into techniques of socialization, the ideals of unity, diversity, and efficiency had specific effects on the ideal team player's personality.

ORGANIZED PLAY AND THE "FEMINIZATION" OF MORALITY

What were the rights and duties of the individual and society?

This philosophical question with which play organizers grappled took on psychological implications in the organized playground. How were moral judgments made? Where and how did the individual receive his moral cues? Did they reside in wholly personal, idiosyncratic norms? Or did they impinge upon the individual from public sources in the form of significant others like the peer group?

Not surprisingly, play organizers wanted the adolescent to receive his moral cues from his peer group. What is surprising is that they viewed peer-oriented morality as a "feminine" style of moral consciousness, and contrasted it to what they called a private or "masculine" moral style.

It should not be assumed that this feminine-masculine moral dichotomy was a consequence of the significant roles played by women in Progressive Era reform movements, including the play movement, although some female reformers tended to view the struggle between reform and reaction as a reflection of a deeper existential rift between "feminine" and "masculine" moral and social styles. For instance, Jane Addams implied that ideals like social cooperation, empathy, loyalty, and solicitude for the weak and dispossessed—in short, the sentiments that inspired the reform movement—were distinctly feminine virtues. By contrast, uncontrolled competitive individualism and the ideal of the "survival of the fittest" were supposedly rooted in a masculine style of social and moral consciousness. Some female reformers suggested that the infusion of so-called female attributes into the sociopolitical process would mitigate the suffering and anxiety produced by masculine entrepreneurial aggressiveness.[2]

In the play movement, however, many male reformers held similar views. Gulick, for instance, divided human motives into the "stomach hungers" and the "love" or "friendship" hungers. Stomach hungers, symbolizing "masculine" drives, were the sources of economic self-interest, ambition, competitiveness, material production, and accumulation. Love hungers, symbolizing "feminine" impulses, inspired empathy, solicitude for the disadvantaged, and self-sacrifice.[3]

While stomach hungers dominated childhood, when personal security and comfort were the individual's main interests, love hungers erupted "with a rush" during adolescence and, if properly cultivated by traditional maternal solicitude, infused the youth's psyche with the so-called feminine sentiments: self-sacrifice and social cooperation. Because the city environment disrupted traditional parent-child interactions, however, the transmission of love hungers from mother to child was threatened.[4] Consequently, nonfamilial institutions like the organized playground and the Camp Fire Girls had to transmit and cultivate "feminine" virtues in the urban young, "and make of our cities the abode of love which women and children have made of the home."[5]

Gulick's perception of the relationship between feminine nurture and social amelioration was significant because he equated reform with the infusion of a "feminine" moral consciousness into male children. In this sense the movement to organize children's play was an attempt to "feminize" the moral style of urban male youths. The question, of course, is why did play organizers dichotomize morality into feminine and masculine styles? In effect, the ideas of femininity and masculinity had been transmuted into cultural symbols of moral bipolarity under which antithetical values, like empathy and individualism, were subsumed. Why did the idea of gender become morally significant?

The belief in two distinct, gender-related moral styles was in part a legacy of nineteenth-century sex roles. What Barbara Welter has called the "cult of true womanhood" was more than a method of idealizing and controlling women. Its ultimate rationalization for funneling feminine aspirations and passions into idealized domestic channels was the claim that women were morally, as well as physically, distinct from men. Women were more emotional and "loving" than men. Women's propensity for self-sacrifice was rooted in their moral passivity: they were easily influenced by significant environmental (male) figures and interpersonal sensitivity allowed them to empathize with others. By contrast, the ideal-typical male of the mid-nineteenth century systematically pursued private goals of wealth, power, and fame. His singlemindedness was rooted in the availability of definitive, stable, and "rational" moral values; the male of the species knew precisely who he was. Thus, while the male's rational and morally autonomous nature equipped him for the ruthless competition of nineteenth-century industrial society, the female's emotional and morally empathic nature made her an ideal domestic worker.[6]

This masculine-feminine moral dichotomy was applied to child-rearing practices. Many Americans, particularly the reform-minded, believed that the female monopolization of child nurture would fortify male children against what they saw as the crass materialism of mid-century society. If mothers could instill in their sons even small doses of "feminine" sentiments, the aggressive pursuit of wealth and power might become a lesser threat to social and psychic stability.[7]

The problem confronting nineteenth-century nurture experts was how to instill the penchant for economic individualism in male children while simultaneously encouraging them to adhere to moral sentiments that were symbolized as "feminine."[8] How far could male children be morally "feminized" without becoming "de-masculinized" as well? However subversive entrepreneurial aggressiveness may have been of social order and moral rectitude, it was nonetheless essential for American economic growth and territorial expansion.

This problem was portrayed, though not resolved, by one of the most influential nurture writers of the mid-century period, the liberal New England theologian Horace Bushnell. Bushnell was ambivalent about the "spatial" sources of the child's moral judgments. He excoriated what he termed the "extreme individualism" of his society, and he believed that moral character consisted to a great extent of ideals "previously wrought in us" through an imitative "organic" interaction between parents, particularly mothers, and their children. Bushnell, however, was never explicit about the precise spheres of influence controlled by individualism and organicism during the processes of moral judgment. Were moral judgments rooted in individual autonomy and personal, idiosyncratic moral principles (individualistic, "masculine" sources), or were they linked to the subtle pressures exerted upon the person by significant environmental figures (social, "feminine" sources)? Bushnell was not sure:

> To a certain extent and for certain purposes, we are individuals, acting each from his own will. Then to a certain extent and for other purposes, we are parts or members of a common body, as truly as the limbs of a tree. We have an open side in our nature, where a common feeling enters, and through which we are actuated by a common will. There we are many—here we are one.[9]

In any case, the emphasis on propagating the "softer" virtues supposedly inherent in women was never pushed to the point where it negated "masculine" traits like ambition and competitiveness. Even Bronson Alcott's "radical" vision of the child as an innocent transcendent idealist was compromised by his desire to instill in his children a kind of "worldly asceticism" based to a degree on respect for private property.[10] And Bushnell himself was seldom specific about where or when the child was "many" or "one." Thus, socialization techniques stressed a series of contrapuntal, bipolar, feminine-masculine moral and social attributes. The ideal child was expected to harmonize within his personality bipolarities like aggression and benevolence, self-interest and cooperation, self-direction and awareness of the social consequences of his behavior, and a penchant for social mobility mingled with a commitment to social unity and equality.[11]

Play organizers not only inherited this dilemma, along with the tendency to use gender as a symbol of moral style, but had to deal with it in a radically different social setting. Balancing the countervailing tendencies between order and freedom in social-training techniques is difficult in any context, but the problem was compounded for Progressive Era reformers by the quantity and ethnic diversity of urban school-age children. Between 1890 and 1918, the urban high school population increased by 711 percent, and in the most populous cities after 1900, including New York, Boston, Chicago, Cleveland, and San Francisco, the majority of school-age children had foreign-born fathers.[12]

This situation helped blur traditional meanings of freedom and order. To mid-nineteenth-century Americans, who lived in what they saw as a *relatively* homogeneous society, ideas of personal freedom, social order, and national unity had definite meanings—at least when applied to Anglo-Saxon males. But what did these ideas mean when applied to the children of immigrants? Did "freedom" mean the right to immerse oneself in the moral and cultural world of one's parents?

How could one speak about national unity and social order in a society where scores of nationalities lived together in congested cities, in what some reformers perceived as a state of mutual hostility? But the problem of defining freedom and order in social-training methods went beyond the problem of immigrant acculturation. Children of all classes and ethnic backgrounds had to be equipped with the intellectual skills necessary for living in a dynamic industrial society. The task of social training was not made easier for Progressive Era child savers and educators by the fact that methods had to be devised for initiating adolescents into the adult world of work and social responsibility.

On organized playgrounds, play advocates tried to resolve these problems by integrating selected masculine and feminine character traits in social training. Thus, they attempted to instill a penchant for social cooperation by encouraging a group-directed, "feminine" moral style. Simultaneously, they encouraged players to cultivate idiosyncratic cognitive skills and personal initiative by creating a team experience that compelled the successful player to acquire proficiency in analyzing and interpreting the "facts" of the game action. The ideal team player, then, was morally intuitive and empathic, yet "rational" and empirically oriented at the same time. He was, in short, a blend of those masculine and feminine traits that play organizers thought essential for individual stability and social order in a society that was complex, rapidly changing, and increasingly bureaucratic.

THE TEAM EXPERIENCE:
MORAL COMPLIANCE THROUGH SHAME

The ideal team player had a shame-prone conscience. When he violated, or thought about violating, a team or playground rule, the youth was threatened by shame anxiety and compelled to make amends or experience the painful, isolating emotion of shame. But shame-proneness is more than a moral sanction. It forces the person to organize ego aims and defenses to avoid the eruption of this particularly unpleasant affect, and to be highly sensitive to, and to take his moral cues from, an external source, in this case the peer group, rather than from "inner," idiosyncratic principles. Thus, a shame-prone conscience is similar to the so-called feminine moral style extolled by nineteenth-century nurture writers. By instilling a shame-prone conscience in urban adolescents, play organizers hoped to transform the social and moral meanings of adolescence. To understand the implications of their strategy, it is necessary to discuss briefly some aspects of the psychoanalytic theory of morality, and the distinctions between shame and guilt.[13]

In contemporary psychoanalytic theory, the "superego," which includes the elements of conscience and moral judgment, is a system of internalized motivations. The child's moral acculturation and compliance are based on his emotional "understanding" of what motivates others to approve or disapprove of his behavior. That is, his compliance to authority is premised on motives that are not available for his conscious examination. Parents' approval or disapproval is affectively imparted to the child through their vocal tones and facial expressions, and his dependence on their care and love compels him to try to live up to their expectations. The child thus perceives, and ultimately internalizes, cultural mandates about behavior.[14] Failure to adhere to these mandates mobilizes unpleasant feelings such as shame, guilt, and remorse. The measures taken to avoid the eruption of these unpleasant sensations affect one's style of dealing with the external world.[15]

Another significant dimension of superego, the ego ideal, represents the idealized people, groups, and values that the person has chosen as models. In effect, ego ideal is a projected ethical future. The difference between what the person is and what ego ideal standards suggest he should strive to become often causes shame, that is, unpleasant sensations derived from the exposure of a self that has failed to live up to expectations.[16]

Ego ideals define, among other things, the values that a person should cherish and help him evaluate his success in making his behavior coincide with those values. The values and goals subsumed under the rubric "ego ideal" may in fact be impossible to achieve realistically, or may simply point toward an idealized future. Nonetheless, however unrealistic these behavioral and ethical standards may be, they exert "a tremendous influence on our realistic behavior."[17]

Ego ideals are subject to change. One cause of change is adolescence, the period during which social and psychological pressures force the youth to question many childhood ideals. During this process the validity of the original ego ideal, based on parental ideals, is questioned, and the youth often becomes confused about his ethical commitments. It is at this stage that peer-group morality can make itself felt, and the youth may turn to it as an alternative to discarded or weakened parental ideals. Thus, "a gang leader or teenage idols may replace the adolescent's parental introjects in determining the content of the ideal self."[18]

There are important phenomenological differences between shame and guilt. Both are punishments inflicted on a person when he violates his moral code, but whether shame or guilt is threatened depends upon the "style" of the person's superego. Guilt most often erupts when the person violates a *specific* aspect of his prohibitive (thou shalt not) moral code, while shame frequently appears when he falls short of ego ideal aspirations. It is possible for an individual's superego to operate predominantly along one of these routes—to use the sanction of either shame or guilt as the principal means of compelling the person to comply with his moral values.[19] Whether shame or guilt predominates depends upon which identifications are stirred by the violation. Thus:

> shame and guilt are highly important mechanisms to insure social-ization of the individual. Guilt transfers the demands of society through the early primitive parental images. Social conformity achieved through guilt will essentially be one of submission. Shame can be brought to the individual more readily in the process of comparing and competing with the peers (siblings, schoolmates, gang, professional group, social class, etc.). Social conformity achieved through shame will essentially be one of identification.[20]

Since shame is evoked when a person fails to live up to ideals that he identifies with his "self," it threatens his self-esteem and identity. Shame is nonspecific and diffuse; it is mobilized to punish the person's failure to measure up to the idealized, projected image he has of him-self, and which others have of him. In other words, shame deals with the self's generalized failure per se rather than with a violation of a specific, identifiable moral prohibition such as the mandate against theft, for example. The individual threatened with shame affect is faced with the possibility of being confronted by internalized "images" which remind him that he has failed to become what he and "they" believed and expected he would become.[21]

> In shame, the internalized admired imago functions . . . as the referent "in whose eyes" shame is experienced; a "shadow" of the imago falls on the self. These "watching" thoughts may include the awareness that the person is thinking about what the other person is thinking about him. In this kind of instance, the self is both participant and watcher in its own fantasy.[22]

Shame also evokes bodily reactions like blushing, sweating, and increased heart rate. The shame-prone individual may feel physically exposed to the gaze and criticism of the internalized "other."[23] Shame isolates its victim. Because it exposes a deficient self, shame subverts the person's image of what he is and what he believes others think he is. Thus, shame tends to arouse feelings of alienation, isolation, abandonment, and self-contempt. Anxiety aroused by fear of being shamed evokes images of "social expulsion" and "ostracism."[24] Finally, shame is extremely difficult to assuage because the self *qua* self has been indicted.[25]

In contrast to the nonspecificity of shame, guilt ensues when the person has violated a specific aspect of his moral code. The act, not the self, is condemned, and expiation usually entails explicit, culturally prescribed modes of atonement. Guilt is a personal sensation because there is no question, as there is with shame, of the social exposure of an inadequate self. The guilty person has *done* something wrong; the shamed person has *become* something wrong:[26]

> the imagery of the self *vis à vis* the "other" is absent in guilt. In the experience of guilt, the self is doing the judging; the experience is thus self-contained and self-propelled. Guilt is about something specific about which the self is critical, in contrast to shame, where criticism or disapproval seems to emanate from the "other" and to envelop the whole self. Guilt thus tends to have a more specific content, which can be put in words. It is intrinsically a more ideational experience than shame, which tends to be a wordless, acute feeling.[27]

The team experience encouraged a shame-prone style of making moral judgments and complying with superego values. Play organizers pointed out that team membership could not instill a moral style suited to modern life if it stressed solely obedience to game rules, that is, if it emphasized the legalistic, negative side of morality. During the team game, moral sanctions resided in the external "watching thoughts" of one's teammates. "The essential rules," declared Gulick, "even of later life are expressed in public opinion," rather than in prohibitive personal values or "rational" legal codes.[28]

The player who violated rules or disregarded the rights of teammates was not reprimanded, but humiliated; he was supposed to experience an acutely painful, unlocalized sensation that exposed him as a traitor to both ego ideals and his peers. The "disloyal," selfish player was "hissed and called a fool,"[29] and exposed to the "keen and silent" judgment of teammates.[30] Abandonment, isolation, and shame were the penalties for disloyalty and individualism.

It was clearly the ego ideal rather than an isolated element in the prohibitive moral code that was betrayed by disloyal conduct. The team player's ego ideal was an internalized representation of his peer-group team and its aspirations. The individual's identity and self-esteem were linked to his own and his teammates' expectations of how an ideal player should behave. The focus was on his attitude, not his conduct alone. In short, the team experience mandated congruence between ego ideal and conduct, between his idealized self-image and his behavior. His "self," not just his behavior, was the focus of playground social training. Since his peer group and his self-image were "fused," as play organizers liked to say, his behavior was controlled by the need to measure up to public or group standards and by anxiety over falling short of those values.[31] Gulick put it more succinctly: "a large part of conduct is undoubtedly controlled by the ideals our friends have of us."[32]

There was also a nexus between the physical quality of team games and the peculiarly physical nature of the experience of shame, between the shame-prone individual's fear of exposure and the belief that the ideal team player's character was revealed by his behavior. As Addams and Gulick observed, physically rigorous play activities compelled the player to "merge" his values (that is, his true self) and his conduct: he was "revealed" through his behavior because his muscles showed peers what he really was.[33] Physical conditioning, in short, was an ideal medium for instilling shame-proneness.

The team player's moral style was not the only facet of his personality affected by shame-proneness. Because shame-proneness compels the individual to be especially sensitive to cues from peers, it has a profound impact upon the ego function of visual perception.[34] Persons with a shame-prone superego are likely to be visually field-dependent. According to the psychoanalyst Helen Lewis, the field-dependent have a fluid or indeterminate sense of their self-boundaries, especially with regard to those whose values and opinions they admire; they not only approximate what David Riesman called "other-direction," but perceptually they are, as play organizers liked to put it, "fused" to admired others.[35] Because his ideals are embodied in the activities and aspirations of others, the field-dependent perceiver sees himself and "their" selves not as discrete entities but as more or less fluid phenomena intertwined on a time-space continuum. The field-dependent person has a "global, relatively unarticulated conception of the human body."[36]

For a shame-prone person, field-dependence is a highly adaptive form of visual perception. It provides him with a public, "objective" embodiment of his ego ideal. Since the field-dependent person experiences himself as a reflection of significant others, an incessant reminder of how he measures up to or falls short of his ego ideals is before him. In Lee's words, the player is compelled to conform because of the "pattern" established between "the inexorable pressure of the ideal within him and the obdurate resistance of outer fact"—the team.[37]

Field-dependent perception is an ideal defense against the eruption of shame because it guarantees that violations of ego ideals will find an immediate social echo. Because shame involves exposure of an inadequate self, field-dependent perception is the perfect complement to a shame-prone superego style. To avoid the alienating consequences of shame, the person must measure himself against those in the outer world who reflect his internalized ideals. Perceptual field-dependence ensures that he will do just that.

Play organizers had a more succinct way of describing this relationship as it applied to the team. Joseph Lee called it a "belonging instinct":

> Just what this feeling of belonging is defies analysis. An accessory to it, included in the consciousness of the efficient member, is a sense of the mechanical working of the team, the extension of the personality so as to include the team as a piece of mechanism. But the thing itself is not mechanical: membership is not a question of physical combining, nor on the other hand, is it merely a matter even of spiritual cooperation. It does not simply consist of helping each other nor of working together for the same end. It means working not coincidentally but as a unit, acting not merely together but as one person, as though from a common soul and consciousness.[38]

Shame-proneness and field-dependence are ideal characteristics for a group-directed individual. But group direction was not the only personality trait that play organizers wished to propagate on the playground. They understood that modern society was rooted in a technical-scientific ethos, that the industrial development and economic prosperity of the United States was in no small measure dependent upon the efficiency and expertise of its labor force and administrators, and, therefore, that young people had to be made competent, efficient, and knowledgeable in the techniques of modern production and administration. Inseparable from the scientific-administrative temper, at least as play organizers perceived it, was the capacity to analyze and scientifically control and administer complex situations and interactions.

Playground socialization reflected these assumptions. The efficient team player had to master three complex aspects of the game. He had to know the meaning of every event that occurred during a game and the behavior it demanded: a sacrifice bunt, an outfield throw to second or third. He had to know the rules of the game and obey them even at the cost of victory; as a corollary, he had to be a gracious winner and a good loser. Finally, he had to judge his teammates' appraisal of his attitude and performance.

Each of these operations required the ability to treat complex problems analytically, that is, idiosyncratically. The ideal team player could not respond quickly and effectively to the innumerable and often unexpected circumstances that arose in the course of games by seeing with his teammates' eyes. A certain amount of cognitive autonomy had to be woven into the fabric of moral conformity.

Organized team sports were attractive social-training devices precisely because they balanced moral conformity with cognitive autonomy. Team games are not unlike what S. N. Eisenstadt has called "totalistic," or closed, experiences.[39] While these games promoted autonomous cognitive evaluations, their structures to a great extent limited, indeed determined, the kind of evaluations the player could make. No matter how varied, complex, and contingent a game situation might be, it demanded a predetermined, "correct" response from the player. For example, whether an outfielder should throw to second or third involved an autonomous act of evaluation, but the judgment's range and independence were narrowed because there was a correct base to throw to in that and every other case. With proper training, practice, and experience, the young outfielder should learn to throw automatically, almost instinctively, to the correct base.

Thus, while the player had the responsibility of interpreting the meaning of a game situation, his freedom of response was narrowed by the closed nature of the system: the game situation contained its own resolution. Once the player learned what response each situation called for, all he had to do, ideally, was efficiently execute the "game plan." Team games honed cognitive skills without threatening the conformist propensities of the ideal team player.

Precisely for this reason, team sports were thought to be ideal means of training the young for life in modern society. Participation in team sports taught young people to be efficient and orderly members of a "team," whether on the playground or in society. If progressives believed that social efficiency, scientific industrial management, and bureaucratic organization were the waves of the future, they also realized that these waves would barely make a splash unless the young were systematically trained to think "efficiently." Team sports promoted efficient thinking by instilling in young people the capacity to make "almost instantaneous and accurate motor reactions to situations,"[40] and by compelling the player to "think quickly, accurately, and conclusively if he is to be successful."[41] Indeed, as Curtis observed, team sports were "the best training that we know for the type of instant decision and execution that virtue requires," because decision —moral or cognitive judgments—and execution were combined in a fluid muscular process.[42] It was unnecessary for the player to make subjective moral or cognitive evaluations during a game. All he had to do was analyze the meaning of the "facts." As in John Dewey's theory of moral knowledge, a correct cognitive evaluation of the game was the equivalent of a moral judgment.

In one sense, then, the organized play experience was a resolution of the nineteenth-century social-training dilemma. Playground socialization emphasized the "feminine," publicly oriented ideals of selfless service, sacrifice, cooperation, and empathy with one's fellows. It also stressed the exercise, however limited in scope, of private "masculine rationality" in the areas of "objective" analyses of reality and the development of technical skills. Significantly, the balance that play organizers fashioned between cognitive autonomy and moral conformity systematically excluded affect from the process of making moral and cognitive judgments. The player based his judgments upon the facts of the game, rather than upon a personal, emotionally charged value system. In effect, the closed system of team game action removed passion and subjectivity from the judgmental process. In psychoanalytic terms, it made the superego function of moral judgment a subcategory of the ego function of cognition.

The social implications of an emotionless, "cognitive morality" are disturbing. As Stanley Milgram pointed out in his book *Obedience to Authority,* once superego operations are reduced to cognitive assessments "of how well or poorly one is functioning in a system of authority," the individual can commit acts in the name of the company, nation, or team from which he would normally shrink:[43]

> Language provides numerous terms to pinpoint this type of morality: loyalty, duty, discipline, all are terms heavily saturated with moral meaning and refer to the degree to which a person fulfills his obligations to authority. They refer not to the "goodness" of the person per se but to the adequacy with which a subordinate fulfills his socially defined role. . . . For a man to feel responsible for his actions, he must sense that the behavior has flowed from the "self."[44]

There was no "self" on the organized playground. What did exist, at least in the minds of play organizers, was the peer group, the "facts" of the game, and the overwhelming desire to reduce the individual to his behavior by destroying his subjective awareness of himself as a being distinct from his social roles and duties. In a sense, the team experience created an intellectual atmosphere analogous to the one described by Thomas Kuhn in his paradigm theory of science. Like Kuhn's practitioner of "normal" science, the ideal team player could "see" only what the game's closed structure and his commitment to peer values allowed him to see.[45]

In the final analysis, one overarching idea pervaded playground social training: a value-free, objective analysis of the "facts" was the premise for social efficiency, social order, and democratic vitality. The fact that play organizers tried to achieve these worthy goals by eliminating moral subjectivity, by reducing morality to a cognitive analysis of technical facts, and by elevating their version of the scientific method from a means to an end, serves as eloquent testimony to their perceptions of science, social order, and democracy.

An important feature of playground socialization was the attempt to control the adolescent experience by manipulating the youth's penchant for group direction. As we saw in chapter 4, play organizers were well aware of the peer orientation of urban youth. What bothered them was the peer group's asocial or antisocial character. By making the "social" aspects of team membership the keynote of playground training, play advocates hoped to cultivate those aspects of peer direction, especially loyalty and cooperation, that they thought essential to the social and economic progress of the country. In effect, the cooperative utopia that they believed existed on playgrounds was a blueprint for ideal social relations in the rest of society.

Adolescents had been peer-oriented before 1890; in both Europe and the United States, peer groups had exercised a significant, though intermittent, control over young people since at least the eighteenth century.[46] Moreover, compulsory mass education after 1880 made the development of a youth culture almost inevitable by creating an institutionalized hiatus between childhood and adulthood. In effect, compulsory mass education defined social roles according to age and forced young people to cope collectively with collective problems.

What made the social-training methods of play organizers and other Progressive Era educators significant was the attempt to turn an unorganized and rather ill-defined tendency toward peer loyalty into an extreme form of peer direction.[47] This is an important point because peer direction, especially the extreme form promoted on playgrounds, is not necessarily a dominant trait of adolescence. but merely one of several devices that the youth can employ to surmount the difficulties arising from his metamorphosis into an adult. Other things being equal, he might choose instead to withdraw into himself and sublimate his energies into intellectual development or hobbies, or he might become peer-oriented in some respects but relatively immune to peer promptings in others.[48]

Other things were not equal, however, on the organized playground, and peer direction was made the eye of the adolescent storm. Some of the reasons for the play organizers' substitution of peer direction for adult authority, such as the role of ostracism in moral development, have already been discussed. Another reason is that the peer group was seen by reformers as a substitute for the family.

Play organizers were convinced that the family was incapable of preparing the child for the psychological and intellectual demands of modern society.[49] The increasingly affectionate and protective tone of middle-class family life in the nineteenth century was hardly an ideal way to prepare the young to absorb the shock of living in a world that appeared more impersonal and capricious with each passing year.[50] As the family became more a refuge from than a means of preparing for the strife and uncertainty of urban-industrial society, outside agencies, most notably the public school, assumed familial prerogatives in the moral and intellectual training of the young.

By 1900 many concerned citizens believed that such responsibility was more than the public schools could bear. There were simply too many students, too few teachers, and not nearly enough time for the schools to do an adequate job in both the intellectual and moral areas. Many people believed that the youth received his formative moral training neither in school nor at home but rather in the "street" as a member of an urban gang. The rise in the juvenile crime rate seemed to confirm such apprehensions. Consequently, concerned citizens created a host of agencies designed to structure the youth's activities and values when he was neither at home nor in school. In various ways, these agencies made the peer group the moral center of the youngster's life. Such agencies included the Boy Scouts, the Camp Fire Girls, juvenile court systems and reformatories, extracurricular school activities, particularly sporting events and student self-government experiments, a wide variety of boys' clubs, and the organized playground. As we have seen, on organized playgrounds the peer-group team not only fostered moral conformity but also was responsible for ensuring that the team player was prompt, acted correctly, got along with teammates, and effectively fulfilled his "assigned task" within the team "organization." All of these elements were important for his successful adaptation to a corporate-bureaucratic-democratic society. The peer group was supposed to serve a "functional" role in socializing young people: it was a mediator between the family and society, and as such it exposed the youth to both the harsh realities and the potential rewards offered by the world outside the family.[51]

Another function of peer direction was to subvert the immigrant child's allegiance to parental authority. Even the cultural pluralists among play organizers doubted that immigrant parents could instill in their children an aptitude for democratic interaction and a commitment to social unity. The peer group was an ideal vehicle for these purposes because it accomplished its tasks without arousing the suspicion that youngsters were being encouraged to emulate adults other than their parents. Play organizers could thus use the peer group to promote Americanization without exposing themselves to charges of cultural condescension; it was the peer group that made kids act that way. And there could be no doubt about the meaning of how they acted on most of the organized playgrounds. Daily activities began not with volleyball or basketball, but with the singing of patriotic songs by peer group teams, followed by flag ceremonies in which youngsters collectively pledged their minds and hearts to "one flag, one nation, one language."[52]

All human vicissitudes are, in the end, melted down into reminiscences.—Jane Addams

6
Playground Training and Sex Roles: Jane Addams and the Play Movement

It may seem incongruous to conclude a volume on the history of male-oriented playground programs with a chapter on the life of a prominent female social reformer renowned more for her role as a social settlement activist than as a play organizer. But the events, issues, and problems that dominated the first three decades of Jane Addams's life —the subject of this chapter—are decisively tied to major issues discussed in previous chapters. From her birth in 1860 in a rural Illinois village to her founding in 1889 of the Hull House social settlement in the heart of Chicago's working-class neighborhoods, Addams's experiences as an adolescent, as a woman, and, most significantly, as a college-educated woman with nondomestic ambitions, shed light on the ideology and the social-training practices of play organizers. Our understanding of the ideal team player's personality, of play organizers' perceptions of adolescence, and of the organizers' attraction to the theory of recapitulation will be enhanced by discussing the events of Addams's early years. More important, Addams's adolescent struggle with competing masculine and feminine moral and social styles was the sex role equivalent of the guilt-shame dichotomy discussed in chapter 5. It is, in short, *necessary* to conclude this volume with a discussion of this important woman's life through early adulthood.

Of course, by analyzing the life of only one play organizer we cannot learn all that there is to know about the complex relationship between the play organizers' social backgrounds and involvement in the play movement.[1] The material on Addams is suggestive rather than conclusive; it will not tell us everything we want to know about the motivations of play organizers. Neither will it establish a nexus between their personalities and the character traits of the ideal team player. Certainly, it will not allow us to assume that Addams's experiences and motivations were representative. Just as the backgrounds and political perspectives of play advocates varied, so too did their reasons for participating in the play movement. We have to take the Addams material for what it is: a suggestive glance into the life of an important play organizer.

The focus of this chapter is on the sex role confusion Addams experienced from childhood to the opening of Hull House. I argue that the resolution of this confusion was implicit in both her decision to become a social reformer and in the personality dynamics of the ideal team player. The team player's personality was the psychological equivalent of the resolution of Addams's deeply seated and culturally determined sex role confusion—a confusion she shared with many educated middle-class women of the late nineteenth century.

In saying that for most of her first thirty years Addams experienced an acute masculine-feminine role confusion, I do not mean to imply that she was uncertain of her feminine identity. Rather, she was uncertain about the social, moral, and political implications of womanhood. As middle-class women like Addams attended college in increasing numbers during the last third of the nineteenth century,[2] many of them became disenchanted with the restrictive social roles assigned them by the domestic piety syndrome discussed in chapter 5. The facile dualisms implied by mid-nineteenth-century perceptions of masculine and feminine characteristics—worldliness-domesticity, aggressiveness-passivity, rationality-emotionalism—were rendered problematical, at least for educated women.

In 1880, for example, Addams, as one of the ablest members of the Rockford College debating team, addressed her schoolmates on a subject that in one way or another would engage the curiosity, passion, and anxiety of Americans for the next hundred years: the "new woman." Addams told her audience at this small northern Illinois women's college that educated women should see themselves as more than future homemakers and mothers. Though more "intuitive" and emotional than men, educated women had the same responsibility as their male counterparts to direct their intellectual energies into the mainstream of modern empirical and scientific thinking. Addams told her listeners that new social roles and new careers would embellish rather than diminish the new woman's femininity. Far from denying her femininity, the new woman

> wishes not to be a man, nor like a man, but she claims the same right to independent thought and action. . . . On the one hand, as young women of the nineteenth century, we gladly claim these privileges, and proudly assert our independence, on the other hand we still retain the old ideal of womanhood—the Saxon lady whose mission it was to give bread unto the household.[3]

As the last lines indicate, young Addams, along with many Americans of her day, adhered to the tenets of the domestic piety configuration: women, no matter how educated, were constitutionally domestic, while men were existentially worldly. But the problem with Addams's "independent" new woman was that she did not mesh with these prevailing sexual stereotypes. Clearly, Addams was exhorting her young female listeners to summon the courage to venture into what for too long had been a man's world. Their educational attainments entitled these woman to a place in that world. At the same time, Addams demanded that they retain and refine their commitment to their "households." But how could these women be both "independent" and "Saxon ladies"? How could they maintain the delicate balance between domesticity and worldliness? At what point would worldly ambition and involvements lead to a diminution of "true womanhood" and pose a threat to their feminine identities? This thorny problem generated pain, anxiety, and disillusionment among late nineteenth-century middle-class women like Addams.[4]

But women were not the only ones disturbed by the apparent irrelevance of mid-century sex roles to late-century social realities. As we saw in chapter 5, male play organizers like Gulick believed that traditional family functions, such as moral transmission and educational preparation, were too complex to be left to the modern nuclear family. These functions had to be assumed by the community and the state. Hence, according to Gulick, the feminine penchant for compassion and empathy, heretofore expressed within the private confines of the home, had to be "socialized." Women, in his words, had to "go into the world," where their publicly oriented feminine traits were desperately needed to counteract economic and moral anarchy.[5] Earlier in the century women had supposedly created an atmosphere in the home that gave children and husbands a feeling of comfort, security—a sense that they "belonged." Now women had to generate the same cohesiveness in an urban-industrial society racked by ethnic, economic, and political factionalism. Robert Woods, Addams's colleague in both the settlement and play movements, wrote revealingly that settlement workers must attempt to revive the flow of "moral menstruum" in the city's morally desiccated streets and politically corrupt wards. Here Woods sounds every bit the mid-nineteenth-century purveyor of the true womanhood cult. In the same volume, however, he claims that the settlement must be a "scientific laboratory" that devises social policies based on a hard-headed analysis of pertinent social facts.[6] Settlement workers, in short, had to exhibit both the moral inclinations of the female and the empirical orientation of the male. But how could they do so?

Progressive Era reformers, both male and female, seemed confused about the relevance of traditional masculine and feminine spheres and characteristics.[7] The ideal team player, like the ideal settlement worker, was a blend of idealized masculine and feminine traits. This confluence of culturally prescribed gender characteristics becomes understandable if we approach the concept of culture from the perspective provided by the sociologist Kai T. Erikson. Erikson defines culture as a "moral space" that shapes and delimits behavior. Culture is a cluster of inhibitions, rules, languages, and values "that promote uniformity of thought and action."[8]

What makes Erikson's definition of culture unique is his argument that other forces in addition to those generating uniformity are at work in all cultures. Culture affects not only how people think and feel, but how and what they imagine as well, and "it is one of the persisting curiosities of human life that people are apt to imagine the complete contrary of the ideas and attitudes that figure most significantly in their view of the world." That is, the opposite of a value is implicit in the minds of its adherents, so that wherever "people devote a good deal of emotional energy to celebrating a certain virtue . . . they are sure to give thought to its counterpart." Value and countervalue, then, become cultural partners, forming what Erikson calls an "axis of variation that cuts through the center of a culture's space" attracting "attention to the diversities arranged along it."[9]

The stereotyping of feminine and masculine moral and social styles that was common in nineteenth-century America can be seen as an example of Erikson's axis of variation hypothesis. The demand that men be assertive and ambitious implied the possibility that they might fall short of these ideals and succumb to a "feminine" passivity. The notion that women were emotionally and intellectually suited to be mistresses of the household contained, however implicitly, the fear that under certain circumstances they might aspire to be masters of the world outside the home. In short, these stereotypes inevitably generated ambiguity. Erikson has discussed how individuals and societies deal with this type of ambivalence:

> These contrary tendencies are reflected at many different levels within the social order. At the individual level . . . they are experienced as a form of ambivalence. When a person is caught between two competing strains in his cultural surround and can find no way to resolve the dilemma, he can be said to suffer from inner conflict. When he is able to attune himself comfortably to one or another of these strains, or *manages somehow to combine them into a new and more coherent whole,* he can be said to have achieved ego-integration. [Italics added.][10]

From early childhood Jane Addams was exposed to cultural ambivalence toward masculine and feminine moral styles. The ambivalence was implicit in her broader cultural milieu as well as in her idiosyncratic family setting. Her decision to become a social reformer constituted, for her and her society, a creative integration of these stereotypical gender styles. The personality of the ideal team player was the psychological equivalent of that integration: the player's shame-prone moral style was stereotypically "feminine," while his relatively emotionless mode of cognition represented masculine rationality and objectivity. Addams herself, during childhood and adolescence, walked the tightrope of a masculine-feminine "axis of variation"; she experienced intense moral and social conflict because she could not integrate competing feminine and masculine moral prescriptions within her personality. She was not sure when or how to act like a "true" woman. But as her personal crisis deepened during the 1880s, so did the social and moral crisis of urban America. Her response to the urban crisis not only led to the founding of Hull House and her participation in the play movement, but also helped her to achieve what Erikson calls "ego integration." For Addams, ego integration consisted of a synthesis of feminine and masculine ethical strains into a new and dynamic moral vision of urban America. Her vision combined a commitment to what she called a "social," that is, feminine, morality with an equally intense faith in the social and political utility of masculine empiricism—the scientific method and bureaucratic techniques. The ideal team player's personality embodied that synthesis.

Addams was born in 1860 in Cedarville, Illinois, a small town in the northwestern corner of the state. Her mother, Sarah Weber Addams, who died two years later while giving birth to her ninth child, came from a middle-class background. Although Sarah Addams entertained "no thought of a 'career' excepting that of mother and homemaker," she had attended boarding school and had obtained what in those days was considered a good education for a woman.[11]

Because her mother died when Addams was two years old and her father did not remarry until 1868, she centered upon him "all that careful imitation which a little girl ordinarily gives to her mother's ways and habits." By her own account, John Addams became the "dominant influence" in her life. Her idealized image of his character, behavior, and status first drew her "into the moral concerns of life."[12] This attachment to her father was so intense that her nephew said it amounted to a "possession."[13] As a child she was constantly ashamed of her physical appearance and the contrast between herself and her father. She was horrified at the thought that strangers might guess that "the ugly, pigeontoed little girl, whose crooked back obliged her to walk with her head held very much to one side," was the daughter of such a dignified, respected, and handsome man. This feeling of inferiority toward her father was a constant theme of Addams's childhood ruminations. One Sunday during her eighth year (it may be significant that it was the same year John Addams planned to remarry) she appeared before him in a new cloak "gorgeous beyond anything I had ever worn before." For some reason, she needed to appear particularly attractive when they went to church together. Her father, however, admonished her that the new cloak was too ostentatious and might make the other girls at Sunday school feel inferior. Sorely disappointed, Addams agreed to leave the cloak at home.[14]

The man whose character his daughter idealized was in many respects the embodiment of his era's ideal of success. John Addams had been a miller's apprentice, but after settling in Cedarville in the 1840s he quickly took advantage of the many opportunities offered by a burgeoning economy. By the late 1850s he was president of the Second National Bank of nearby Freeport. In addition, he was president of a life insurance company and the owner of lumber and flour mills. Politically, he was conservative and immensely influential. He was a friend and political ally of Lincoln, and served as a Republican member of the Illinois legislature from 1854 to 1870. Addams was a "practical" man who spurned political and religious extremism. His political philosophy revolved around the ideals of equal opportunity, individual initiative, and local control of the economy. He is described as "austere" in his relations with his family: he expected, and usually received, the obedience and loyalty of his children.[15]

In fact, John Addams exemplified the virtues of the nineteenth-century "rugged individualist." While a young pioneer, he exhorted himself in his diary to ignore opinions and enticements that threatened his principles. He was a man who took advice "only from his own conscience." Since he seldom troubled himself over questions of religious dogma, his description of himself as a Quaker assumes meaning only when viewed from the perspective of his moral individualism. He offered no advice to others, except in business affairs. Accustomed to living by his private "inner light," and convinced that the great duty of a man was the preservation of moral integrity, " 'Honorable John Addams' refused to interfere with the spiritual affairs of others."[16]

As she neared adolescence, Addams's moral precepts were dominated by her idealized image of her father's character. She identified with, admired, and tried to emulate those facets of his character which made him socially and economically successful: "I doubtless contributed my share to that stream of admiration which our generation so generously poured forth for the self-made man. I was consumed by a wistful desire to apprehend the hardships of my father's earlier life in that faraway time when he had been a miller's apprentice."[17] Accordingly, she sought out the books, ideas, and ideals that had influenced him in his youth. She emulated him whenever possible. Sometimes this passion for emulation assumed an extreme form, such as awakening at three in the morning because he did so. Addams assumed that by exposing herself to her father's experiences she would eventually "understand life as he did."[18]

Her father's ideals may have dominated Addams's childhood values and behavior, but they did not monopolize them. Although she died when Jane was two years old, Sarah Addams, or at least her death, had a considerable influence on her daughter. People often died young in the world in which Addams grew up. Only four of the nine children born to Sarah and John Addams lived beyond sixteen years of age.[19] But death's pervasiveness did not lessen the effect of Sarah's death on Jane Addams. Indeed, according to her nephew James Weber Linn, Addams never forgot her mother's final hours, when, in her desire to be at her mother's side, she had pounded on the bedroom door.[20]

Half a century later Addams provided indirect evidence of the impact Sarah's death had had on her. In 1916, at the age of fifty-six, she published a book entitled *The Long Road of Woman's Memory,* a sensitive, moving description of the physical and psychic degradation experienced by Western women. In the final chapter Addams discussed an eerie experience she had had while visiting Egypt some years after the founding of Hull House. The ancient Egyptians' religious and artistic responses to death aroused within her "an unexpected tendency to *interpret racial and historic experiences through personal reminiscences"* [italics added].[21] Perhaps this sense of recapitulation was a natural response to the artistic splendor of Egyptian tombs.

> Nevertheless, what I, at least, was totally unprepared to encounter, was the constant revival of primitive and over-powering emotions which I had experienced so long ago that they had become absolutely detached from myself and seemed to belong to some one else—to a small person with whom I was no longer intimate, and who was certainly not in the least responsible for my present convictions and reflections. It gradually became obvious that the ancient Egyptians had known this small person quite intimately and had most seriously and naively set down upon the walls of their temples and tombs her earliest reactions in the presence of death.[22]

In their tombs the Egyptians "painstakingly portrayed everything that a child has felt in regard to death." In their ardor to overcome the finality of death, the ancient Egyptians and the modern child "often become confused" and "curiously interrelated." Children and "primitive" peoples shut out death, the latter by erecting "massive defences" like the pyramids, the former through magical thinking. Both primitives and children believed in eternal life, that the dead are not really dead but possess a "double" form that defies destruction.[23]

These thoughts, sprinkled with images of racial recapitulation, sparked another memory in Addams. When she was six or seven the mother of a classmate had died, and the students were brought to the cemetery to take part in the final rites. Young Addams had believed the dead went straight to heaven and was "totally unprepared to see what appeared to be the person herself put deep down into the ground." She became "suddenly and brutally" aware of the finality of death, and for weeks her "days were heavy with a nameless oppression and the nights filled with horror." During these painful weeks the question of what her motherless classmates could do to help themselves haunted her. That dread, however, was soon "translated into a demand for definite action on the part of the children against this horrible thing which had befallen their mother."[24]

It may seem odd that Addams remembered her first confrontation with death's finality as occurring at the funeral of someone else's mother, but it is understandable. It was unlikely, for two reasons, that Addams's Egyptian experience would lead to a direct confrontation with her mother's death.

First, a two-year-old is not mature enough to experience fully the loss of a love object, although the child's psychic development can be retarded by such a loss. What a child of that age loses because of her mother's "absence" is not a fully internalized object—that is, a part of her superego motive system, which at age two is in a primitive state of development—but rather a comforting nurturer. If the child is fortunate enough to have competent "mother surrogates" at hand, as Addams did in her older sisters and her father, the effect of the loss may be lessened. The child might experience something akin to grief, rather than mourning, but permanent psychological damage can be avoided.[25]

Second, the memory awakened in Egypt was that of her classmate's mother because the visual impact of the interment "suddenly and brutally" brought six-year-old Addams face to face with something she may have hitherto denied: the finality of the loss of her own mother. It also resuscitated the memory of her response to that loss. Her feelings were translated, as she put it, into definite "action." Now a child of six or seven, she was infinitely more capable than she had been four years earlier of feeling adrift in the absence of a mother, of feeling different from children whose mother had not "deserted" them, and of feeling vaguely culpable that she was somehow unworthy of having a mother.

Such feelings are not unusual in a motherless or fatherless six-year-old.[26] What was significant was Addams's capacity to cope with her crisis, to respond realistically—within the parameters allowed by her society—to the fact that she and her siblings were motherless and her father was a widower. She coped by identifying with the virtues, attitudes, and duties that her society associated with femininity and motherhood.

As we have seen, she doted on her father, adored him, and wanted to appear attractive for him. In her autobiography she recalled having "a curious sense of responsibility" during her sixth or seventh year. Her almost missionary sense of responsibility was pervaded by feelings of maternal solicitude, and was made even more intense because it coincided with Oedipal tensions and with her recent discovery at the "other" mother's funeral that Sarah Addams was gone forever.

I dreamed night after night that everyone in the world was dead excepting myself, and that upon me rested the responsibility of making a wagon wheel. The village street remained as usual, the village blacksmith shop was "all there," even a glowing fire upon the forge and the anvil in its customary place near the door, but no human being was within sight. They had all gone around the edge of the hill to the village cemetery, and I alone remained alive in the world. I always stood in the same spot in the blacksmith shop, darkly pondering as to how to begin, and never once did I know how, although I fully realized that the affairs of the world could not be resumed until at least one wheel should be made. The next morning would often find me, a delicate little girl of six, with the further disability of a curved spine, standing in the doorway of the village blacksmith shop, anxiously watching the burly, red-shirted figure at work. I would store my mind with such details of the process of making wheels as I could observe, and sometimes I plucked up courage to ask for more. "Do you always have to sizzle the iron in water?" I would ask, thinking how horrid it would be to do so.[27]

This recurring dream and her recollections of her confrontation with death in the *Long Road of Woman's Memory* indicate that however strongly Addams indentified with her father's private, austere, "masculine" moral style, she also was influenced from an early age by its "feminine" counterpart. One need not be a Freudian to discern the sexual symbolism in her dream, along with the not very subtle hints that she had taken her mother's place in the household. Of much greater significance, however, is the impression that Addams's dream conveys of one way in which socially prescribed feminine roles became intertwined with the idiosyncratic experiences of a female child left "alone" with her widower father.

This does not indicate that Addams had "neurotic" inclinations. Her attempts to cope with death appear to have been adaptive, given the society in which she lived. By the time she was fifteen Addams viewed death as a "relentless and elemental" force. Whatever anguish it might evoke, death was inevitable: "once to be young, to grow old and to die, everything came to that!"[28] But as we shall see, this was not her last brush with the anguish of death, and it was only the beginning of her confusion over masculine and feminine moral styles.

At seventeen Addams entered Rockford Seminary, a nondegree women's college that specialized in missionary training. She had wanted to go to Smith College because it was one of the few institutions that offered the bachelor of arts degree to women, but her father insisted that she attend nearby Rockford, and, as usual, she obeyed him.[29]

On the surface at least, Addams appeared to be as attached as ever to the moral, social, and political ideals of John Addams through most of her four years at Rockford. She resisted her teachers' attempts to "convert" her, because she believed that she, like her father, could live a morally upright life without adhering to externally imposed denominational dogma. Her social and political ideals, as expressed in her school work, also largely reflected the crucial elements of the elder Addams's world view: hard work, personal initiative, and asceticism. As late as the mid 1880s, she still considered herself a high-tariff Republican.[30]

Alongside these "masculine" identifications, "feminine" counter-identifications were reawakened during the Rockford years. Perhaps it would be more precise to say that her feminine identification developed and began to assume a form quite alien to the pliant, would-be mother of the blacksmith dream. Addams could no more accept Rockford's conventional teaching that woman's social role was restricted to home-making or mission work than she could accept the seminary's conventional religious wisdom. Her exposure to the major intellectual currents of the day, particularly Darwinism, convinced her that the study of science might open social and political doors that had formerly been closed to women. Through the study of science, the "intuitive" mind of women could be disciplined and taught to function empirically and concretely. The educated woman must not limit her aspirations to traditional social roles, but must "convert" her "wasted force to the highest use."[31]

Although Addams's vision of women's role in American society was very different from the prevailing "domestic piety" model, the difference, as J. O. C. Phillips has pointed out, was social rather than sexual. While higher education provided some women with skills that allowed them to seek work and rewards outside the home, it also extended the scope of their alleged innate nurturant tendencies to perplexing social and political issues.[32]

Once she began to think of feminine nurturance as a political force instead of a means of exerting a benign influence on children and husband within the home, Addams ran the risk of openly rejecting her father's moral style. In almost every way the nurturant propensities of what Addams called the "truest womanhood" that "can yet transform the world,"[33] clashed with the moral consciousness of John Addams. The notion of feminine nurturance was far removed from the morally privatized world of her father. Indeed, the public, "feminine" morality with which she increasingly identified during her college years was

explicitly opposed to a "masculine" moral style based upon individualism, unrestrained ambition, and a subjective "inner light." Thus, even
before her graduation from Rockford in 1881—the year of her father's
death—Addams was already reassessing her commitment to his moral
style. Consequently, she found herself in the midst of a struggle between antipodal masculine and feminine moral styles.

It is difficult to pinpoint the reasons for the surfacing of this
conflict at Rockford. Undoubtedly, the missionary school was permeated with visions of woman's destiny as savior of a forlorn, materialistic world. Although Addams was relatively immune to Rockford's
religious-messianic ambiance, she was highly receptive to feminine
nurturant themes that could be applied to social and political issues.

A more compelling reason for the surfacing of the conflict in these
years may have been the very fact that Addams was in college. She was
a member of the first generation of middle-class women to attend college in significant numbers.[34] It was because she was a college student
that she could develop skills and ambitions that would make her dis-
satisfied with traditional feminine social roles. In fact, her college
training may have made traditional feminine roles singularly unat-
tractive to her, and may have sparked a desire to explore vocational
possibilities that had previously been monopolized by men.

Had Addams resigned herself to becoming a mother and homemaker, she might have handled conflicting masculine-feminine moral
styles with relative ease. Her nurturant propensities would have been
exercised within the home. There would have been little sex role conflict in her believing in a high tariff, since this was a worldly, nondomestic issue that fell within the masculine, nonnurturant sphere.
On the other hand, if for some reason Addams the homemaker opposed a high tariff, she could exert her feminine influence in the
home by trying to change the opinions of "her men." In either case,
she would remain within the bounds of the assigned feminine sphere.
But once Addams confronted the possibility that as a college trained
woman she might have to find a place for herself in the masculine
world, the struggle between masculine and feminine moral styles
could become acute. If her college experience broadened her vocational horizons and created the potential for a career previously un-
available to a woman, it inevitably forced Addams to deal head-on
with the conflict between masculine and feminine roles and values.
Could she be a "true" woman and work in the "outside" world? Could
she adhere to John Addams's moral style and maintain her femininity? If she went into the "masculine" world armed with publicly oriented nurturant values, would she have to turn away from her

beloved father's insular moral style—a style that since childhood she had cherished and tried to emulate?

The dilemma was made more acute by the crisis of adolescence. The adolescent experience must have been far more painful for young women in Addams's situation than it had been for women in earlier years or in other classes. An educated, adolescent middle-class female living in the last quarter of the nineteenth century was confronted with the difficult task of becoming something other than what her mother had been, and perhaps something other than what she herself had previously envisioned becoming. In Addams's case, the combination of moral ambivalence and adolescent uncertainty provided the foundation for an existential crisis that began in 1881 and persisted until 1889.

The death of her father in 1881 exacerbated her confusion. In that year she entered a phase in which she felt "absolutely at sea as far as any moral purpose was concerned." After a one-year residence at the Woman's Medical College of Philadelphia, Addams became mired in a prolonged period of lassitude and "melancholy." Her suffering derived in part from her chronic spinal problem, but the depth of her depression and her profound confusion about vocational goals and moral styles convinced her that her malaise was not caused by ill health:[35] "However, it could not have been due to my health for as my wise little notebook sententiously remarked, 'In *his* own way each *man* must struggle, lest the moral law become a far-off abstraction utterly separated from *his* active life.' "*[36]

Year by year during the 1880s she became less able to transcend her depression or to make her moral life less "abstract." In a letter of 1884 to her former Rockford classmate Ellen Gates Starr, Addams confided that her ill health and vocational uncertainty were symbols of a failure of will: she could not make a vocational choice because of an overwhelming failure of self-confidence.[37] In 1886 she complained to Starr that her "faculties, memory, receptive faculties and all" had become "perfectly inaccessible locked up away from me."[38] That year marked "the nadir of my nervous depression and sense of maladjustment."[39]

Passivity and inertia were accompanied by a revulsion against the cultural attainments of young men and women of her class. The literary and artistic world to which she was exposed at school and during trips to Europe enhanced her alienation from the real world. Literary and artistic endeavors seemed to "cloud the really vital situation

*Italics added. It is significant that Addams used masculine pronouns to describe her moral dilemma and vocational uncertainty.

spread before our eyes," especially when intellect was viewed as differing from moral concerns and consequences.[40]

During her crisis Addams was unable to make vocational plans, which is to say she was unable to confront her future. Why? Is there a connection between her inability to face her future on the one hand, and on the other, her adolescent crisis and the masculine-feminine moral conundrum that left her morally at sea?

There is an intimate connection between psychic time and the moral dilemmas confronting adolescents. The superego, particularly the ethical values of the ego ideal, stands for the person's future. Conscience "speaks to us from the viewpoint of an inner future," pointing toward what the person should become, and generating anxiety and loss of self-esteem should she fall short of the idealized future. In this sense, superego represents the young person's future.[41]

Addams's prolonged time of troubles represented a need to suspend her future. It was, therefore, a profoundly moral crisis. She was unable to make a final choice between the moral style characteristic of feminine nurturance and the style reflected in her father's individualistic moral consciousness. Consequently, she lacked the will to be anything but passive and inert. Not only were her cognitive and moral faculties "inaccessible," but she was pendant in time, unable to respond autonomously or actively to the external world. The psychoanalyst Paul Seton has described the relationship between this passivity and the crumbling of parental ideals during adolescence:

> Without past or future or both, there can be no experience of duration and no sense of one's own history. The timelessness has not been an eruption of the unconscious or a decomposition of ego functioning, but is frequently a suspension of superego operations because one needs to suspend a sense of closure, which nothing can convey as ineluctably as time does. Adolescence is a psychedelic period, a time of dedifferentiation and expansion beyond the up-until-then abiding constrictions of the parental superego and ego ideal.[42]

In Addams's case these normal difficulties were compounded by her father's death. This occurred in the midst of her period of moral reassessment, and the feelings of guilt, loss, and mourning inherent in the adolescent task of turning away from at least some parental ideals were exacerbated for her. Addams's sense of guilt may have been intensified because his death appeared to fulfill her desire to rid herself of part of the paternal value system.[43] This desire may have seemed tantamount to a wish for the death of her father. Because Addams could neither let go of the paternal style nor subscribe to it, she suffered her long bout with depression.

While her moral dilemma was not fully resolved until she and Starr opened Hull House in 1889, the outline of its resolution had appeared by the mid-1880s. As we have seen, mid-nineteenth-century nurture writers associated John Addams's privatized moral conscious-ness with "masculine" traits of entrepreneurial and social aggressive-ness. By contrast, the "feminine" virtues were considered social because they were rooted in an intuitive, empathic insight into the needs and feelings of others. Thus, mid-century ideas about moral styles not only associated gender with specific forms of moral evalua-tion, but also viewed these forms in spatial terms—"inner," or mascu-line, and "outer," or feminine. Addams commented on this bipolarity in 1883 when she wrote Starr that from "babyhood" female children were encouraged to follow their altruistic impulses. Girls were "taught to be self-forgetting and self-sacrificing, to consider the good of the [social] whole before the good of the ego."[44] As Addams took the first tentative steps to resolve her dilemma, she tended to broach her ideas about moral evaluation in bipolar spatial terms.

The spatial parameters of her crisis were poignantly revealed in her correspondence with Starr during the 1880s, especially in letters dealing with religion. "I am always blundering," wrote Addams:

> when I deal with religious nomenclature . . . simply because my religious life has been so small;—for many years it was my ambi-tion to reach my father's moral requirements, and now when I am needing something more, I find myself approaching a crisis.[45]

The significance of Addams's religious speculations lies in her spa-tial imagery. In another letter to Starr she confessed that whereas Starr desired to experience an inner, "beautiful faith," she herself felt only the need for "religion in a practical sense," as a guide to *social* behavior.[46] The same inner-outer bipolarity was reflected in her discus-sion of the Incarnation:

> I don't think God embodied himself in Christ to reveal himself, but that he did it considering the weakness of man; that while man might occasionally comprehend an abstract deity he couldn't live by it, it came to him only in his more exalted moments, and it was impossible for his mind to retain his own conception of God. . . . If a man can once see God through Christ then he is saved for he can never again lose him as Christ is always with him.[47]

In other words, a God that is wholly other and can be "seen" only through an abstract and blind act of faith is inadequate as an ethical guide. Only a divinity embodied in Jesus—that is, in the life of a real person engaged in a network of social and moral relationships—could be relevant to ethics because the individual can "see" Jesus and use the facts of his life as a behavioral model. "I believe more and more," she wrote to Starr in 1885, "in keeping the . . . facts of Christ's life before us and letting the philosophy go."[48] Facts were inexorably "outer." They were far removed from the inner-directed subjectivity of faith.

Addams's agony, at least on the religious front, was eased somewhat in 1885 when she became a Presbyterian. Although her "conversion" was bereft of emotional upheaval, joining the church alleviated to some degree her morbid sense of a discrepancy between "what I am and what I ought to be." Significantly, Addams also felt that she had entered a community of "fellowship" that was "almost early Christian in its simplicity." This bond of fellowship allowed her to "give up one's conceit or hope of being good in one's own right," a "conceit" that John Addams would never have surrendered. By opting for a modern counterpart to primitive Christianity, instead of becoming a Quaker like her father, Addams in effect rejected her father's inner light perception of moral rectitude. Instead, she chose a church in which her craving for "an *outward*, public symbol of fellowship, some bond of peace, some blessed spot where unity of spirit might claim right of way over all differences," could be satisfied [italics added].[49]

The most striking and significant insight into Addams's adolescent crisis was provided by a letter she wrote to Starr in August 1879. Addams, characteristically, was discussing her moral dilemma: how could personal religious values be related to everyday social activities? She then described a short-lived psychic experience of "peace" during which the dualisms and conflicts of her moral malaise had been temporarily eased. Her description provides us with precious insights into the phenomena at the root of her crisis:

> Lately it seems to me that I am getting back of it—superior to it, I almost feel—Back to a great Primal Cause, not Nature exactly, but a fostering mother, a necessity, brooding and watching over all things, above every passion and yet not passive, the mystery of creation . . . the idea embodied in the Sphinx—peace.[50]

It is essential to understand what an adolescent torn between conflicting moral configurations meant when she said that she was going "back to a Primal Cause . . . a fostering mother." However fleeting were those moments when Addams experienced reunion with a feminine "mystery of creation," they indicated she was indeed re-evaluating her commitment to John Addams's moral style. What, then, is the connection between her experience of being pulled back to a "Primal Cause" and her masculine-feminine conflict?

Adolescent regression to pre-ego-ideal states is both common and normal.[51] The reasons for the regression are manifold. Because the superego becomes less efficient in fulfilling its roles as a regulator of self-esteem and an appraiser of behavior during adolescence, the ego, whose task is to guide the person through the maze of often conflicting demands made by the "inner voice" and external reality, is "left weak, isolated, and inadequate."[52] Set adrift with little or no guidance from the superego, the ego may seek refuge at one or another preadolescent level of development, probably at a period when the person had not been racked by doubt and conflict. This form of regression is necessary for the youth's stability and future development. It allows her to re-visit, and in a sense relive, those infantile interactions with parental figures that generated the superego in the first place.[53] In effect, regres-sion allows the adolescent to reevaluate past identifications and com-mitments in light of her present needs.

Addams's regression took the form of going back to a fostering mother because the "earliest wishful fantasies of merging and being one with the mother" are "the foundations on which all object relations as well as all future types of identifications are built."[54] Once the primal union of mother and child begins to crumble during the second half of the child's first year, and once the infant begins to realize that she is in fact an entity separate from what Addams called her "Primal Cause," the ego ideal emerges as a substitute for the loss of the primary ideal state. From this point on, the child's self-esteem is based on the congruence between her behavior and her internalized "omnipotent" parental images.[55]

By feeling she had gotten "back of it all" through reunion with a "fostering mother" and also through her subsequent conversion to Presbyterianism, Addams re-created the experience of union, separa-tion, and reunion that preceded the formation of her ego ideal. Stated differently, Addams's adolescent regression to her "fostering mother" was a *recapitulation* of her moral birth. Regression and recapitulation allowed her to discard the paternal superego, reexternalize it, as it were, as a first step in reevaluating her commitment to his moral style.[56]

Given this situation, it is hardly surprising that Addams's adult analysis of the adolescent experience in *The Spirit of Youth and the*

City Streets and in other essays was informed by the recapitulation theory. She was no doubt influenced by Hall, but her conviction that adolescence recapitulated the past was based less on intellectual constructs than upon personal experiences: during her own adolescence, she had creatively used her "regressive" recapitulation to overcome her moral crisis.

Adolescence for Addams was disturbing and disorienting, and her subsequent involvement with the play movement was a way of interpreting and controlling the adolescent crisis. The congruence of "play stages" and "life stages" imposed meaning and order on this otherwise confusing psychosocial experience. Organizing children's play made it possible to control and to direct the youth's moral and emotional confusion into socially useful channels, and simultaneously to create an institution, the playground, that helped to reduce the young person's anxieties by providing a model of moral rectitude and certainty—the peer-group team. The fact that Addams knew from personal experience that adolescence was a moral watershed makes understandable her belief that organized play instilled permanent moral tendencies in impressionable youths.

Addams's paternal moral tendencies were gradually replaced by "feminine" social-organic tendencies. Her conversion to a denomination that evoked images of early Christian communitarianism symbolized her desire to live by "the simple proposition that man's action is found in his social relationships in the way in which he connects with his fellows."[57]

Through what she called a "code of social ethics," or a "social," nonidiosyncratic, morality, she was able to resolve the dualisms at the heart of her crisis. Addams was convinced that these dualisms caused many of her middle-class contemporaries to experience the same difficulties that she had suffered in relating private ideals to social behavior. Years after her crisis had passed, she summarized the cause of this malaise.

> They fail to be content with the fulfillment of their family and personal obligations, and find themselves striving to respond to a new demand involving a social obligation; they have become conscious of another requirement, and the contribution they would make is toward a code of social ethics. The conception of life which they hold has not yet expressed itself in social changes or legal enactments, but rather in a mental attitude of maladjustment, and in a sense of divergence between their consciences and their conduct. They desire both a clearer definition of the code of morality

adapted to present day demands and a part in its fulfillment, both a creed and a practice of social morality.[58]

Addams's moral crisis was rooted in her unusual childhood and family experiences, but the moral vocabulary of her crisis was social as well as personal. Changes in her moral vocabulary had echoes in the changing structure of American society. The increasingly corporate tendency of American business, the monumental problems spawned by overcrowded and unsanitary conditions in cities, and the social and educational problems generated by the presence of new immigrants affected the sensibilities of this intelligent young woman. Specifically, these conditions indicated that the country was becoming too complex and, as Addams put it, too "interdependent," to accommodate her father's moral individualism. The old frontier virtues of "thrift, industry, and sobriety," she later wrote, pertained only to the individual and to a decentralized economy in which "each man had his own shop." As society and industry became more organized, moral values had to emphasize the needs of society "as a whole." It was Addams's desire to extend her own empathic morality as a means of making "social intercourse express the growing sense of economic unity" that prompted her to open Hull House and participate in the play movement.[59]

Jane Addams (1860–1935). Renowned social settlement worker, winner of the Nobel Peace Prize, and a founder of the Playground Association of America. (Library of Congress)

ADDAMS AS REFORMER
AND PLAY ORGANIZER

Addams found an ideal forum to express what she called "both a creed and a practice of social morality" in 1889 when she and Starr opened Hull House. Unquestionably, the social settlement symbolized for Addams the domestication of her worldly skills. She and Starr were "ready to perform the humblest" services, "wash the new-born babies, and prepare the dead for burial, nurse the sick and mind the children."[60] When discussing the role of the settlement in urban society, she often employed images consistent with her adolescent recreating of union with her "fostering mother." Hull House workers, Addams wrote, must be "swallowed" and "digested" and "disappear into the bulk of the people."[61] They must persuade city dwellers that "individual morality" and pride in purely personal achievements were irrelevant "in an age demanding social morality and social adjustment."[62] Addams was certain these aspects of the reform impulse were rooted in maternal sentiments:

> Maternal affection and solicitude, in woman's remembering heart, may at length coalesce into a chivalric protection for all that is young and unguarded. This chivalry of women expressing protection for those at the bottom of society, as far as it has already developed, suggests a return to that idealized version of chivalry which was the consecration of strength to the defense of weakness.[63]

Hull House represented Addams's rejection of her father's moral insularity. On the other hand, her belief that social settlement workers should undertake "objective" analyses of social data constituted a rejection of the stereotypically passive, emotional female role in favor of "masculine" rationality. Settlement workers should make scientific, objective evaluations of the underlying causes and social consequences of poverty, political corruption and the like, because only unprejudiced and rational analyses of the "facts" could uncover the underlying causes of urban problems. More significantly, residents must focus their attention on the concreteness, factuality, and immediacy of the social experience of their clients, for "we do not believe that genuine experience can lead us astry [sic] any more than scientific data can."[64]

Thus, Addams's social philosophy blended a spatially outward, or public (feminine), moral style with a (masculine) empirical orientation. Both tendencies pointed in the same direction: each emphasized, in its unique way, the centrality of facts, objectivity, and public experiences, while implicitly denigrating the private and the subjective in the areas of morality and social analysis. "Action," Addams wrote, "is indeed the sole medium of expression for ethics."[65] What people did, in contrast to what they felt or thought, was what mattered ultimately—as any play organizer would agree—because "the deed often reveals when the idea does not." What the deed reveals is the actor; and what the abstractions of personal morality and intellectual ideas often conceal are the private, insular causes of behavior. Addams's "pragmatic" interest in results, her quest to have the settlement "test the value of human knowledge by action, and realization," was a reflection of the shift from private control to public conformity that occurred in her moral and social perspectives during the 1880s.[66]

This shift from masculine inner control to feminine social morality was implicit in Addams's moral crisis. But feminine empathy was not incongruous with a (masculine) empirical orientation, for both stressed the moral and social relevance of animate and inanimate environments. Indeed, the emphasis on people as "actors," and morality as a network of social "facts" must have seemed a highly adaptive response to the chaotic social and economic circumstances of late nineteenth-century America.

The personality of the ideal team player integrated these feminine and masculine orientations. Shame-proneness feminized and made public his moral style. Like the domesticated "true" woman of the nineteenth century, the player was exquisitely sensitive to the needs and values of significant others. His willingness to empathize with others—which was the most glaring mandate of playground socialization—would supply cohesiveness in an otherwise factionalized society. The shame-prone player spoke the same moral language as the idealized mid-nineteenth-century woman. "These public games," Addams wrote,

> would also perform a social function in revealing *men* to each other, for it is in moments of pleasure, of emotional expansion that men do this most readily. Play, beyond any other human activity fulfills this function of revelation of character and is therefore most useful in modern cities which are full of devices for keeping men apart and holding them ignorant of each other. [Italics added.][67]

But the ideal team player spoke a different cognitive language, that of the twentieth-century social analyst. The player's penchant for fact hounding, his tendency to take a cool, objective view of his environ-

ment, and his predisposition to let the facts speak for themselves reflected the hard-headed rationalism that the nineteenth century associated with masculinity. His analysis of external events was
relatively emotionless, but objectivity was vital in an urban-industrial
society in dire need of organization and stability. In any event, the
team player's cognitive cold-bloodedness was more than offset by his
emotionally charged shame-prone moral style. His personality thus
combined the quests for social organization and social cohesiveness, for
order and feeling. The player's character, like that of Addams, wedded
characteristics that in the nineteenth century had been sundered into
idealized and stereotypical masculine or feminine attributes.

Once these styles had been wedded, especially in social-training
techniques on organized playgrounds, it was but a short step to the idea
that "scientific" control of the youth's animate and inanimate environments could determine his personality development and, could, therefore, create an atmosphere conducive to social reform. "We don't
expect to change human nature," Addams said of reformers shortly
before her death in 1935, "but we do expect to change human behavior."[68] Her statement could have served as the credo for the movement
to organize children's play.

Conclusion:
Implications of the Play Movement

My purpose in this concluding section is to synthesize the major ideological currents in the play movement by discussing how playground social training was supposed to create what I call a public orientation in the urban young. In addition, because I have simply used interdisciplinary methods rather than justified their use, I will discuss both my rationale for using them and how they influenced my interpretations of Progressive Era social reform.

On the question of playground social training and its promotion of a public orientation, it is important to remember that the movement to organize children's play was an attempt to forge a new equilibrium among a series of cultural bipolarities. Literally and symbolically, play organizers spoke a language of countervailing binaries: individualism versus social cooperation, private versus public, selfishness versus loyalty, masculine versus feminine, guilt versus shame. To play organizers these binaries were closely related. Individualism and cooperation were not just economic categories; they had sex role (masculine-feminine) and ethical (inner-direction–other-direction or shame-guilt) equivalents. For play organizers, these sets of binaries were connected layers of cultural imperatives: each binary related to specific forms of social interaction, and together they formed the intricate cultural weave that determined the texture of social relations.

For a variety of reasons, play organizers believed the nineteenth-century balance within these binaries was inadequate for meeting the needs of an ethnically heterogeneous, dynamic, urban-industrial society. The supposedly individualistic—that is, private—values espoused by nineteenth-century pioneers of geographical and industrial frontiers were unsuitable, they thought, for the spatially and psychologically compact—public—world of the modern city.

Neither the cultural implications of the play movement nor the effectiveness of playground social training methods can be understood unless viewed as attempts to alter the balance within and between binaries relating to sex roles, economic activity, and ethics. The best approach for understanding this issue is through Kai T. Erikson's theory of culture, discussed briefly in chapter 6. According to Erikson, the moral imperatives of a culture are not one-dimensional values to which all citizens comply all the time in every situation. If this were the case, moral, social, and ideological diversity could not exist. "The identifying motifs of a culture," writes Erikson:

> are not just the *core values* to which people pay homage but also the lines of *point and counterpoint* along which they diverge. That is, the term "culture" refers not only to the customary ways in which a people induce conformity in behavior and outlook but the customary ways in which they organize diversity.[1]

Political, social, economic, and sexual core values seldom attain hegemony in the individual or in the society. A society might mandate sexual monogamy but for a variety of reasons allow certain segments of the population to practice the opposite with relative impunity. It might glorify the "rugged" individualism of the entrepreneurial genius while permitting direct and indirect governmental subsidies to corporations. Erikson's point is that countervalues originate neither in the abyss of original sin nor in the calculations of corrupt individuals. Countervalues thrive in the imaginations of those who espouse core values; they are implied by their opposites. Core value and countervalues might exist on opposite ends of the moral spectrum, but in between there is an area where ethical nuances and moral ambiguity thrive. Here core value and countervalues exist in a state of tension, and countervalues may rise to prominence when core values are found wanting or when moral experimentation is deemed necessary. Ambiguity, diversity, and even the blending of apparently contradictory values are inherent in value systems.[2]

Play organizers rebelled against some nineteenth-century core values, especially the cult of economic individualism, the equations of masculinity with public life and femininity with domesticity, and the ideal of the morally autonomous individual. They did not, however, wish to eradicate these values and replace them with their opposites. Although playground social training stressed "feminine," nurturant sensibilities, opposing "masculine" postures were muted rather than destroyed. As we saw in chapter 5, the personality of the ideal team player incorporated aspects of each set of apparently contradictory values. Play organizers, in short, engaged in a delicate act of moral balancing.

Playground social training was the means used by play advocates to forge new moral equations. Team spirit, for example, was supposed to foster immigrant acculturation and enhance democratic values. The team was a nurturant (feminine) and functional counterpart to the family. It was a new world peer commonwealth and a sort of halfway house between family and society that exposed youngsters to the give and take of the public world. But the team was also a metaphor for a new ideal of community built on the ruins of the moral and economic individualism that, correctly or incorrectly, play organizers perceived as the credo of a less ethnically diverse, less urban and less industrial nineteenth-century world. On the organized team all players, regardless of their ethnic or class origins, were equal, and each player had a task to perform, a role to play in securing the goals of the team. Each player was instilled with analytic skills needed for competence in an organizational society, and all were equally subordinated to the aspirations of the team (or "social whole" as play advocates would have said). The team, in short, was an island of stability, continuity, and community in an urban sea of alienation, crime, and flux.

At the same time, however, the team experience enhanced the individual initiative that play organizers believed essential for economic and scientific progress. Each player on the baseball or basketball team was encouraged to sharpen and display his skills, though not to the point where personal ambition and egotism endangered the team's success. On organized playgrounds individual achievement was supposed to augment public goals and become a servant of collective progress rather than a slave of personal aggrandizement. As a social-training mechanism, the team experience was designed to create a new balance between individualism and cooperation and between masculine and feminine sensibilities.

This new balance was ultimately designed to force the youth to look toward the public sector for the resolution of his private problems. Nearly all of the value bipolarities that have been discussed in these chapters—particularly the basic masculine-feminine binary—symbolize a dichotomy between private and public spheres. Play organizers, for example, were not afraid of masculinity because it evoked images of nineteenth-century aggression and unrestrained ambition, which supposedly led to political and economic turmoil. Masculinity frightened them because its characteristic psychological processes—the mechanisms through which ambition and aggression were translated into economic or political behavior—were private and idiosyncratic. By infusing masculine sensibilities with feminine nurturance, that is, with a public display of concern and affection for others, play organizers were not simply taming adolescent boys. They were making boys public beings, individuals whose desires and aspirations had meaning only insofar as they were reenforced by public approval. What play organizers disliked about the nineteenth century, then, was its supposed commitment to privacy, whether expressed in the notion of the family as a "haven" from the pressures of the outside world, or in the realms of economic and moral individualism. Playground social training salvaged some important elements associated with the private self, such as desires for personal success and social mobility, by linking them indissolubly to public encounters and commitments.

The shift from a private to a public orientation can be seen most clearly in the dynamics of team games. On the surface, the elements of a team game, its rules, the camaraderie of the players, the game's status as a closed system of action, created a unique blend of subjectivity and collectivity, of private and public spheres. There was room on the organized playground for competition, idiosyncratic behavior, and personal achievement. But these subjective elements were contained by, and given meaning through, overarching shared meanings implied by commitment to the rules of the game and the goals of the team. In the context of the limited range of choices inherent in a team game, private or subjective evaluations of the game-action and the display of individual skills could flourish without disrupting shared social meanings and goals. Competition and subjectivity were harnessed to collective ends.

A second reason for the popularity of team games was that the player's commitment to collective ends was expressed through his body. The player who hit away when the game situation called for a sacrifice bunt could not conceal his lack of team, or public, spirit: it was etched in his bodily movements. When a player did sacrifice himself in the appropriate situation, it really did not matter what his private thoughts or motives were: his behavior bore witness to his apparent commitment to collective ends. In team games the focus of moral concern and evaluation was objectified—made public.

At the same time, team games created a theater of action in which events and contingencies contained their own resolutions. The number of possible game-events was finite and the analyses of their meanings were relatively unambiguous, especially if perceived as technical problems. Solutions to these problems could be diagrammed, rehearsed, and drilled into players during practice. Cognitive assessments of events, therefore, were shaped by the events themselves, with a minimum of subjective input, at least as far as play organizers were concerned. Physical drill and practice were supposed to condition the player to respond decisively to appropriate external signals. In this fashion reformers in the play movement tried to secure control over a relentlessly heterogeneous and stimulating urban environment. They trained young people to approach life as a series of technical, public problems that called for suspension of competing and private ethical meanings. Objective analysis, along with team spirit, was the new basis for social cohesion, for it compelled the player, regardless of his ethnic or class background, to see life in the same way as his fellows and to bear witness to that sameness by objectifying his perceptions in his physical bearing.

The intellectual inspiration for this approach to social training was the implicit behaviorism of the child psychologies discussed in chapter 2. In distinctive ways, and to varying degrees, the theories of child psychology presented by Hall, Dewey, Baldwin, and Thorndike emphasized the moral significance of the public environment and denigrated the importance of autonomous, private moral deliberation. These theories were rooted in a perception of evolution that emphasized the catalytic quality of environmental events in individual development and social progress. Whether this sentiment was expressed in terms of the muscular primitivism of the recapitulation theory (Hall), the centrality of imitation in the development of moral ideas and social competence (Baldwin), the instrumentalist notion that knowledge was rooted in "objective" analyses of "things" (Dewey), or the stimulus-response theory of social adaptation (Thorndike), the ultimate implication was clear: an orientation toward public life could be instilled in the young through physical activities, including play.

This is why the play movement existed. The ideal team player embodied the assumptions of publicly oriented, physicalistic child psychologies. His feminized, shame-prone superego and perceptual field-dependence made him aware of the moral cues radiated by his human environment—the peer group. At the same time, his masculine empirical orientation toward the game, and his ability to transmute analytical objectivity into moral necessity, locked his cognitive faculties securely into the public environment. Morally, socially, and intellectually the ideal team player *was* his environment. In his public life, he lacked an internal preserve shielded from the critical gaze of peers or the compelling moral force of his physical environment. It is, then, not surprising that Jane Addams associated social reform with changes in behavior rather than changes in human nature: by manipulating the environment, reformers could control behavior. The movement to organize children's play was the institutionalized expression of that sentiment.

My discussion of methodology will focus on the historiographical implications of the psychological profile of the ideal team player. Because the profile was informed by psychoanalytic theories of morality, I shall begin with a few remarks on psychohistory.

My approach to psychohistory was informed by Cushing Strout's sage advice on the use of psychology in historical research. Strout recommended that psychologically informed analysis be avoided unless the ambiguous nature of the data clearly called for its use.[3] Using the psychological profile of the team player seemed to me a necessary strategy for isolating key elements in play organizers' ideology. I was also convinced that the ambiguities, tensions, and problems faced by Jane Addams could be understood adequately only with the aid of psychoanalytic theory. In both instances, particularly in the Addams material, I tried to remember the historian's obligation to respect rather than to clinically dissect the lives, feelings, and behavior of his subjects.

The significance of the psychological profile of the ideal team player rests on its ability to shed light on the motives of the Progressive Era reformers who participated in the play movement. The profile was a psychological sketch of collective symbols. Each aspect of the profile was gleaned from ideas of individual play advocates, and the profile itself was a collective representation of play organizers' ideology.

By approaching ideology in this manner one can avoid a pitfall of psychoanalytic theory: psychological reductionism. The psychological profile refers to the intentions of play organizers, to their collective goals, and to their stated or implied values. It does not, however, relate their adult values and goals to their individual childhood problems or familial settings.* The profile technique permits one to make psychologically informed statements about play organizers without referring to their individual life histories.

Because the ideal-typical team player was a collective representation, however, he did not conform to the ideological perspective of any

---

*I did link childhood settings and adult values in Addams's case, but neither reduced one to the other, nor claimed that her youthful experiences were similar to those of other play advocates.

individual play advocate. The intellectual efficiency of the player, for example, would have warmed the hearts of bureaucratic progressives like Curtis and Gulick but left Lee rather cold. For Lee, whose major preoccupation was the resurrection of community control over the individual, the player's extreme peer orientation and shame-proneness were most important. While Lee visualized team camaraderie as a symbol of community and of a uniquely American melting pot, Addams perceived the player's resourcefulness and personal achievements as evidence of pluralism in action. The team player and the team game represented multiple socio-ethical orientations; a play organizer could emphasize the ones that most comported with his or her values and vision of the ideal American society and citizen. The ideal team player's personality thus highlights the heterogeneous quality of the play movement. Even when play organizers agreed on the importance of a particular virtue—for example, group loyalty—it meant something different to Addams, a pacifist, than to Lee, a vigorous supporter of American involvement in World War I.

This ideological diversity highlights what Peter Filene said about Progressive Era reform: it "lacked unanimity of purpose either on a programmatic or on a philosophic level."[4] Progressives differed on the most fundamental social, political, and economic questions of the age, including immigration restriction, government regulation of the economy, and prohibition.[5] These divisions were found among reformers in the play movement. Even if it is true that most Progressive Era reformers were middle class, college educated, urban, and WASP, we are still left with the problem of why all middle-class, college-educated, urban WASPs did not become reformers. Categories of class, regional origin, and religious affiliation did not by themselves determine who became a reformer.

If this is true, then how did the *movement* to organize children's play originate? How could a self-described Deweyan pragmatist like Gulick join forces with a philosophical idealist like Lee? How did a proponent of unrestricted immigration like Addams team with Lee, a notorious advocate of immigration restriction, to found the Playground Association of America? This is a complex question, and the answer, if there is one, goes far beyond the purpose of this study and the ability of its author. It might prove useful, however, to make a few remarks about this issue within the context of the play movement.

Once again I shall draw on Kai T. Erikson's perceptive insights into the nature of culture. Erikson contends that the interplay between moral opposites characterizes societies as well as individuals. Whereas individuals experience the strain of opposing values as ambivalence and adaptive synthesis as "ego integration," societies experience value strain as social conflict and ideological differentiation, respectively. According to Erikson, people divide themselves, or are divided, into a variety of religious, social, and economic camps, "each of them sharing something of the larger culture at the same time that each tries to fashion modes of being peculiar to itself."

> When these differences develop into competition for power or goods or are based on antagonisms of long standing, the result is apt to be social conflict; but when these differences develop into an implicit agreement to apportion the work of the culture as well as its rewards on the basis of the contrasting qualities that each group represents, the result is apt to be a form of complementarity.[6]

This applies to sensibilities and values as well as to social activities. By "complementarity" Erikson means that individuals can think or feel "different things in the service of an over-all pattern of coordination."[7] Complementarity implies that people whose values appear to exist on opposite ends of the moral spectrum can unite in the pursuit of common goals and provide societies and social movements with useful "portions" of each moral orientation.

The ideal team player embodied value complementarity. He was (from the perspectives of play organizers) a socially adaptive blend of competitive-cooperative and masculine-feminine sensibilities. In spite of their philosophical and political diversity, play advocates could band together and organize a play movement because they held one vital thing in common. Play organizers shunned extreme forms of economic and social competition, such as laissez-faire capitalism, and extreme forms of economic and social cooperation, like communism, as solutions to the problems of urban disorder and class conflict. Their ideological differences were played out in that vast theater of the middle ground called liberalism. Their collective vision of the ideal twentieth-century citizen blended a number of nineteenth- and twentieth-century values that in their extreme form might be contradictory but that, when pulled toward the middle of the moral spectrum, could be effectively united in a personality. The ideal team player was at once a nineteenth-century achiever and a twentieth-century conformist, a cool masculine analyst of "hard" facts and a feminized, nurturant teammate. Moral complementarity, symbolized by the player's diverse sensibilities, made him appealing to the liberal reformers in the play movement.

The idiom of team games allowed play organizers to see in them the language of modern liberalism. These games emphasized a consensual approach to social interaction: all players had to agree beforehand to play the game according to the rules, and all had to agree that rules applied equally to every player. Competing teams, like competing classes or interest groups, wanted to win, but if they lost they did not overhaul the rules, but "waited till next year" and another chance to get their piece of pie and glory. Most important, regardless of skill and ambition, a player without a team was like a modern city dweller without a group affiliation: action devoid of context, potential without hope of realization. Team games symbolized the key goals of modern liberalism: harmony between classes, orderly competition between interest groups, and individual achievement within frameworks of group and social progress.[8]

Thus the need to organize a play movement and the personality of the ideal team player dovetailed. Play organizers wanted to develop forms of social training that effectively blended contrasting sensibilities. They tried to produce personalities that were homogeneous enough to ensure social unity and differentiated enough to meet the diverse challenges and stresses of a fluid, ever-changing society.

And what of the youngsters, the denizens of organized playgrounds, who were the targets of these wishes? We will never know what they thought or how they responded to playground social training. Their reaction, like the cloud formed by a player sliding into home plate, is dust in the wind. What really happened to the young people on city playgrounds of long ago? Did they become what play organizers would make of them? Or was it just a game they played?

NOTES

INTRODUCTION: THE MOVEMENT TO ORGANIZE
CHILDREN'S PLAY

1. Anthony Platt, *The Child Savers: The Invention of Delinquency* (Chicago, 1969); Roy Lubove, *The Professional Altruist* (Cambridge, Mass., 1965); Joseph Hawes, *Children in Urban Society* (New York, 1971); William D. Murray, *The History of the Boy Scouts of America* (New York, 1937); Jack M. Holl, *Juvenile Reform in the Progressive Era: William R. George and the Junior Republic Movement* (Ithaca, 1971).

2. The best analysis of the play movement is found in Paul Boyer, *Urban Masses and Moral Order in America, 1820–1920* (Cambridge, Mass., 1978); see also Lawrence Finfer, "Leisure as Social Work in the Urban Community: The Progressive Recreation Movement, 1890–1920" (Ph.D. diss., Michigan State University, 1974); Richard Knapp, "Play for America: The National Recreation Association, 1906–1950" (Ph.D. diss., Duke University, 1971).

3. Eugen Weber, "Gymnastics and Sports in Fin-de-Siècle France: Opium of the Classes?" *American Historical Review* 76 (1971): 70.

4. Jane Addams, *Twenty Years at Hull House* (New York, 1910), pp. 208–10.

5. On the student self-government movement see Joel Spring, *Education and the Rise of the Corporate State* (Boston, 1972), pp. 113–17.

6. Henry Curtis, *Education Through Play* (New York, 1915), pp. 55–56.

7. For reformers' reactions to the city, see Jane Addams, *The Spirit of Youth and the City Streets* (New York, 1909) and *Twenty Years at Hull House;* Robert Woods, *The City Wilderness* (Boston, 1895); Woods, *The Neighborhood in Nation-Building* (Boston, 1923); Jacob Riis, *How the Other Half Lives* (New York, 1890).

8. It must be emphasized that play organizers did not invent peer direction but simply tried to direct its social manifestations. Progressive Era child savers were well aware that peer direction and group activity could be spontaneous among young people. See Henry Sheldon, "The Institutional Activities of American Children," *American Journal of Psychology* 9 (1898): 425–47. On the uses of peer direction in the kindergarten, see Dominick Cavallo, "The Politics of Latency: Kindergarten Pedagogy, 1860–1930" in Barbara Finkelstein, ed., *Regulated Children, Liberated*

Children (New York, 1979); Cavallo, "From Perfection to Habit: Moral Training in the American Kindergarten, 1860–1920," *History of Education Quarterly* 16 (1976): 147–61.

9. John Demos and Virginia Demos, "Adolescence in Historical Perspective," *Journal of Marriage and the Family* 31 (1969): 632–38. For a different view of the origins of adolescence in America see N. Ray Hiner, "Adolescence in Eighteenth-Century America," *History of Childhood Quarterly* 3 (1975): 253–80; Ross W. Beales, "Cares for the Rising Generation: Youth and Religion in Colonial New England" (Ph.D. diss., University of California, 1971).

10. Joseph Kett, *Rites of Passage: Adolescence in America, 1790 to the Present* (New York, 1977), pp. 144–244.

11. On the socializing role of youth groups, see S. N. Eisenstadt, "Archetypal Patterns of Youth," in Erik H. Erikson, ed., *The Challenge of Youth* (New York, 1964), pp. 29–50.

12. In addition to playgrounds, adult-dominated youth institutions included the public school, the social center, and a variety of boys' and girls' associations and clubs.

13. Paula Fass, *The Damned and the Beautiful: American Youth in the 1920s* (New York, 1977).

14. In one guise or another, peer direction characterizes most situations when the young are institutionally segregated from society, for example, as students or apprentices. See John R. Gillis, *Youth and History* (New York, 1974).

15. Spring, *Education and the Rise of the Corporate State,* pp. 1–21; Christopher Lasch, *The New Radicalism in America* (New York, 1965), pp. 13–15; Marvin Lazerson, "Urban Reform and the Schools: Kindergartens in Massachusetts, 1870–1915," in Michael Katz, ed., *Education in American History* (New York, 1973), pp. 228–36.

16. Peter Gabriel Filene, *Him, Her, Self: Sex Roles in Modern America* (New York, 1974); Ann Douglas, *The Feminization of American Culture* (New York, 1977); Barbara Welter, "The Feminization of American Religion," in Mary Hartman and Lois W. Banner, eds., *Clio's Consciousness Raised* (New York, 1974), pp. 137–57; Welter, "The Cult of True Womanhood," *American Quarterly* 18 (1966): 151–74; Lasch, *New Radicalism,* pp. 3–68.

17. Organized team sports were aimed at male youths. While young girls were allowed to play preadolescent games with boys on organized playgrounds, team games were played only by adolescent boys. This study consequently reflects this orientation.

18. Robert Wiebe, *The Search for Order, 1877–1920* (New York, 1967).

CHAPTER 1: THE ORGANIZATION OF CHILDREN'S PLAY

1. Newton Baker, "Invisible Armor," *Playground* 11 (1918): 473, 478.

2. For the most part, the play movement was an urban phenomenon, although

some efforts were made to organize the play of rural children. These efforts were few and far between, however, since the problems addressed by the play movement—juvenile crime, immigrant acculturation, physical congestion—were for the most part urban problems. Consequently, the issue of rural play is not addressed in this book. For a typical example of the differences in play organizers' perceptions of urban and rural play, see Fred Eastman, "Rural Recreation through the Church," *Playground* 6 (1912): 232–38.

3. Baker, "Invisible Armor," pp. 476–77.
4. Ibid.
5. For a full discussion of these differences over the child's nature, see chapter 2.
6. Bernard Mergen, "The Discovery of Children's Play," *American Quarterly* 27 (1975): 399–420; Clarence Rainwater, *The Play Movement in the United States* (Chicago, 1922); Everett Mero, ed., *American Playgrounds* (New York, 1908).
7. Foster R. Dulles, *America Learns to Play* (New York, 1940), p. 150.
8. Henry Adams, *The Education of Henry Adams* (New York, 1931), p. 38.
9. Quoted in John A. Lucas, "A Prelude to the Rise of Sport: Ante-Bellum America, 1850–1860," *Quest* 11 (1968): 53.
10. Ibid., p. 54.
11. Guy Lewis, "The Muscular Christianity Movement," *Journal of Health, Physical Education and Personality* 37 (1966): 27.
12. Ralph Slovenko and James Knight, eds., *Motivation in Play, Games and Sports* (Springfield, Ill., 1967), p. 5; James McLachlan, *American Boarding Schools* (New York, 1970), pp. 169–70.
13. Nancy Struna, "Puritans and Sport: The Irretrievable Tide of Change," *Journal of Sport History* 4 (1977): 6.
14. Ibid., pp. 18–19; Edmund Morgan, *The Puritan Family* (New York, 1966); Peter Wagner, "Puritan Attitudes toward Physical Recreation in Seventeenth-Century New England," *Journal of Sport History* 3 (1976): 139–51. As Struna, Morgan, and Wagner point out, Puritans hardly immersed themselves in the joyless, playless world of the so-called Puritan work ethic. Morgan has argued persuasively that New England Calvinists had a more balanced outlook on matters such as play and recreation than is implied by historical stereotypes of Puritanism. My point, however, is that regardless of their opinions about the nature of play, most antebellum Americans did not view supervised play as a medium of political socialization.
15. Richard A. Swanson, "The Acceptance and Influence of Play in American Protestantism," *Quest* 11 (1968): 59.
16. Mero, *American Playgrounds,* p. 245; Erich Geldbach, "The Beginning of German Gymnastics in America," *Journal of Sport History* 3 (1976): 239.
17. Quoted in Peter Levine, "The Promise of Sport in Ante-Bellum America"

(paper delivered at the Brockport Conference on the Social History of Sport, October 1978), p. 13.

18. Quoted in Lucas, "Prelude to the Rise of Sport," p. 54; see also Melvin Adelman, "Academicians and Athletics: Historians' Views of American Sport," *Maryland Historian* 4 (1973): 123–37; Lawrence W. Fielding, "Reflections from the Sports Mirror: Selected Treatments of Civil War Sport," *Journal of Sport History* 2 (1975): 133.

19. George M. Frederickson, *The Inner Civil War* (New York, 1965), pp. 222–24.

20. Dominick Cavallo, "The Politics of Latency," pp. 163–68; Cavallo, "From Perfection to Habit," pp. 148–52.

21. Roberta Park, "The Attitudes of Leading New England Transcendentalists Toward Healthful Exercise, Active Recreation and Proper Care of the Body: 1830–1860," *Journal of Sport History* 4 (1977): 34–50.

22. Geoffrey Blodgett, "Frederick Law Olmsted: Landscape Architecture as Conservative Reform," *Journal of American History* 62 (1976): 878–79, 884–89.

23. Lewis, "Muscular Christianity Movement," p. 27.

24. Leslie Bruce, "The Responses of Four Colleges to the Rise of Intercollegiate Athletics," *Journal of Sport History* 3 (1976): 213–22. During these years the YMCA was also active in promoting "wholesome" leisure activities for young men exposed to the "evils" of the city. See Howard Hopkins, *History of the YMCA in North America* (New York, 1951), pp. 245–48.

25. Benjamin G. Rader, "Subcommunities and the Rise of Sport," *American Quarterly* 29 (1977): 355–69.

26. Ibid. On the issue of status anxiety among members of the nineteenth-century upper class, see Stow Persons, *The Decline of Gentility* (New York, 1973).

27. Swanson, "Acceptance and Influence of Play," p. 59.

28. John R. Betts, "Sporting Functions in Nineteenth-Century America," *American Quarterly* 5 (1953): 47–52.

29. Frederickson, *Inner Civil War,* pp. 222–24; Swanson, "Acceptance and Influence of Play," p. 59; Mero, *American Playgrounds,* chap. 1.

30. Joseph Lee, *Constructive and Preventive Philanthropy* (New York, 1902), pp. 125–26; Rainwater, *Play Movement,* pp. 22, 51–53.

31. Rainwater, *Play Movement,* pp. 133–38.

32. Ibid., pp. 3–4, 53–54.

33. Spring, *Education and the Rise of the Corporate State,* pp. 65–66; Lee, *Constructive and Preventive Philanthropy,* pp. 112–17; Clarence Perry, *The Wider Use of the School Plant* (New York, 1910), pp. 134–48.

34. Henry Curtis, "Vacation Schools and Playgrounds," *Harpers* 105 (1902): 25–27; George Johnson, "An Educational Experiment," *Pedagogical Seminary* 6 (1899): 513.

35. Evangeline Whitney, "Vacation Schools, Playgrounds, and Recreation Centers," *National Education Association Proceedings* 43 (1904): 299.

36. Lee, *Constructive and Preventive Philanthropy*, p. 145; Perry, *Wider Use of the School Plant*, pp. 181–82.
37. E. B. DeGroot, "The Management of Park Playgrounds," *Playground* 8 (1914): 272.
38. Cornelius Stevenson and Jane Hubbard, "Vacation Schools in Philadelphia," *Playground* 2 (1908): 6.
39. Charles M. Robinson, "The Ideal Playground," PAA Pamphlet, no. 22 (New York, 1909), p. 9.
40. DeGroot, "Management of Park Playgrounds," p. 272.
41. Ibid., pp. 271–76; E. B. DeGroot, "Playground Equipment," *Playground* 7 (1914): 439–45.
42. Mero, *American Playgrounds*, p. 22. There was an effective play movement on the West Coast, however. By 1910 Los Angeles had seven playgrounds and a politically independent Playground Commission. Playground management was so efficient in Oakland that one prominent play organizer called it the most "completely organized system" in the country. As for the Midwest, with the exception of Chicago, the playground system in Gary, Indiana, was the only notable one. While play organizers were concerned about the recreation needs of rural children, they devoted the bulk of their time, energy, and funds to play programs related to the problems of city, especially ethnic, children. The play movement, therefore, never took hold in the South, where the immigrant "problem" was less acute, or at least less visible. See Henry Curtis, *The Significance of the Play Movement* (New York, 1917), pp. 72–75.
43. J. K. Paulding, *Charles B. Stover* (New York, 1938), pp. 17–18, 43; Charles Stover, "Playground Progress in Seward Park," *Charities* 6 (1901): 386.
44. Stover, "Playground Progress," p. 386; Paulding, *Charles B. Stover*, pp. 45–46; Jacob Riis, *The Battle with the Slum* (New York, 1902), pp. 275–76.
45. Lillian Wald, *The House on Henry Street* (New York, 1915), p. 84.
46. Riis, *Battle with the Slum*, p. 304.
47. Allen Davis, *Spearheads for Reform* (New York, 1967), pp. 63–67; Wald, *House on Henry Street*, p. 85; Paulding, *Charles B. Stover*, pp. 46–58.
48. Henry Curtis, *The Practical Conduct of Play* (New York, 1915), p. 2.
49. Paulding, *Charles B. Stover*, pp. 60, 83.
50. Graham Taylor, *Chicago Commons Through Forty Years* (Chicago, 1936), pp. 57–58.
51. Lee, *Constructive and Preventive Philanthropy*, pp. 165–75; Addams, *Second Twenty Years*, p. 366.
52. Zueblin quoted in Sophonisba Breckinridge, ed., *The Child in the City* (Chicago, 1912), p. 449.
53. Ernest Poole, "Chicago's Public Playgrounds," *Outlook* 87 (1907): 775–81; Mero, *American Playgrounds*, pp. 212–18; Charles Zueblin, "Municipal Playgrounds in Chicago," *American Journal of Sociology* 4 (1898): 145–58. The South Park System was governed by a board of five members who were appointed by the fourteen judges of the circuit court. The system was

financed by a special tax on the residents of the South Side. From 1903 to 1906 over six million dollars were spent on the system. Nor were other areas of the city neglected. The West Chicago Park Commission, for example, was authorized by the city to spend one million dollars per year on playground development and staffing.

54. Lee, *Constructive and Preventive Philanthropy,* p. 175.
55. Joseph Lee, "Boston's Playground System," *New England Magazine* 27 (1903): 529; Stoyan Tsanoff, *Educational Value of Children's Play* (Philadelphia, 1897), p. 129; Benjamin Chace, "The Playground Movement in Rochester," *Playground* 2 (1908): 251; C. Arthur, "History of Playground Beginnings in Detroit, Michigan," *Playground* 3 (1909): 2.
56. "Toll of the Neglected Playground," *Playground* 4 (1910): 310.
57. Rainwater, *Play Movement,* p. 241.
58. Ben Lindsey, "Public Playgrounds and Juvenile Delinquency," in Arthur Leland and Lorna Leland, eds., *Playground Techniques and Playcraft* (New York, 1910), pp. 38–42.
59. Mero, *American Playgrounds,* p. 247.
60. Henry Curtis, "How it Began," *Playground* 25 (1931): 71; Curtis, *Practical Conduct of Play,* pp. 20, 88.
61. Ethel Dorgan, *Luther Halsey Gulick* (New York, 1934), pp. 1–4.
62. Ibid., p. 5.
63. Ibid., pp. 6, 43, 105–6; Hopkins, *YMCA,* pp. 29–37.
64. Hopkins, *YMCA,* pp. 29–36.
65. Joseph Lee was born in Brookline, Massachusetts, in 1862. His father was Colonel Henry Lee, one of Boston's leading bankers; his mother, Elizabeth Perkins Cabot, was a member of one of the city's leading families. Lee entered Harvard at sixteen and graduated in 1887. Instead of joining his father's firm after graduating from Harvard Law School, Lee traveled through Europe, had an inspiring visit with Tolstoy, and returned to Boston intent upon helping the city's poor. During the 1890s he became convinced that unrestricted immigration was a prime cause of urban poverty, and he helped organize the Immigration Restriction League, whose goal was to persuade Congress to forbid entrance into the United State to illiterate immigrants. As for those immigrants already in the country, Lee's goal was to help Americanize them as quickly and completely as possible. See Allen Sapora, "The Contributions of Joseph Lee to the Modern Recreation Movement and Related Social Movements in the United States" (Ph.D. diss., University of Michigan, 1952); Barbara Soloman, *Ancestors and Immigrants* (Cambridge, Mass., 1956).
66. Sapora, "The Contributions of Joseph Lee," pp. 279–80.
67. Curtis, "How it Began," p. 71.
68. Sapora, "The Contributions of Joseph Lee" pp. 285–87.
69. "Statement of Purpose," *Playground* 1 (1908): 3.
70. "The Playground Association of America: Purpose," *Playground* 4 (1910): 73.

71. Luther Gulick to John Glenn, 30 April 1908, Russell Sage Foundation Archives (hereafter cited as *RSF*); "Report of the Playground Extension Committee," RSF; John Glenn to Luther Gulick, 27 September 1907, RSF; "Minutes of PAA Board of Directors Meeting, 15 November 1907," National Recreation and Parks Association Archives (hereafter cited as *NRPA*).

72. "Minutes of Executive Committee Meeting of the PAA," 5 November 1908, NRPA.

73. Luther Gulick, *Morals and Morale* (New York, 1919), p. 83.

74. Curtis, *Practical Conduct,* pp. 129–30.

75. "Minutes of the Executive Committee Meeting of the PAA," 12 December 1907, 5 November 1908, NRPA; "Report of the Secretary of the PAA," 1 October 1911, Social Welfare History Archives Center, University of Minnesota (hereafter cited as *SWHAC*); Henry Curtis to Luther Gulick, 6 April 1908, NRPA.

76. Rainwater, *Play Movement,* pp. 20–21.

77. Gustavus Kirby, "The Recreation Movement: Its Possibilities and Limitations," *Playground* 5 (1911): 221–22.

78. Luther Gulick, "Popular Recreation and Public Morality," *Annals of the American Academy of Political and Social Sciences* 35 (1910): 39–40.

79. Ibid., p. 41.

80. Rowland Haynes, "Making a Recreation Survey," *Playground* 7 (1913): 20–25.

81. Rowland Haynes, "Recreation Survey, Milwaukee, Wisconsin," *Playground* 6 (1912): 55–56.

82. Ibid., pp. 45–46, 55.

83. Addams, *The Spirit of Youth,* pp. 82–83.

84. Haynes, "Recreation Survey, Milwaukee," p. 56.

85. This was not an unusual situation in American cities. In a survey by the Russell Sage Foundation in 1911, it was discovered that in New York City pool halls, saloons, burlesque houses, and motion picture theaters collectively outnumbered supervised playgrounds by nearly a hundred to one. Play organizers not only wanted city young people off the streets, but were equally intent upon removing them from the clutches of all unsupervised leisure activities. See Michael M. Davis, *The Exploitation of Pleasure: A Study of Commercial Recreation in New York City* (New York, 1911), pp. 19–57.

86. Haynes, "Recreation Survey, Milwaukee," pp. 58–61.

87. Curtis, *Education Through Play,* p. 270.

88. Clark Hetherington, "Playground Directors—Sources from Which They May Be Obtained," *Playground* 5 (1911): 225; John Chase, "How a Playground Director Feels," *Playground* 3 (1909): 15.

89. DeGroot, "Management of Park Playgrounds," pp. 275–76.

90. George Dickie, "Organization and Management of Playgrounds and Recreation Centers," *National Education Association Proceedings* 54 (1915): 972.

91. Chase, "How a Play Director Feels," p. 13.
92. Whitney, "Vacation Schools," p. 299.
93. Clark Hetherington, "The Training of Physical Education and Play Directors," *Educational Review* 48 (1914): 242.
94. Hetherington, "Playground Directors," pp. 226–29.
95. Hetherington, "Training of Physical Education and Play Directors," p. 243.
96. Curtis, *Practical Conduct,* pp. 160–61, 128–31.
97. Ibid., pp. 129–36.
98. Ibid., pp. 168–73.
99. Orson Ryan, "Class Athletics for Boys," *Playground* 9 (1915): 164–67; Lee Hanmer, "Athletics for the Playground," *Playground* 5 (1911): 274–77.
100. William Burdick, "Athletic Standards for Boys," *Playground* 8 (1914): 105–8.
101. "Children's Festivals," *Playground* 3 (1909): 1–22; Alice Corbin and Edna Fisher, "The Making of a Play Festival," *Playground* 5 (1912): 355–60.
102. Addams, *Spirit of Youth,* pp. 98–100.
103. Otto Mallory, "Field Day," *Playground* 2 (1908): 12.
104. John Gillin, *Poverty and Dependence* (New York, 1921), p. 669; Mero, *American Playgrounds,* pp. 20–21.
105. "Yearbooks," *Playground Association of America* (1912, 1918). There may have been as many as twice the reported number of supervised playgrounds during these years but, for one reason or another, play directors failed to report to PAA officials.
106. Mero, *American Playgrounds,* pp. 20–21.
107. Curtis, *Significance of Play Movement,* p. 31.
108. Zueblin, "Municipal Playgrounds in Chicago," pp. 147–54.
109. Nor did construction of playgrounds in ethnic wards guarantee interaction between various ethnic groups. Precise attendance figures for major cities are difficult to find, but Roy Rosenzweig's data on playground attendance in Worcester, Massachusetts, for 1910 indicate that 82 percent of the children who attended a specific playground lived within one-quarter mile of it. If, therefore, the surrounding neighborhood was ethnically homogeneous, the playground's clientele was likely to reflect that homogeneity. Organized playgrounds, in short, may have promoted rather than discouraged ethnic exclusivity—at least in playgrounds constructed in ethnically homogeneous quarters. See Roy Rosenzweig, "Reforming Working Class Play: The Development of Parks and Playgrounds in Worcester, Massachusetts, 1870–1920" (paper presented at the Brockport Conference on the Social History of Sport, October 1978).
110. David Blaustein, "The Schoolhouse Recreation Center as an Attempt to Aid Immigrants in Adjusting to American Conditions," *Playground* 6 (1912): 330.
111. Luther Gulick, "Municipal Aspects of Health and Recreation," *Life and Health* 25 (1910): 546; Curtis, *Significance of Play Movement,* p. 31.

112. Edward Ward, *The Social Center* (New York, 1913).
113. Curtis, *Education Through Play,* p. 185.
114. Gulick, "Popular Recreation," pp. 39–41.
115. "Report on the Present Status of the Recreation Movement," RSF, August 1916.

CHAPTER 2: CHILD PSYCHOLOGY, PHYSICALISM, AND
THE PLAY MOVEMENT

1. Luther Gulick, *A Philosophy of Play* (New York, 1920), p. 167.
2. G. Stanley Hall et al., *Aspects of Child Life and Education* (Boston, 1907), p. 26; Hall, "Recreation and Reversion," *Pedagogical Seminary* 22 (1914): 510.
3. For American child-rearing practices in the seventeenth, eighteenth, and nineteenth centuries, see Philip Greven, ed., *Child-Rearing Concepts, 1628–1861* (Itasca, Ill., 1973); Greven, *Four Generations* (Ithaca, 1970); Greven, *The Protestant Temperament* (New York, 1977); Michael Katz, *The Irony of Early School Reform* (Cambridge, Mass., 1968); Anne Kuhn, *The Mother's Role in Childhood Education: New England Concepts, 1830–1860* (New Haven, 1947); Hawes, *Children in Urban Society;* Charles Strickland, "A Transcendentalist Father: The Child-Rearing Practices of Bronson Alcott," *History of Childhood Quarterly* 1 (1973): 4–51; Bernard Wishy, *The Child and the Republic* (Philadelphia, 1968); Daniel Calhoun, *The Intelligence of a People* (Princeton, 1973); John Demos, *A Little Commonwealth* (New York, 1970); Peter Slater, *Children in the New England Mind* (New York, 1977).
4. Hawes, *Children in Urban Society,* p. 53.
5. Calhoun, *Intelligence of a People,* pp. 156–60; Katz, *Irony of Early School Reform,* pp. 43–48; Wishy, *Child and the Republic,* pp. 47–58.
6. Cavallo, "From Perfection to Habit," pp. 43–58.
7. John Dewey, *The Influence of Darwin on Philosophy and Other Essays in Contemporary Thought* (New York, 1910), p. 15.
8. Kett, *Rites of Passage,* pp. 171–72.
9. Michael O'Shea, "The Purpose, Scope and Method of Child Study," *Journal of Pedagogy* 2 (1898): 11–12.
10. Dewey, for example, vehemently disagreed with Hall's theory of recapitulation, while Baldwin agreed with Hall on some aspects of this issue but disagreed on others. On the other hand, Edward L. Thorndike strenuously took issue both with Baldwin's reliance on imitation as the key element in socialization and with Hall's theory of recapitulation. See John Dewey, *Democracy and Education* (New York, 1916), p. 85; James Mark Baldwin, *Mental Development in the Child and the Race* (New York, 1894), p. 24; Edward L. Thorndike, *Educational Psychology,* vol. 1 (New York, 1913), pp. 117, 254.
11. Luther Gulick, "Miscellaneous Papers, 1893–1912" (Gulick Papers, Spring-

field College); Addams, *Twenty Years at Hull House,* pp. 172–73; Jill Conway, "Jane Addams: An American Heroine," *Daedalus* 93 (1964): 775; George Johnson, *Education by Play and Games* (New York, 1907), chap. 1; Johnson, "Play as a Moral Equivalent of War," *Playground* 6 (1912): 113–23; Sapora, "The Contributions of Joseph Lee," chaps. 1–4.

12. See Dorothy Ross, *G. Stanley Hall: The Psychologist as Prophet* (Chicago, 1972); G. Stanley Hall, *Life and Confessions of a Psychologist* (New York, 1923), for details of Hall's life.

13. Sarah Wiltse, "A Preliminary Sketch of Child Study in America," *Pedagogical Seminary* 3 (1895): 191.

14. Linus Kline, "A Study in Juvenile Ethics," *Pedagogical Seminary* 10 (1903): 239–66.

15. For example, see G. Stanley Hall and F. H. Saunders, "Pity," *American Journal of Psychology* 11 (1900): 534–91; Earl Barnes, "Punishment as Seen by Children," *Pedagogical Seminary* 3 (1895): 235–45; Linus Kline and Clemens France, "The Psychology of Ownership," *Pedagogical Seminary* 6 (1899): 421–70.

16. G. Stanley Hall, *Adolescence,* 2 vols. (New York, 1904), 1: x; 2: 152. For a history of the recapitulation theory, see Charles Strickland, "The Child and the Race" (Ph.D. diss., University of Wisconsin, 1963).

17. Strickland, "Child and the Race," pp. 85–86, 70–72.

18. Cephas Guillet, "Recapitulation and Education," *Pedagogical Seminary* 7 (1899): 404–5.

19. Hall, *Adolescence,* 2: 65–66.

20. Ross, *G. Stanley Hall,* pp. 250–53. For a history of the child study movement, see James Hendricks, "The Child Study Movement in America, 1880–1910" (Ph.D. diss., Indiana University, 1968).

21. G. Stanley Hall, "Morale in War and After," *Psychological Bulletin* 15 (1918): 367.

22. Hall, *Adolescence,* 1: 407.

23. Charles Strickland and Charles Burgess, eds., *Health, Growth and Heredity* (New York, 1965), p. 135; see also Edgar Swift, *Youth and the Race* (New York, 1915), p. 126.

24. Hall, *Adolescence,* 1: 169.

25. Ibid., pp. 131–32, 183.

26. G. Stanley Hall, "Moral Education and Will Training," *Pedagogical Seminary* 2 (1892): 75.

27. Strickland and Burgess, *Health,* pp. 156–57; Hall, *Adolescence,* 1: 132.

28. Michael O'Shea, "Notes on Ethical Training," *Educational Review* 33 (1907): 371.

29. Hall, *Aspects of Child Life,* pp. 74–80, 115–16.

30. Ibid., pp. 79–80.

31. Baldwin, *Mental Development,* pp. 266–74, 265, 340.

32. Ibid., pp. 158–61.

33. Ibid., pp. 205, 452.

34. Ibid., pp. 205–8, 263–64, 456.
35. James Mark Baldwin, *Social and Ethical Interpretations in Mental Development* (New York, 1897), pp. 46–47.
36. Baldwin, *Mental Development,* pp. 318–21.
37. Ibid., p. 325.
38. Ibid., pp. 324–25.
39. Baldwin, *Social and Ethical Interpretations,* pp. 42–43, 54, 309.
40. Ibid., pp. 58–59.
41. Ibid., pp. 148–55.
42. Ibid.
43. Ibid.
44. Ibid.
45. John Dewey, *The School and Society* (Chicago, 1899), pp. 111–12.
46. Ibid., p. 113.
47. Dewey, *Democracy and Education,* p. 229.
48. Ibid., p. 230.
49. Ibid., pp. 33–35, 321.
50. Ibid., pp. 153–54; John Dewey and Evelyn Dewey, *Schools of Tomorrow* (New York, 1915), pp. 115–20.
51. Dewey, *Democracy and Education,* pp. 153–54, 120.
52. Dewey, *School and Society,* p. 27.
53. Dewey and Dewey, *Schools of Tomorrow,* pp. 119–20.
54. Dewey, *School and Society,* p. 123.
55. Dewey and Dewey, *Schools of Tomorrow,* p. 114.
56. Dewey, *Democracy and Education* p. 415.
57. Morton White, *Social Thought in America* (Boston, 1947), pp. 212–16.
58. The pamphlet is reproduced in Reginald Archambault, ed., *John Dewey on Education* (New York, 1964), pp. 22–60.
59. Ibid., p. 25.
60. Ibid., p. 30.
61. Ibid., pp. 29, 48–53.
62. Ibid., p. 57.
63. Ibid., p. 58.
64. William James, *Principles of Psychology,* vol. 1 (New York, 1890), pp. 108–22. James could not fathom how new habits were formed in the older child or adult "de novo of a simple reflex or path in a pre-existing nervous system." See *Principles of Psychology,* 1:108. The problem was resolved by Edward L. Thorndike in his stimulus-response, habit formation psychology.
65. James, *Principles of Psychology,* 1:114–16.
66. Ibid., 1:122.
67. Thorndike, *Educational Psychology,* 1:102.
68. Ibid., 1:1, 89, 227.
69. Edward L. Thorndike, *Notes on Child Study* (New York, 1903), p. 133.

70. Cavallo, "From Perfection to Habit," pp. 154–57.
71. See note 10.

CHAPTER 3: PLAY AND SOCIALIZATION

1. Lee, *Constructive and Preventive Philanthropy,* chaps. 1–3; Lee, "Work and Citizenship," *Survey* 30 (1913): 611; Lee, "Growth Through Achievement," *School Review* 17 (1909): 352–62.

2. Joseph Lee, "Play and Congestion," *Charities and the Commons* 20 (1908): 43–48; Lee, "Kindergarten Principles in Social Work," *Charities* 11 (1903): 532–37.

3. Josiah Royce, *Race Questions, Provincialism, and Other American Problems* (New York, 1908), p. 272; Joseph Lee, "Assimilation and Nationality," *Charities and the Commons* 19 (1908): 43–48.

4. Luther Gulick, "The New Spirit of Efficiency," *Independent* 80 (1914): 328.

5. G. T. W. Patrick, "The Psychology of Play," *Pedagogical Seminary* 21 (1914): 471.

6. Curtis, *Education Through Play,* pp. 55–61.

7. Addams, *The Spirit of Youth,* pp. 27–28, 53.

8. Wald, *House on Henry Street,* p. 95.

9. Luther Gulick, "The Social Function of Play" (Gulick Papers, Springfield College); Johnson, *Education by Play and Games,* p. 16.

10. Curtis, *Education Through Play,* pp. 1, 7, 56–59.

11. Edward A. Ross to Joseph Lee, 25 May 1915, Lee Papers, NRPA. Johnson's theories were expounded in *Education by Play and Games,* and Gulick's in *Philosophy of Play.*

12. Joseph Lee, *Play in Education* (New York, 1915), pp. 5, 7.

13. Ibid., p. 65.

14. Ibid., p. 78.

15. Ibid., pp. 86–90.

16. Ibid., p. 91.

17. Ibid., p. 98.

18. Ibid., pp. 111–17.

19. Ibid., pp. 139–40.

20. Ibid., pp. 134–42.

21. Ibid., pp. 162–67.

22. Ibid., pp. 143, 159–61.

23. Ibid., pp. 235–39.

24. Ibid., pp. 308–9.

25. Luther Gulick, "Notebook on the Philosophy of Physical Training" (Gulick Papers, Springfield College); idem, "Some Psychical Aspects of Muscular Exercise," *Popular Science Monthly* 53 (1898): 803.

26. Gulick, "Psychical Aspects of Exercise," p. 797.

27. Luther Gulick, *Mind and Work* (New York, 1908), pp. 80–82.

28. Ibid.

29. Gulick, "Psychical Aspects of Exercise," p. 797.

30. Gulick, *Mind and Work,* p. 67.

31. Lee, *Play in Education,* pp. 24–30.

32. George Johnson, "Why Teach a Child to Play?" PAA Pamphlet, no. 76 (New York, 1909), p. 5.

33. Frank Nagley, "A Study in the Psychology of Play," *Playground* 3 (1909): 19.

34. Stoyan Tsanoff, *Educational Value of Children's Play* (Philadelphia, 1897), pp. 47–52.

35. Johnson, "Play as a Moral Equivalent of War," p. 114.

36. Ibid., pp. 115–22.

37. Ibid., p. 122.

38. Curtis, *Education Through Play,* pp. 55–58.

39. Spring, *Education and the Rise of the Corporate State,* pp. 73–75.

40. Woods Hutchinson, "The Evil Influences of School Conditions Upon the Health of School Children," *National Education Association Proceedings* 48 (1906): 263; Curtis, *Practical Conduct,* p. 142.

41. Louis Rapeer, "The School Playground as a National Playground Factor," *Playground* 3 (1909): 16.

42. Luther Gulick and Leonard Ayres, *Medical Inspection of Schools* (New York, 1908), p. 8.

43. Curtis, *Education Through Play,* p. 192.

44. Ibid., p. 75.

45. David B. Tyack, *The One Best System* (Cambridge, Mass., 1974), pp. 178–82.

46. Jacob Riis, "Playgrounds in Washington and Elsewhere," *Charities and the Commons* 20 (1908): 101–4; Curtis, *Education Through Play,* p. 62.

47. Curtis, *Education Through Play,* pp. 77–78; Addams, *Spirit of Youth,* p. 159.

48. Curtis, *Education Through Play,* p. 221.

49. Rapeer, "The School Playground," p. 17.

CHAPTER 4: TAMING THE WILD ANIMAL

1. Addams, *Spirit of Youth,* pp. 53–54; Johnson, *Education by Play,* p. 79. For contemporary theories of adolescence, see Erik H. Erikson, *Identity, Youth and Crisis* (New York, 1968); Peter Blos, *On Adolescence* (New York, 1962); Helene Deutsch, *Selected Problems of Adolescence* (New York, 1967).

2. Leland and Leland, *Playground Techniques and Playcraft,* p. 34.

3. Lee, *Play in Education,* pp. 319–20.

4. Luther Gulick, "Games and Gangs," *Lippincott's Monthly Magazine* 88 (1911): 87.

5. Henry Curtis, *The Significance of Play* (New York, 1917), p. 251; Joseph Lee, "Playground Education," *Educational Review* 22 (1901): 465; Henry Curtis, "Inhibition," *Pedagogical Seminary* 6 (1899): 71.

6. Addams, *Spirit of Youth,* p. 154.

7. Joseph Lee, "Play as a School of the Citizen," *Charities and the Commons* 18 (1907): 491.

8. Luther Gulick, "Team Games and Civic Loyalty," *School Review* 14 (1906): 677; Gulick, *Philosophy of Play* (New York, 1919), p. 191; George Johnson, "Games Every Boy and Girl Should Know," PAA Pamphlet, no. 1 (New York, 1908), 6; Lee, *Play in Education,* pp. 330–34.

9. Luther Gulick, "Psychological, Pedagogical, and Religious Aspects of Group Games," *Pedagogical Seminary* 6 (1899): 142.

10. Curtis, *Practical Conduct,* p. 207.

11. Ibid., p. 209.

12. Ibid., p. 213.

13. E. B. DeGroot, "The Boy in Competition," *Playground* 3 (1909): 10.

14. Johnson, "Games Every Boy and Girl Should Know," p. 7.

15. Luther Gulick, *The Healthful Art of Dancing* (New York, 1910), p. 16.

16. Gulick, *Philosophy of Play,* pp. 190–93.

17. Curtis, *Practical Conduct,* p. 212.

18. Lee, *Play in Education,* p. 336.

19. Lee, "Playground Education," p. 466.

20. George Johnson, "An Experiment in Athletics," *Playground* 7 (1913): 17.

21. Royce, *Race Questions,* pp. 235–37.

22. Ibid., p. 238.

23. Ibid., pp. 239–41, 272.

24. Ibid., pp. 257–58.

25. E. B. DeGroot, "Players and Officials," *Playground* 2 (1908): 5–7.

26. Ibid., p. 6.

27. Rainwater, *The Play Movement in the United States,* p. 285.

28. Curtis, *Practical Conduct,* p. 267; Caroline Bergen, "Relation of Play to Juvenile Delinquency," *Charities and the Commons* 18 (1907): 562.

29. Lee, *Play in Education,* p. 382.

30. Ibid., p. 260.

31. Gulick, *Philosophy of Play,* p. 193; Gulick, *The Dynamic of Manhood* (New York, 1917), p. 50.

32. Lee, *Play in Education,* p. 340.

33. Foster Warren, "Organized Recreation," *National Education Association Proceedings* (1916): 49.

34. Howard Braucher, "Miscellaneous Writings" (Braucher Papers, NRPA).

35. Lee, *Play in Education,* p. 276.

36. Addams, *Spirit of Youth,* p. 96; Addams, "Recreation as a Public Function in Urban Communities," *American Journal of Sociology* 17 (1912): 618; Addams, *Second Twenty Years,* pp. 365–67.

37. Curtis, "Inhibition," p. 71.

38. Johnson, "Games Every Boy and Girl Should Know," p. 6.

39. Gulick, *Morals and Morale,* p. 53; Joseph Lee, "Play as an Antidote to Civilization," *Playground* 5 (1911): 111; Lee, "Play as Medicine," *Playground* 5 (1911): 294.

40. Lee, "Play as Medicine," p. 294.
41. Jacob Riis, *How the Other Half Lives* (New York, 1957), pp. 88–109.
42. Luther Gulick, "Camp Fire Girls," *Playground* 6 (1912): 209.
43. Addams, *Spirit of Youth*, pp. 20–31; Curtis, *Education Through Play*, pp. 72, 226.
44. Gulick, *Philosophy of Play*, p. 79.
45. C. M. Mayne, "What a Corporation Can and Does Do for the Recreation of Its Employees," *Playground* 7 (1914): 449; Charles Weller, "Recreation in Industries," *Playground* 11 (1917): 250; Graham Taylor, "Planning Recreation in an American Industrial Community," *Playground* 7 (1913): 196.
46. Joseph Lee, "The Educational Possibilities of Democracy," *Ethical Record* 2 (1900–1901): 57.
47. Addams, *Spirit of Youth*, p. 127.
48. Elizabeth Rafter, "Playgrounds and Playground Equipment," *Playground* 2 (1908): 11.
49. Addams, *Spirit of Youth*, p. 99.
50. Woods, *The City Wilderness*, pp. 114–22; Addams, "Recreation as a Public Function," p. 617.
51. Curtis, *Practical Conduct*, pp. 129–30; John Gillin, "The Sociology of Recreation," *American Journal of Sociology* 19 (1914): 833.
52. Joseph Lee, "Americanization and Recreation" (Lee Papers, NRPA).
53. Graham Taylor, "City Neighbors at Play," *Survey* 24 (1910): 548; David Blaustein, "The Schoolhouse Recreation Center as an Attempt to Aid Immigrants in Adjusting Themselves to American Conditions," *Playground* 6 (1912): 331; Perry, *Wider Use of the School Plant*, p. 177; Gillin, "Sociology of Recreation," p. 833.
54. Curtis, *Education Through Play*, p. 80.
55. Playgrounds may not have deterred juvenile crime, but they did contribute to a decrease in the juvenile arrest rate, a very different thing. A study of juvenile crime sponsored by the Russell Sage Foundation in 1914, for example, found that of 463 juvenile arrests in a New York ward in 1909, 112 were for truancy, begging, selling newspapers and "general incorrigibility," 125 youths were apprehended for playing in the streets, and 28 for upsetting trash cans. Only 57 of the 463 were arrested for committing serious crimes like assault and substantial theft. In an analysis of data compiled by the Pennsylvania Children's Aid Society in 1890, Homer Folks found a similar disproportion between commission of serious crime and the juvenile arrest rate. These studies indicated that juvenile crime was whatever city police and magistrates said it was. Young people in slum areas were often arrested because they had nowhere to congregate or play except the street. It is no wonder that construction of a playground in a slum ward led to a dramatic diminution in the juvenile arrest rate: youths formerly liable to arrest for playing or standing about in the street were breaking no law by doing the same on a playground. Thus, organized playgrounds reduced the arrest rate rather than serious crime. See Ruth

True et al., *Boyhood and Lawlessness* (New York, 1914), pp. 16–19; Homer
Folks, "The Care of Delinquent Children," *Proceedings of the National
Conference on Charities and Correction* (1891): 139–40. On attitudes toward
juvenile crime during the period under discussion, see Anthony Platt, *The
Child Savers* (Chicago, 1969); Steven Schlossman, *Love and the American
Delinquent: The Theory and Practice of "Progressive" Juvenile Justice,
1825–1920* (Chicago, 1977).

56. Oscar Handlin, *The Uprooted* (Boston, 1973); Eisenstadt, "Archetypal Patterns of Youth," in Erikson, ed., *The Challenge of Youth.*

57. Thomas Kessner, *The Golden Door: Italian and Jewish Immigrant Mobility
in New York City, 1880–1915* (New York, 1977); Virginia Yans-McLaugh-
lin, *Family and Community: Italian Immigrants in Buffalo, 1880–1930*
(Ithaca, 1977); Humbert S. Nelli, *Italians in Chicago, 1880–1930* (New
York, 1970); Richard Gambino, *Blood of My Blood: The Dilemma of the
Italian-Americans* (New York, 1974); Moses Rischin, *The Promised City:
New York's Jews, 1870–1914* (New York, 1962); Alfred Kazin, *A Walker in
the City* (New York, 1951); Rudolph J. Vecoli, "Contadini in Chicago: A
Critique of *The Uprooted,*" *Journal of American History* 51 (1964): 404–17.

58. Roy Rosenzweig, "Reforming Working-Class Play," p. 56.

59. This is not to say that ethnic youths were paragons of virtue. They formed
youth gangs, committed serious crimes, and contributed their share to the
disorder that plagued American cities in this period. The issue, however,
is whether the reality of misbehavior among ethnic youths justified play
organizers' rhetoric of doom. It did not. Violence in general, and urban
violence in particular, were hardly unknown in the United States before
the arrival of eastern and southern Europeans in great numbers. What
disturbed play organizers was the existence of more or less autonomous
ethnic enclaves and the apparent viability of ethnic cultures in an American setting. For many play organizers, ethnic separatism implied violence
against the American body politic. This was the violence that concerned
play organizers. On the issue of ethnic disorder, see note 57 above and Sam
Bass Warner, Jr., *The Private City* (Philadelphia, 1968), pp. 137–47.

CHAPTER 5: THE ANATOMY OF MORAL CHANGE

1. John Higham, *Send These to Me: Jews and Other Immigrants in Urban
America* (New York, 1975), pp. 198–99.

2. J. O. C. Phillips, "The Education of Jane Addams," *History of Education
Quarterly* 14 (1974): 50–63; see also Lasch, *New Radicalism in America,* pp.
38–68.

3. Luther Gulick, "The Social Function of Play" (Gulick Papers, Springfield
College); Gulick, *Dynamic of Manhood,* p. 5. Dorothy Ross has suggested
that G. Stanley Hall experienced severe conflict over paternal and maternal identifications that were never resolved. See Ross, *G. Stanley Hall,* pp.
256, 338–39.

4. Gulick, "Social Function of Play."

5. Gulick, "Camp Fire Girls," p. 210.

6. Kuhn, *Mother's Role in Childhood Education*, chap. 1; Calhoun, *Intelligence of a People*, pp. 135–55; Welter, "The Cult of True Womanhood," pp. 224–25.

7. Kuhn, *Mother's Role*, p. 4; Douglas, *The Feminization of American Culture*, chaps. 1–3; Welter, "The Feminization of American Religion," pp. 137–57.

8. Kuhn, *Mother's Role*, pp. 150–51; Wishy, *Child and the Republic*, p. 28; John Abbott, "On the Mother's Role in Education," in Greven, ed., *Child-Rearing Concepts*, pp. 113–33.

9. Bushnell quoted in Greven, p. 157.

10. Charles Strickland, "A Transcendentalist Father: The Child-Rearing Practices of Bronson Alcott," *History of Education Quarterly* 1 (1973): 16–17, 40.

11. Wishy, *Child and the Republic*, p. 17; Katz, *Irony of Early School Reform*, pp. 43–58, 117–18, 149.

12. David Tyack, *The One Best System* (Cambridge, Mass., 1974), pp. 183, 230.

13. Manuel Furer, "The History of the Superego Concept in Psychoanalysis," in Seymour Post, ed., *Moral Values and the Superego Concept in Psychoanalysis* (New York, 1972), pp. 12–19; Joseph Sandler, "On the Concept of the Superego," *Psychoanalytic Study of the Child* 15 (1960): 133; David Beres, "Vicissitudes of Superego Functions and Superego Precursors in Childhood," *Psychoanalytic Study of the Child* 13 (1958): 326; Rene Spitz, "On the Genesis of Superego Components," *Psychoanalytic Study of the Child* 13 (1958): 385–93; Roy Schafer, *Aspects of Internalization* (New York, 1968), pp. 229–34; Schafer, "Emotion in the Language of Action," in Merton Gill and Philip S. Holzman, eds., *Psychology Versus Metapsychology*, vol. 9 of *Psychological Issues* (New York, 1976), pp. 106–33; Jane Loevinger, "Origins of Conscience," in vol. 9 of *Psychological Issues*, pp. 265–97.

14. Talcott Parsons, *Social Structure and Personality* (London, 1964), pp. 23–36; Hans Loewald, "The Superego and the Ego Ideal," *International Journal of Psychoanalysis* 43 (1962): 267; Schafer, *Aspects of Internalization*, p. 148.

15. Edith Jacobson, *The Self and the Object World* (New York, 1964), p. 132, 134; Heinz Hartmann, Ernst Kris, and Rudolph Lowenstein, *Papers on Psychoanalytic Psychology*, vol. 14 of *Psychological Issues* (New York, 1964), p. 167.

16. Roy Schafer, "Ideals, Ego Ideal, and Ideal Self," *Psychological Issues* 18/19 (New York, 1967), pp. 129–74; Jeanne Lampl-DeGroot, "Ego Ideal and Superego," *Psychoanalytic Study of the Child* 17 (1962): 99–100; Annie Reich, "Early Identifications as Archaic Elements in the Superego," *Journal of the American Psychoanalytic Association* 2 (1954): 218.

17. Jacobson, *Self and Object World*, p. 111; M. Laufer, "Ego Ideal and Pseudo Ego Ideal in Adolescence," *Psychoanalytic Study of the Child* 19 (1964): 200–201.

18. Laufer, "Ego Ideal," p. 200; Schafer, "Ideals, Ego Ideal," pp. 129–39.

19. Helen Lewis, *Shame and Guilt in Neurosis* (New York, 1971), pp. 21–26, 82.
20. Milton Piers and Gerhard Singer, *Shame and Guilt* (Chicago, 1953), p. 36.
21. Lewis, *Shame and Guilt in Neurosis,* pp. 30–31; Helen Lynd, *Shame and the Search for Identity* (New York, 1958), p. 236.
22. Lewis, *Shame and Guilt in Neurosis,* p. 23.
23. Ibid., p. 34.
24. Piers and Singer, *Shame and Guilt,* p. 16; Lynd, *Shame and Search,* pp. 34, 42, 67.
25. Lewis, *Shame and Guilt in Neurosis,* pp. 25, 507.
26. Ibid., pp. 30–34. It should be emphasized that shame and guilt are not mutually exclusive states. It is, for example, possible for a person to feel ashamed for violating a moral prohibition. In speaking of a shame-prone moral "style," I am referring to a tendency or a prediliction, rather than an absolute state.
27. Ibid., p. 251.
28. Gulick, *Philosophy of Play,* pp. 193–95.
29. Curtis, *Education Through Play,* p. 55.
30. E. B. DeGroot, "Players and Officials," p. 6.
31. Curtis, *Practical Conduct of Play,* p. 207.
32. Gulick, *Dynamic of Manhood,* p. 50.
33. Jane Addams, "Public Recreation and Social Morality," *Charities and the Commons* 18 (1907): 494; Gulick, *Philosophy of Play,* p. xiv.
34. On "ego functions," see Heinz Hartmann, *Essays in Ego Psychology* (New York, 1964), pp. 86, 115–22; Hartmann, *Ego Psychology and the Problem of Adaptation* (New York, 1939), pp. 25, 30–32, 103; Schafer, *Aspects of Internalization,* pp. 11–12, 158.
35. Lewis, *Shame and Guilt in Neurosis,* p. 51.
36. Ibid., pp. 133–35.
37. Lee, *Play in Education,* p. 337.
38. Ibid.
39. Eisenstadt, "Archetypal Patterns," p. 47.
40. Johnson, "Play as a Moral Equivalent of War," p. 120.
41. Nagley, "A Study in the Psychology of Play," p. 10.
42. Curtis, *Education Through Play,* p. 67.
43. Stanley Milgram, *Obedience to Authority* (New York, 1974), p. 146.
44. Ibid.
45. Thomas Kuhn, *The Structure of Scientific Revolutions* (Chicago, 1962).
46. John R. Gillis, *Youth and History* (New York, 1974), pp. 62–65; Kett, *Rites of Passage,* p. 58.
47. On the inculcation of peer-group direction during the Progressive Era, see Spring, *Education and the Rise of the Corporate State,* pp. 44–61.
48. Gregory Rochlin, *Griefs and Discontents* (Boston, 1965), p. 271; Blos, *On Adolescence,* pp. 117, 206–7; Aaron Esman, "Adolescence and the Consolidation of Values," in Post, ed., *Moral Values and the Superego,* pp. 88–89.
49. See chapter 4, pp. 88–91.

50. Cavallo, "The Politics of Latency," pp. 168–71; William Bridges, "Family Patterns and Social Values in America, 1825–1875," *American Quarterly* 17 (1965): 3–11; Fass, *The Damned and the Beautiful,* pp. 53–118.
51. Eisenstadt, "Archetypal Patterns," p. 36.
52. Evangeline Whitney, "Vacation Schools, Playgrounds, and Recreation Centers," *National Education Association Proceedings* 43 (1904): 298.

CHAPTER 6: PLAYGROUND TRAINING AND SEX ROLES

1. I intended to do biographical studies of Gulick and Lee as well as Addams. This became impossible when surviving members of the Gulick and Lee families informed the author that material relating to their adolescent years had either been destroyed (Gulick) or was "too personal" for perusal by outsiders (Lee). John Gulick to author 17 December 1975; Susan M. Lee to author, 2 February 1975.
2. John Rousmaniere, "Cultural Hybrid in the Slums: The College Woman and the Settlement House," in Katz, ed., *Education in American History,* pp. 122–27.
3. Addams quoted in Phillips, "The Education of Jane Addams," p. 63.
4. Addams, *Twenty Years,* p. 94.
5. Gulick, "The Social Function of Play" (Gulick Papers, Springfield College).
6. Woods, *Neighborhood in Nation-Building,* pp. 106–9, 9, 43.
7. Rousmaniere, "Cultural Hybrid," passim; Lasch, *The New Radicalism in America,* pp. 38–68; Ross, *G. Stanley Hall,* pp. 256, 338–39.
8. Kai T. Erikson, *Everything in Its Path* (New York, 1976), p. 81.
9. Ibid., pp. 81–82.
10. Ibid., p. 82. Erikson's definition of culture is compelling because he assumes that cultural mandates are multi-dimensional. In Erikson's view, values are not necessarily sharply defined categorical imperatives: they can intersect with their opposites, thereby generating moral ambiguity in the person and social diversity, and possibly conflict, among social groups. Since each value implies its opposite, one must analyze values as dynamic and shifting binaries, rather than one-dimensional imperatives that are either observed or transgressed. It is precisely this dynamic, binary quality that characterized the child training methods of play organizers.
11. Marcet Halderman-Julius, "The Two Mothers of Jane Addams" (Addams Papers, Swarthmore College Peace Collection, hereafter cited as *SCPC*), pp. 3–5.
12. Addams, *Twenty Years,* pp. 25, 1–2.
13. James Linn, *Jane Addams, A Biography* (New York, 1938), p. 26.
14. Addams, *Twenty Years,* pp. 7, 26–27.
15. Ibid., p. 16; Allen Davis, *American Heroine: The Life and Legend of Jane Addams* (New York, 1973), pp. 4–6.
16. Linn, *Jane Addams,* pp. 16–18.

17. Addams, *Twenty Years,* pp. 12–13.
18. Ibid.
19. Halderman-Julius, "Two Mothers," pp. 4, 11.
20. Linn, *Jane Addams,* p. 22.
21. Jane Addams, *The Long Road of Woman's Memory* (New York, 1916), p. 141.
22. Ibid., p. 142.
23. Ibid., pp. 145–49.
24. Ibid., pp. 154–57.
25. Adele Scharl, "Regression and Restitution in Object Loss," *Psychoanalytic Study of the Child* 16 (1961): 479; Margaret Mahler, "On Sadness and Grief in Infancy and Childhood," *Psychoanalytic Study of the Child* 16 (1961): 337–43.
26. Gregory Rochlin, "The Dread of Abandonment," *Psychoanalytic Study of the Child* 16 (1961): 452–53.
27. Addams, *Twenty Years,* p. 22.
28. Addams quoted in Linn, *Jane Addams,* p. 39.
29. Lionel C. Lane, "Jane Addams as Social Worker" (Ph.D. diss., University of Pennsylvania, 1963), pp. 6–7.
30. Addams, *Twenty Years,* p. 49; Davis, *American Heroine,* pp. 20, 35–36.
31. Addams quoted in ibid., p. 63.
32. Phillips, "Education of Jane Addams," pp. 50–60.
33. Linn, *Jane Addams,* p. 63.
34. Rousmaniere, "Cultural Hybrid," pp. 124–27.
35. Addams to Ellen Gates Starr, 7 January 1883 (Starr Papers, Sophia Smith Collection, Smith College, hereafter cited as *SSC*).
36. Addams, *Twenty Years,* p. 16.
37. Addams to Starr, 8 June 1884 (Starr Papers, SSC).
38. Addams to Starr, 7 February 1886 (Starr Papers, SSC).
39. Addams, *Twenty Years,* p. 77.
40. Ibid., pp. 70–76.
41. Paul Seton, "The Psychotemporal Adaptation of Late Adolescence," *Journal of the American Psychoanalytic Association* 22 (1974): 797–804; Hans Loewald, "The Superego and the Ego-Ideal," *International Journal of Psychoanalysis* 43 (1962): 265.
42. Seton, "Psychotemporal Adaptation," p. 816.
43. Rochlin, "Dread of Abandonment," p. 461; Martha Wolfenstein, "How Is Mourning Possible?" *Psychoanalytic Study of the Child* 21 (1966): 113–15.
44. Addams to Starr, 2 December 1883 (Starr Papers, SSC).
45. Addams to Starr, 6 December 1885 (Starr Papers, SSC).
46. Addams to Starr, 29 January 1880 (Starr Papers, SSC).
47. Ibid.
48. Addams to Starr, 2 December 1885 (Starr Papers, SSC).
49. Addams, *Twenty Years,* p. 78.
50. Addams to Starr, 2 December 1883 (Starr Papers, SSC).

51. Blos, "Character Formation in Adolescence," p. 253; Edith Jacobson, "Adolescent Moods and the Remodeling of the Psychic Structure in Adolescence," *Psychoanalytic Study of the Child* 16 (1961): 180.
52. Blos, *On Adolescence,* pp. 73, 193.
53. Blos, "Character Formation," p. 253.
54. Jacobson, *Self and the Object World,* p. 39.
55. Calvin Settlage, "Cultural Values and the Superego in Late Adolescence," *Psychoanalytic Study of the Child* 27 (1973): 80–81.
56. Jacobson, *Self and the Object World,* p. 121.
57. Addams, *Twenty Years,* p. 96.
58. Jane Addams, *Democracy and Social Ethics* (New York, 1902), p. 4.
59. Ibid., pp. 212–13; Jane Addams et al., *Philanthropy and Social Progress* (New York, 1893), p. 1.
60. Addams quoted in Lane, "Jane Addams as Social Worker," p. 59.
61. Addams quoted in Morton White and Lucia White, *The Intellectual Against the City* (Cambridge, Mass., 1961), p. 154.
62. Addams, *Twenty Years,* p. 100; Addams, *Democracy and Social Ethics,* pp. 2–3.
63. Addams, *Long Road,* pp. 82–83.
64. Addams, *Democracy and Social Ethics,* pp. 64–68, 6–7, 273–75.
65. Ibid., p. 273.
66. Jane Addams, "A Function of the Social Settlement," *Annals of the American Academy of Political and Social Sciences* 13 (1899): 326.
67. Jane Addams, "Public Recreation and Social Morality," p. 494.
68. Addams quoted in Linn, *Jane Addams,* p. 416.

CONCLUSION: IMPLICATIONS OF THE PLAY MOVEMENT

1. Erikson, *Everything in Its Path,* p. 82.
2. Ibid.
3. Cushing Strout, "The Uses and Abuses of Psychology in American History," *American Quarterly* 28 (1976): 342.
4. Peter Filene, "An Obituary for 'The Progressive Movement,'" *American Quarterly* 22 (1970): 27.
5. Ibid., pp. 20–26.
6. Erikson, *Everything in Its Path,* p. 83.
7. Ibid.
8. The nexus between team games and modern liberalism was suggested to me by Professor Mel Albin. For an incisive analysis of the relationship between Progressive Era reform and the origins of modern liberalism see Michael Paul Rogin, *The Intellectuals and McCarthy* (Cambridge, Mass., 1967), pp. 192–215.

SELECTED BIBLIOGRAPHY

A NOTE ON SOURCES

The most valuable guide to the ideology of play organizers is contained in the published works of Luther H. Gulick, Jr., Joseph Lee, Henry Curtis, Jacob Riis, and Jane Addams. These works have been cited in textual references.

Information about the origins of the Playground Association of America, the strategies of its leaders, the sources of its financial backing, and its role in launching War Camp Community Service is located in the minutes of PAA Executive Committee Meetings. Unfortunately, these records are both scattered and incomplete. Most of what survives of these minutes is located in the Social Welfare History Archives Center, University of Minnesota. A limited collection of these records can be found at the National Recreation Association, Arlington, Virginia. An excellent and complete fund of data about the financial and ideological links between the PAA and the Russell Sage Foundation is located in the archives of the Russell Sage Foundation, New York City.

A most important propaganda vehicle for play organizers was the PAA's monthly journal, *The Playground.* Another valuable index of playground progress in the early years of the twentieth century was the PAA's annual *Yearbook.* Among other things the *Yearbook* recorded the amount of money expended by municipalities for playground construction and maintenance, and the number, gender, wages, and educational backgrounds of playground workers.

The private papers utilized in this study are located in the following libraries and collections: Springfield College (Luther H. Gulick, Jr., Papers); Swarthmore College Peace Collection (Jane Addams Papers); Sophia Smith Women's Collection, Smith College (Ellen Gates Starr Papers); Library of Congress (Jacob Riis Papers).

The most complete collection of PAA pamphlets on playground organization and purposes is located in the New York Public Library.

PRIMARY SOURCES: THE PLAY MOVEMENT

Addams, Jane. *The Second Twenty Years at Hull House.* New York: Macmillan, 1930.
————. *Twenty Years at Hull House.* New York: Macmillan, 1910.
————. *The Spirit of Youth and the City Streets.* New York: Macmillan, 1909.
————. "Public Recreation and Social Morality." *Charities and the Commons* 18 (August 1907): 492–97.
————. *Democracy and Social Ethics.* New York: Macmillan, 1902.
Addams, Jane, et al. *Philanthropy and Social Progress.* New York: Crowell, 1893.
American, Sadie. "The Movement for Small Playgrounds." *American Journal of Sociology* 4 (September 1898): 159–70.
————. "The Movement for Vacation Schools." *American Journal of Sociology* 4 (November 1898): 309–25.
Angell, Emmett. *Play.* Boston: Little, Brown, 1910.
Appleton, Lilla. *A Comparative Study of the Play Activities of Adult Savages and Civilized Children.* Chicago: University of Chicago Press, 1910.
Baker, Newton. "Invisible Armor." *Playground* 11 (1918): 473–81.
Bancroft, Jessie. *Games for the Playground, Home, School and Gymnasium.* New York: Macmillan, 1909.
Batchelor, W. C. "Pure Democracy in Playground Management." *Playground* 12 (July 1918): 141–46.
Bergen, Caroline. "Relation of Play to Juvenile Delinquency." *Charities and the Commons* 18 (August 1907): 562–65.
Blunt, H. "Effects of Evil Recreation." *Indiana Bulletin of Charities and Correction* 97 (1914): 188–94.
Bocker, Dorothy. "Social Cleavage and the Playground." *Playground* 9 (June 1915): 87–90.
Boone, Richard. "The Educational Value of Playgrounds." *Proceedings of the National Education Association* 54 (1915): 989–93.
Bradley, John. "Play in Relation to Character." *Education* 19 (March 1899): 406–13.
Bradstreet, Howard. "Does the Influence of the Playground Extend to the Neighborhood?" *Playground* 2 (September 1908): 17–18.
Braucher, Howard. "Why I Believe That Community and Neighborhood Centers, Schools, and Parks Should Be Under Government Direction and Control." *Playground* 10 (June 1916): 83–96.
————. "The Social Worker and the Playground Association of America." *Proceedings of the National Conference of Charities and Corrections* (1910): 219–22.
Brown, Elmer. "Health, Morality, and the Playground." *Russell Sage Foundation Pamphlet,* no. 48 (1910).
Burdick, William. "Athletic Standards for Boys." *Playground* 8 (June 1914): 105–8.
Carr, H. A. "The Survival Value of Play." *Investigations of the Department of*

Psychology and Education of the University of Colorado 1 (November 1902): 3–47.

Chase, John. "How a Director Feels." *Playground* 3 (July 1909): 13–15.

———. "Street Games of New York Children." *Pedagogical Seminary* 12 (December 1905): 503–4.

Corbin, Alice, and Edna Fisher. "The Making of a Play Festival." *Playground* 5 (January 1912): 355–60.

Curtis, Henry. "How It Began." *Playground* 25 (May 1931): 71.

———. *Education Through Play.* New York: Macmillan, 1915.

———. *The Practical Conduct of Play.* New York: Macmillan, 1915.

———. "Public Provision and Responsibility for Playgrounds." *Annals of the American Academy of Political and Social Sciences* 35 (January 1910): 118–28.

———. "The Formation of Playground Associations." *Playground* 2 (June 1908): 8–10.

———. "Vacation Schools and Playgrounds." *Harpers* 105 (1902): 22–29.

DeGroot, E. B. "The Boy in Competition." *Playground* 3 (July 1909): 9–12.

———. "What is a Playground?" *Playground* 3 (October 1909): 12–15.

———. "Players and Officials." *Playground* 2 (May 1908): 5–7.

Devine, Edward. "How Fundamental Is the Play Movement?." *Playground* 8 (March 1915): 422–23.

Edgerton, Hiram. "The Playground and Its Place in the Administration of a City." *Russell Sage Foundation Pamphlet,* no. 26 (1909).

Gillin, John. "The Sociology of Recreation." *American Journal of Sociology* 19 (May 1914): 825–34.

Gulick, Luther. *A Philosophy of Play.* New York: Scribner, 1920.

———. *Morals and Morale.* New York: Association Press, 1919.

———. *The Dynamic of Manhood.* New York: Association Press, 1917.

———. "The New Efficiency of the Spirit." *Independent* 80 (November 1914): 328–29.

———. "Camp Fire Girls." *Playground* 6 (September 1912): 209–16.

———. "The Camp Fire Girls and the New Relation of Women to the World." *Proceedings of the National Education Association* 51 (1912): 322–27.

———. "Games and Gangs." *Lippincott's Monthly Magazine* 88 (July 1911): 84–89.

———. "Municipal Aspects of Health and Recreation." *Life and Health* 25 (September 1910): 544–46.

———. "Popular Recreation and Public Morality." *Annals of the American Academy of Political and Social Sciences* 34 (July 1909): 33–42.

———. *Mind and Work.* New York: Doubleday, 1908.

———. "The Playground." *Playground* 1 (April 1907): 7–8.

———. "Team Games and Civic Loyalty." *School Review* 14 (November 1906): 676–78.

———. "Rhythm and Education." *American Physical Education Review* 10 (June 1905): 164–69.

――――. "Psychological, Pedagogical, and Religious Aspects of Group Games." *Pedagogical Seminary* 6 (March 1899): 135–51.

――――. "Some Psychical Aspects of Muscular Exercise." *Popular Science Monthly* 43 (1898): 793–805.

Hanmer, Lee. "Organizing the Neighborhood for Recreation." *Proceedings of the National Conference of Charities and Corrections* (1915): 70–76.

Haynes, Rowland. "Making a Recreation Survey." *Playground* 7 (April 1913): 19–25.

――――. "Recreation Survey, Milwaukee, Wisconsin." *Playground* 6 (May 1912): 38–66.

Heller, Harriet. "The Playground as a Phase of Social Reform." *American Physical Education Review* 13 (1908): 498–505.

Hermann, Ernst. "Producing Neighborhood Efficiency Through Play." *Playground* 10 (April 1916): 25–27.

Hetherington, Clark. "The Training of the Physical Educator and Play Directors." *Educational Review* 48 (October 1914): 241–53.

Howe, Frederic. *The Modern City and Its Problems.* New York: Scribner, 1915.

Hutchinson, Woods. "Can the Child Survive Civilization?" *Russell Sage Foundation Pamphlet,* no. 11 (1909).

Johnson, George. "An Experiment in Athletics." *Playground* 7 (April 1913): 17–18.

――――. "Play as a Moral Equivalent of War." *Playground* 6 (July 1912): 111–23.

――――. "Why Teach a Child to Play?" *Playground Association of America Pamphlet,* no. 76 (1909).

――――. *Education by Plays and Games.* New York: Ginn and Company, 1907.

Kennard, Beulah. "Playground Marching Song." *Playground* 3 (May 1909): 37.

Lathrop, Julia. "Taking Play Seriously." *Playground* 10 (January 1917): 356–63.

Lee, Joseph. *Play in Education.* New York: Macmillan, 1915.

――――. "The Unknown Basis of Mental Hygiene." *Proceedings of the National Conference of Charities and Corrections* (1915): 236–40.

――――. "Democracy and the Illiteracy Test." *Survey* 35 (January 1918): 497–99.

――――. "American Play Tradition and Our Relation to It." *Playground* 7 (July 1913): 148–59.

――――. "Work and Citizenship." *Survey* 30 (August 1913): 611.

――――. "Play as an Antidote to Civilization." *Playground* 5 (July 1911): 110–26.

――――. "Play as Medicine." *Playground* 5 (December 1911): 289–302.

――――. "Play and Congestion." *Charities and the Commons* 20 (April 1908): 43–48.

――――. "Play as a School of the Citizen." *Charities and the Commons* 18 (August 1907): 486–91.

――――. *Constructive and Preventive Philanthropy.* New York: Macmillan, 1902.

――――. "Playground Education." *Educational Review* 22 (1901): 449–71.

Leland, Arthur, and Lorna Leland, eds. *Playground Technique and Playcraft.* New York: Doubleday, 1910.

Leland, Lorna. "Organizing Sports in Public Schools." *Proceedings of the National Education Association* 48 (1909): 774–77.

Lord, Katherine. "Pageant of the Evolution of Industry." *Playground* 5 (March 1912): 407–10.

Mallory, Otto. "A Builder of the New Democracy." *Playground* 10 (February 1917): 413–15.

McDowell, Mary. "Recreation as a Fundamental Element of Democracy." *Playground* 7 (August 1913): 191–95.

Mero, Everett, ed. *American Playgrounds*. Boston: Dale Association, 1909.

Nagley, Frank. "A Study in the Psychology of Play." *Playground* 3 (July 1909): 18–19.

O'Shea, Michael. "Work and Play in Adjustment to the Social Environment." *American Journal of Sociology* 8 (November 1902): 382–89.

Patrick, G. T. W. "The Psychology of Play." *Pedagogical Seminary* 21 (1914): 469–84.

Perry, Clarence. *Wider Use of the School Plant*. New York: Survey Associates, 1910.

Riis, Jacob. "Playgrounds in Washington and Elsewhere." *Charities and the Commons* 20 (April 1908): 101–4.

———. "The Island Playgrounds of the Future." *Charities* 11 (September 1903): 205–7.

———. "Playgrounds for City Schools." *Century* 58 (September 1894): 657–66.

Robinson, Charles. "Recreation from a City Planning Standpoint." *Playground* 7 (September 1913): 220–27.

———. "Educational Value of Public Recreation Facilities." *Annals of the American Academy of Political and Social Sciences* 35 (January 1910): 134–40.

Royce, Josiah. *Race Questions, Provincialism, and Other American Problems*. New York: Macmillan, 1908.

Stover, Charles. "Playground Progress in Seward Park." *Charities and the Commons* 6 (1901): 386–93.

Taylor, Graham. "Planning Recreation in an Industrial Community." *Playground* 7 (August 1913): 196–200.

———. "City Neighbors at Play." *Survey* 24 (July 1910): 548–59.

Zueblin, Charles. *American Municipal Progress*. New York: Macmillan, 1916.

———. "Municipal Playgrounds in Chicago." *American Journal of Sociology* 4 (September 1898): 145–58.

PRIMARY SOURCES: CHILD PSYCHOLOGY

Archambault, Reginald, ed. *John Dewey on Education*. New York: Modern Library, 1964.

Baldwin, James Mark. *Social and Ethical Interpretations in Mental Development*. New York: Macmillan, 1897.

———. *Mental Development in the Child and the Race*. New York: Macmillan, 1894.

Barnes, Earl. "Punishment as Seen by Children." *Pedagogical Seminary* 3 (October 1895): 235–45.

Bolton, Thaddeus. "Rhythm." *American Journal of Psychology* 6 (January 1894): 145–238.

Bryan, E. B. "Nascent Stages and Their Pedagogical Significance." *Pedagogical Seminary* 7 (1900): 357–96.

Burke, Frederic. "From Fundamental to Accessory in the Development of the Nervous System and of Movements." *Pedagogical Seminary* 6 (October 1898): 5–64.

Burnham, William. "Education from the Genetic Point of View." *Proceedings of the National Education Association* 44 (1905): 727–34.

———. "Suggestions from the Psychology of Adolescence." *School Review* 5 (1897): 652–65.

Chamberlain, Alexander. *The Child: A Study in the Evolution of Man.* London: Scribner's, 1900.

Dawson, George. "A Study in Youthful Degeneracy." *Pedagogical Seminary* 4 (December 1896): 221–58.

Dewey, John. *Democracy and Education.* New York: Macmillan, 1916.

———. *The Educational Situation.* Chicago: University of Chicago Press, 1902.

———. *The School and Society.* Chicago: University of Chicago Press, 1899.

———. "The New Psychology." *Andover Review* 2 (1884): 278–89.

———, and Evelyn Dewey. *Schools of Tomorrow.* New York: Dutton, 1915.

Forbush, William. *The Boy Problem.* Boston: Pilgrim Press, 1901.

Guillet, Cephas. "Recapitulation and Education." *Pedagogical Seminary* 7 (1899): 397–445.

Hall, G. Stanley. *Life and Confessions of a Psychologist.* New York: Appleton, 1923.

———. "Recreation and Reversion." *Pedagogical Seminary* 22 (December 1914): 510–20.

———. *Educational Problems.* 2 vols. New York: Appleton, 1911.

———. "A Glance at the Phyletic Background of Genetic Psychology." *American Journal of Psychology* 19 (1908): 149–212.

———. *Adolescence.* 2 vols. New York: Appleton, 1904.

———. "The Relations Between Lower and Higher Races." *Proceedings of the Massachusetts Historical Society* 17 (January 1903): 4–13.

———. "Child Study: The Basis of Exact Education." *Forum* 16 (December 1893): 429–41.

———. "Moral Education and Will Training." *Pedagogical Seminary* 11 (June 1892): 72–89.

Halleck, Reuben. "Some Contributions of Child Study to the Science of Education." *Proceedings of the National Education Association* 37 (1898): 354–63.

James, William. *Principles of Psychology.* 2 vols. New York: H. Holt and Company, 1890.

O'Shea, Michael. "Notes on Education for Social Efficiency." *American Journal of Sociology* 11 (March 1906): 646–54.

———. *Education as Adjustment.* New York: Longmans, Green, 1903.

Puffer, Joseph. *The Boy and His Gang.* Boston: Houghton, 1912.

Smith, Theodate. "The Questionnaire Method in Genetic Psychology." *Pedagogical Seminary* 10 (1903): 405–9.

Stelzle, Charles. *Boys of the Street.* New York: F. H. Revell, 1904.

Swift, Edgar. *Youth and the Race.* New York: Scribner, 1915.

———. *Learning and Doing.* Indianapolis, Bobbs-Merrill, 1914.

———. *Mind in the Making.* New York: Scribner, 1908.

Thorndike, Edward L. *Educational Psychology,* vol. 1. New York: Teachers College, Columbia University, 1913.

———. *Education: A First Book.* New York: Macmillan, 1912.

———. *Notes on Child Study.* New York: Macmillan, 1903.

Wiltse, Sara. "A Preliminary Study of Child Study in America." *Pedagogical Seminary* 3 (October 1895): 189–212.

SECONDARY SOURCES: PSYCHOLOGY

Adatto, Carl. "Ego Reintegration Observed in Analysis of Late Adolescents." *International Journal of Psychoanalysis* 39 (1958): 172–177.

Beres, David. "Vicissitudes of Superego Functions and Superego Precursors in Childhood." *Psychoanalytic Study of the Child* 13 (1958): 324–51.

Bernfeld, S. "Types of Adolescence." *Psychoanalytic Quarterly* 7 (1935): 243–53.

Blos, Peter. "Character Formation in Adolescence." *Psychoanalytic Study of the Child* 23 (1968): 245–53.

———. *On Adolescence.* New York: Free Press of Glencoe, 1962.

Deutsch, Helene. *Selected Problems of Adolescence.* New York: International Universities Press, 1967.

Erikson, Erik H. *Childhood and Society.* New York: Norton, 1950.

Fairbairn, W. R. D. *An Object-Relations Theory of the Personality.* New York: Basic Books, 1954.

Jacobson, Edith. *The Self and the Object World.* New York: International Universities Press, 1964.

Lampl-DeGroot, Jeanne. "Ego Ideal and Superego." *Psychoanalytic Study of the Child* 17 (1962): 94–106.

Landis, Bernard. *Ego Boundaries.* New York: International Universities Press, 1970.

Laufer, M. "Ego Ideal and Pseudo Ego Ideal in Adolescence." *Psychoanalytic Study of the Child* 19 (1964): 196–221.

Lewis, Helen. *Shame and Guilt in Neurosis.* New York: International Universities Press, 1971.

Loewald, Hans. "The Superego and the Ego-Ideal." *International Journal of Psychoanalysis* 43 (1962): 264–68.

Lynd, Helen. *On Shame and the Search for Identity.* New York: Harcourt, Brace, 1958.

Parsons, Talcott. *Social Structure and Personality.* London: Free Press, 1964.

Piers, G., and M. Singer. *Shame and Guilt.* Springfield, Ill.: Thomas, 1953.

Post, Seymour, ed. *Moral Values and the Superego Concept in Psychoanalysis.* New York: International Universities Press, 1972.

Schafer, Roy. *Aspects of Internalization.* New York: International Universities Press, 1968.

——. "Ideals, Ego Ideal and Ideal Self." *Psychological Issues* 18/19 (1967): 129–74.

Seton, Paul. "The Psychotemporal Adaptation of Late Adolescence." *Journal of the American Psychoanalytic Association* 22 (1974): 795–818.

Settlage, Calvin. "Cultural Values and the Superego in Late Adolescence." *Psychoanalytic Study of the Child* 27 (1973): 74–92.

SECONDARY SOURCES: GENERAL

Cavallo, Dominick. "From Perfection to Habit: Moral Training in the American Kindergarten, 1860–1920." *History of Education Quarterly* 16 (1976): 147–61.

Cremin, Lawrence. *The Transformation of the School: Progressivism in American Education.* New York: Knopf, 1961.

Davis, Allen. *American Heroine: The Life and Legend of Jane Addams.* New York: Oxford University Press, 1973.

——. *Spearheads for Reform.* New York: Oxford University Press, 1967.

Demos, John. *A Little Commonwealth.* New York: Oxford University Press, 1970.

Dorgan, Ethel. *Luther Halsey Gulick.* New York: Teachers College, Columbia University, 1934.

Dulles, Foster R. *America Learns to Play.* New York: Appleton-Century, 1940.

Erikson, Kai T. *Everything in Its Path.* New York: Simon and Schuster, 1976.

Finkelstein, Barbara. *Regulated Children, Liberated Children.* New York: Psychohistory Press, 1979.

Fulk, Joseph. *The Municipalization of Play and Recreation.* University Place, Nebraska: 1922.

Greven, Philip. *The Protestant Temperament.* New York: Knopf, 1977.

Hartman, Mary, and Lois W. Banner, eds. *Clio's Consciousness Raised.* New York: Harper and Row, 1974.

Hawes, Joseph. *Children in Urban Society.* New York: Oxford University Press, 1971.

Hays, Samuel. "The Politics of Reform in Municipal Government in the Progressive Era." *Pacific Northwest Quarterly* 45 (October 1964): 157–69.

Hendricks, James. "The Child-Study Movement in American Education, 1880–1910." Ph.D. dissertation, Indiana University, 1968.

Hofstadter, Richard. *The Age of Reform.* New York: Knopf, 1955.

Huizinga, Johan. *Homo Ludens.* Boston: Beacon Press, 1950.

Katz, Michael. *The Irony of Early School Reform.* Cambridge, Mass.: Harvard University Press, 1968.

——. *Class, Bureaucracy and Schools.* New York: Praeger, 1975.

Kett, Joseph. *Rites of Passage: Adolescence in America, 1790 to the Present.* New York: Basic Books, 1977.

Kuhn, Anne. *The Mother's Role in Childhood Education: New England Concepts, 1830–1860.* New Haven: Yale University Press, 1947.

Lasch, Christopher. *The New Radicalism in America.* New York: Knopf, 1965.

Lubove, Roy. *The Professional Altruist.* Cambridge, Mass.: Harvard University Press, 1965.

Platt, Anthony. *The Child Savers: The Invention of Delinquency.* Chicago: University of Chicago Press, 1969.

Rainwater, Clarence. *The Play Movement in the United States.* Chicago: University of Chicago Press, 1922.

Riesman, David. *The Lonely Crowd.* New Haven: Yale University Press, 1950.

Ross, Dorothy. *G. Stanley Hall, the Psychologist as Prophet.* Chicago: University of Chicago Press, 1972.

Spring, Joel. *Education and the Rise of the Corporate State.* Boston: Beacon Press, 1972.

Strickland, Charles. "The Child and the Race: The Doctrines of Recapitulation and Culture Epochs." Ph.D. dissertation, University of Wisconsin, 1963.

Wiebe, Robert. *The Search for Order, 1877–1920.* New York: Hill and Wang, 1967.

White, Morton. *Social Thought in America.* Boston: Beacon Press, 1947.

———. *The Origins of Dewey's Instrumentalism.* New York: Columbia University Press, 1943.

Wilson, R. Jackson. *In Quest of Community: Social Philosophy in the United States, 1860–1920.* New York: Wiley, 1968.

Wishy, Bernard. *The Child and the Republic.* Philadelphia: University of Pennsylvania Press, 1968.

INDEX